What Readers Are Saying About *Hello, Android*

Learn to develop Android apps with this complete yet gentle introduction to the Android platform. Out of all the books on Android, *Hello, Android* has the best flow and coverage for developers new to this platform. You'll be writing Android apps in no time!

▶ **Marko Gargenta**
CEO, Marakana.com

The third edition of *Hello, Android* gets you on the fast track of Android application development, from the basic concepts to publishing to the Android Market. Ed shows his vast experience on the subject and even covers hard-to-find topics such as multi-touch and OpenGL. This is a must-read for everyone starting on the fascinating journey of Android development.

▶ **Diego Torres Milano**
Android expert and blogger

I thoroughly enjoyed the *Hello, Android* book, and it helped me get on the right track to releasing my first two apps to the Market.

▶ **Nathan Rapp**
Founder, KMBurrito Designs

More than a greeting, *Hello, Android* welcomes both beginners and pros to Android development.

▶ **Michael Martin PMP**
Founder, GoogleAndBlog and Mobile Martin

Hello, Android

Introducing Google's
Mobile Development Platform, 3rd Edition

Hello, Android

Introducing Google's
Mobile Development Platform, 3rd Edition

Ed Burnette

The Pragmatic Bookshelf
Raleigh, North Carolina   Dallas, Texas

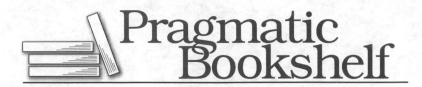

Our Pragmatic courses, workshops, and other products can help you and your team create better software and have more fun. For more information, as well as the latest Pragmatic titles, please visit us at http://www.pragprog.com.

The team that produced this book includes:

Editor:	Susannah Davidson Pfalzer
Indexing:	Seth Maislin
Copy edit:	Kim Wimpsett
Layout:	Steve Peter
Production:	Janet Furlow
Customer support:	Ellie Callahan
International:	Juliet Benda

ISBN-10: 1-934356-56-5
ISBN-13: 978-1-934356-56-2
Printed on acid-free paper.
P3.0 printing, November 2010
Version: 2010-11-4

Contents

Acknowledgments

I'd like to thank the many people who made this book possible, including the readers of the previous editions for all their great suggestions; my editor, Susannah Pfalzer, for her attention to detail; Javier Collado, Marilynn Huret, and Staffan Nöteberg for providing valuable review comments; and especially Lisa, Michael, and Christopher for their continued patience and support.

Preface

Android is an open source software toolkit for mobile phones that was created by Google and the Open Handset Alliance. It's inside millions of cell phones and other mobile devices, making Android a major platform for application developers. Whether you're a hobbyist or a professional programmer, whether you are doing it for fun or for profit, it's time to learn more about developing for Android. This book will help you get started.

What Makes Android Special?

There are already many mobile platforms on the market today, including Symbian, iPhone, Windows Mobile, BlackBerry, Java Mobile Edition, Linux Mobile (LiMo), and more. When I tell people about Android, their first question is often, Why do we need another mobile standard? Where's the "wow"?

Although some of its features have appeared before, Android is the first environment that combines the following:

- *A truly open, free development platform based on Linux and open source*: Handset makers like it because they can use and customize the platform without paying a royalty. Developers like it because they know that the platform "has legs" and is not locked into any one vendor that may go under or be acquired.

- *A component-based architecture inspired by Internet mashups*: Parts of one application can be used in another in ways not originally envisioned by the developer. You can even replace built-in components with your own improved versions. This will unleash a new round of creativity in the mobile space.

- *Tons of built-in services out of the box*: Location-based services use GPS or cell tower triangulation to let you customize the user experience depending on where you are. A full-powered SQL database lets you harness the power of local storage for occasionally con-nected computing and synchronization. Browser and map views can be embedded directly in your applications. All these built-in capabilities help raise the bar on functionality while lowering your development costs.

- *Automatic management of the application life cycle*: Programs are isolated from each other by multiple layers of security, which will provide a level of system stability not seen before in smart phones. The end user will no longer have to worry about what applications are active or close some programs so that others can run. Android is optimized for low-power, low-memory devices in a fundamental way that no previous platform has attempted.

- *High-quality graphics and sound*: Smooth, antialiased 2D vector graphics and animation inspired by Flash are melded with 3D-accelerated OpenGL graphics to enable new kinds of games and business applications. Codecs for the most common industry-standard audio and video formats are built right in, including H.264 (AVC), MP3, and AAC.

- *Portability across a wide range of current and future hardware*: All your programs are written in Java and executed by Android's Dalvik virtual machine, so your code will be portable across ARM, x86, and other architectures. Support for a variety of input methods is included such as keyboard, touch, and trackball. User interfaces can be customized for any screen resolution and orientation.

Android offers a fresh take on the way mobile applications interact with users, along with the technical underpinnings to make it possible. But the best part of Android is the software that you are going to write for it. This book will help you get off to a great start.

Who Should Read This Book?

The only requirement is a basic understanding of programming in Java or a similar object-oriented language (C# will do in a pinch). You don't need any prior experience developing software for mobile devices. In fact, if you do, it's probably best if you try to forget that experience. Android is so different that it's good to start with an open mind.

What's in This Book?

Hello, Android is divided into four parts. Roughly speaking, the book progresses from less advanced to more advanced topics, or from more common to less common aspects of Android.

Several chapters share a common example: an Android Sudoku game. By gradually adding features to the game, you'll learn about many aspects of Android programming including user interfaces, multimedia, and the Android life cycle.

In Part I, we'll start with an introduction to Android. This is where you'll learn how to install the Android emulator and how to use an integrated development environment (IDE) to write your first program. Then we'll introduce a few key concepts like the Android life cycle. Programming in Android is a little different from what you're probably used to, so make sure you get these concepts before moving on.

Part II talks about Android's user interface, two-dimensional graphics, multimedia components, and simple data access. These features will be used in most programs you write.

Part III digs deeper into the Android platform. Here you'll learn about connecting to the outside world, location-based services, the built-in SQLite database, and three-dimensional graphics.

Part IV wraps things up with a discussion on using advanced input techniques including multi-touch and extending your home screen with widgets and live wallpaper. Finally, we'll explore making your app compatible with multiple Android devices and versions and then publishing it on the Android Market.

At the end of the book, you'll find an appendix that covers the differences between Android and Java Standard Edition (SE), along with a bibliography.

What's New in the Third Edition?

The third edition has been updated to support all versions of Android from 1.5 through 2.2 and beyond. Here's a summary of the new features introduced in each version and the corresponding sections that cover those features.

New for Cupcake

Android 1.5 (Cupcake) introduced a large number of enhancements to the Android platform including support for soft (onscreen) keyboards, video recording, and application widgets. Under the covers, there were more than 1,000 changes to the Android API between 1.1 and 1.5.[1] Widgets are covered in Section 12.1, *Hello, Widget*, on page 229.

New for Donut

Android 1.6 (Donut) added support for high- and low-density displays, plus a number of minor changes that don't affect most developers.[2] You can learn how to support these different device form factors in Section 13.5, *All Screens Great and Small*, on page 264.

New for Eclair

Android 2.0 (Eclair) added support for multi-touch, virtual keys, centralized account management, synchronization APIs, docking, HTML5, and more.[3] The 2.0 version was quickly replaced by Android 2.0.1 (also called Eclair), which contains all the changes in the 2.0 version plus a few bug fixes.[4] Multi-touch is covered in Chapter 11, *Multi-Touch*, on page 215.

New for Eclair MR1

Android 2.1 (Eclair Maintenance Release 1) added support for live wallpapers, more HTML5 support, and other minor improvements.[5] Home screen enhancements, including live wallpapers and widgets, are covered in Chapter 12, *There's No Place Like Home*, on page 229.

New for FroYo and Beyond

Android 2.2 (FroYo) supports application installation on external storage (SD cards), a much faster Java virtual machine, OpenGL ES 2.0 APIs, and more.[6] Section 13.6, *Installing on the SD Card*, on page 265 explains how to set up your program to install on external storage and when you should and shouldn't do that.

---

1. http://d.android.com/sdk/api_diff/3/changes.html
2. http://d.android.com/sdk/api_diff/4/changes.html
3. http://d.android.com/sdk/api_diff/5/changes.html
4. http://d.android.com/sdk/api_diff/6/changes.html
5. http://d.android.com/sdk/api_diff/7/changes.html
6. http://d.android.com/sdk/api_diff/8/changes.html

Android 1.5 (or newer) is now available for all shipping Android devices. All new devices have it installed, and Google says that almost all older devices have upgraded. See the Android Device Dashboard[7] for the latest market share of active Android devices in the wild. This edition of the book does not cover version 1.1 or earlier.

Note: It may be a while before all devices are upgraded to the latest version of Android (if ever), so Chapter 13, *Write Once, Test Everywhere*, on page 253 covers how to create a single program that supports multiple versions. All the examples in this book have been tested on versions 1.5 through 2.2.

Online Resources

At the website for this book (http://pragprog.com/titles/eband3), you'll find the following:

- The full source code for all the sample programs used in this book

- An errata page, listing any mistakes in the current edition (let's hope that will be empty!)

- A discussion forum where you can communicate directly with the author and other Android developers (let's hope that will be full!)

You are free to use the source code in your own applications as you see fit. Note: If you're reading the ebook, you can also click the little gray rectangle before the code listings to download that source file directly.

Fast-Forward >>

Although most authors expect you to read every word in their books, I know you're not going to do that. You want to read just enough to let you get something done, and then maybe you'll come back later and read something else to let you get another piece done. So, I've tried to provide you with a little help so you won't get lost.

Each chapter in this book ends with a "Fast-Forward >>" section. These sections will provide some guidance for where you should go next when you need to read the book out of order. You'll also find pointers to other resources such as books and online documentation here in case you want to learn more about the subject.

---

7. http://d.android.com/resources/dashboard/platform-versions.html

So, what are you waiting for? The next chapter—Chapter 1, *Quick Start*, on page 3—drops you right into the deep end with your first Android program. Chapter 2, *Key Concepts*, on page 17 takes a step back and introduces you to the basic concepts and philosophy of Android, and Chapter 3, *Designing the User Interface*, on page 31 digs into the user interface, which will be the most important part of most Android programs.

Your ultimate goal will be to make your apps available for sale or free download in the Android Market. When you're ready, Chapter 14, *Publishing to the Android Market*, on page 269 will show you how to take that final step.

Part I

Introducing Android

Chapter 1

Quick Start

Android combines the ubiquity of cell phones, the excitement of open source software, and the corporate backing of Google and other Open Handset Alliance members like Motorola, HTC, Verizon, and AT&T. The result is a mobile platform you can't afford *not* to learn.

Luckily, getting started developing with Android is easy. You don't even need access to an Android phone—just a computer where you can install the Android SDK and phone emulator.

In this chapter, I'll show you how to get all the development tools installed, and then we'll jump right in and create a working application: Android's version of "Hello, World."

1.1 Installing the Tools

The Android software development kit (SDK) works on Windows, Linux, and Mac OS X. The applications you create, of course, can be deployed on any Android devices.

Before you start coding, you need to install Java, an IDE, and the Android SDK.

Java 5.0+

First you need a copy of Java. All the Android development tools require it, and programs you write will be using the Java language. JDK 5 or 6 is required.

It's not enough to just have a runtime environment (JRE); you need the full development kit. I recommend getting the latest Sun JDK SE 6.0

update from the Sun download site.[1] The 32-bit version seems to work best (see the "32-bit vs. 64-bit" sidebar). Mac OS X users should get the latest version of Mac OS X and the JDK from the Apple website.

To verify you have the right version, run this command from your shell window. Here's what I get when I run it:

```
C:\> java -version
java version "1.6.0_14"
Java(TM) SE Runtime Environment (build 1.6.0_14-b08)
Java HotSpot(TM) Client VM (build 14.0-b16, mixed mode, sharing)
```

You should see something similar, with version "1.6.something" or later.

Eclipse

Next, you should install a Java development environment if you don't have one already. I recommend Eclipse, because it's free and because it's used and supported by the Google developers who created Android.

The minimum version of Eclipse is 3.3.1, but you should always use whatever is the most up-to-date production version. Go to the Eclipse downloads page,[2] and pick "Eclipse IDE for Java Developers." Note that you need more than just the standard Eclipse SDK "classic" platform. Download the package into a temporary directory, unpack it (usually this is just a matter of double-clicking it), and move the entire unpacked directory to a permanent location (like C:\Eclipse on Windows or /Applications/Eclipse on Mac OS X).

If you don't want to use Eclipse (there's always one in every crowd), support for other IDEs such as NetBeans and JetBrains IDEA is available from their respective communities. Or if you're really old-school, you can forgo an IDE entirely and just use the command-line tools.[3] The rest of the book will assume you're using Eclipse, so if you're not, you'll need to make adjustments as necessary.

Android SDK Starter Package

Starting with Android 2.0, the Android SDK has been broken into two parts: the SDK Starter Package and the SDK Components. First, use your web browser to get the starter package. The Android download

---

1. http://java.sun.com/javase/downloads
2. http://www.eclipse.org/downloads
3. See http://d.android.com/guide/developing/tools for documentation on the command-line tools.

> ### 32-bit vs. 64-bit
>
> If you're using a 64-bit version of Windows, you may be tempted to install the 64-bit version of the Java Development Kit instead of the 32-bit version. Older versions of Eclipse had issues running with a 64-bit JDK, but that has been fixed as of Eclipse 3.6 ("Helios").* However, some browsers still require the 32-bit version of the Java plug-in. Unless you really need 64-bit Java, you may find it easier to just use the 32-bit version of both Java and Eclipse for now.
>
> *.   https://bugs.eclipse.org/bugs/show_bug.cgi?id=293969

page[4] has packages for Windows, Mac OS X, and Linux. After downloading the package that's right for you, unpack the .zip file to a temporary directory.

By default, the SDK will be expanded into a subdirectory like android-sdk-windows. Move that subdirectory underneath a permanent directory such as C:\Google or /Applications/Google. Then make a note of the full path so you can refer to it later as your *SDK install directory.*

No special install program is needed for either Eclipse or the SDK, but I do recommend you add the SDK's tools directory to your PATH.

Android SDK Components

Next, invoke the SDK Setup program. On Windows, run SDK Setup.exe. On Linux and Mac OS X, run the tools/android program, select Available Packages, put a check mark next to every package, and click Install Selected.

The Setup program will now display a list of available components including documentation, platforms, add-on libraries, and USB drivers (see Figure 1.1, on the following page). Select Accept All and then click Install. All the components listed will be downloaded and installed into your SDK install directory. Note: this can take a long time to complete. To make it go faster, you can accept or reject the individual components separately instead of installing them all.

---

4. http://d.android.com/sdk

Figure 1.1: INSTALLING THE ANDROID SDK COMPONENTS

If you get an HTTPS SSL error, then cancel the window and select Settings from the main SDK and AVD Manager window. Select the option Force https:// sources to be fetched using http://, and then click Save & Apply. Exit the Setup program and start it again.

The next step is to start Eclipse and configure it.

Eclipse Plug-In

To make development easier, Google has written a plug-in for Eclipse called the Android Development Toolkit (ADT). To install the plug-in, follow these steps (note these directions are for Eclipse 3.5—different versions may have slightly different menus and options):

1. Start Eclipse by running eclipse.exe on Windows or eclipse on Mac OS X or Linux. If you're prompted for a workspace directory, just accept the default and click OK.

2. Select the Help menu and then select Install New Software... (Help > Install New Software...). See the *Joe Asks...* on page 8 if you get a connection error.

3. Click the Available Software Sites link in the dialog that appears.

Figure 1.2: INSTALLING THE ANDROID DEVELOPMENT TOOLKIT

4. Click the Add... button.

5. Enter the location of the Android Development Tools update site: https://dl-ssl.google.com/android/eclipse/.

   Once you've filled it out, the dialog box should look like Figure 1.2.

6. Click OK to return to the Sites list, and click Test Connection to verify the site you just entered. If you have trouble with this address, try using **http** in the location instead of **https**. Once you're satisfied the address is correct, click OK again to return to the Install New Software dialog.

7. Type the word "android" in the Work With field and press Return. "Developer Tools" should now appear in the list below.

8. Select the checkbox next to Developer Tools and then click Next. If you get an error message at this point, then you may not have the right version of Eclipse. I strongly recommend using either the prebuilt Eclipse IDE for Java Developers or the Eclipse IDE for Java EE Development package, version 3.5 or newer.

   If you have a custom install of Eclipse, then to use the Android editors, you will also need to install the Web Standard Tools (WST) plug-in and all its prerequisites.

```
 \ /
 ;*{   Joe Asks...
 ~
      It Says "Connection Error," So Now What?
```

If you get a connection error, the most likely cause is some kind of firewall erected by your system administrators. To get outside the firewall, you'll need to configure Eclipse with the address of your proxy server. This is the same proxy server you use for your web browser, but unfortunately Eclipse isn't smart enough to pick up the setting from there.

To tell Eclipse about the proxy, select Window > Preferences > General > Network Connections (Eclipse > Preferences on Mac OS X), turn on the option for Manual proxy configuration, enter the server name and port number, and click OK. If you don't see the option, you may be running an older version of Eclipse. Try looking under Preferences > Install/Update, or search the preferences for the word *proxy*.

See the Web Tools platform home page[5] for more details and download links. These are already built into the recommended packages mentioned earlier.

9. Review the list of items to be installed, click Next again, accept the license agreements, and then click Finish to start the download and install process.

10. Once the install is done, restart Eclipse.

11. When Eclipse comes back up, you may see a few error messages because you need to tell it where the Android SDK is located. Select Window > Preferences > Android (Eclipse > Preferences on Mac OS X), and enter the SDK install directory you noted earlier. Click OK.

Whew! Luckily, you have to do that only once (or at least once every time a new version of ADT or Eclipse comes out). Now that everything is installed, it's time to write your first program.

---

5. http://www.eclipse.org/webtools

1.2 Creating Your First Program

ADT comes with a built-in example program, or template, that we're going to use to create a simple "Hello, Android" program in just a few seconds. Get your stopwatch ready. Ready? Set? Go!

Select File > New > Project... to open the New Project dialog box. Then select Android > Android Project, and click Next.

Enter the following information:

```
Project name: HelloAndroid
Build Target: Android 2.2
Application name: Hello, Android
Package name: org.example.hello
Create Activity: Hello
Min SDK Version: 8
```

When you're done, it should look something like Figure 1.3, on the next page.

Click Finish. The Android plug-in will create the project and fill it in with some default files. Eclipse will build it and package it up so it will be ready to execute. If you get an error about missing source folders, select Project > Clean to fix it.

OK, that takes care of writing the program; now all that's left is to try running it. First we'll run it under the Android emulator.

1.3 Running on the Emulator

To run your Android program, go to the Package Explorer window, right-click the HelloAndroid project, and select Run As > Android Application. If you're following along in Eclipse, you may see an error dialog like the one in Figure 1.4, on page 11. This indicates we haven't told the emulator what kind of phone to emulate.

Creating an AVD

To do this, you need to create an Android Virtual Device (AVD) using either Eclipse or the android avd command.[6] It's easier to use Eclipse, so select Yes in the AVD Error dialog to open the AVD Manager. You can open the manager again later by selecting Window > Android SDK and AVD Manager.

---

6. http://d.android.com/guide/developing/tools/avd.html

Figure 1.3: NEW ANDROID PROJECT

Keeping Up with the Plug-In

The Android Eclipse plug-in is a work in progress that changes much more often than the Android SDK. The version you download may be different from the one I used when writing this book, and it may contain a few, shall we say, idiosyncrasies. I recommend you check the plug-in site monthly to pick up any new features and fixes.

Figure 1.4: MISSING ANDROID VIRTUAL DEVICE (AVD)

Click the New... button, and then fill out the fields for the new AVD as follows:

```
Name: em22
Target: Android 2.2 - API Level 8
SDCard: 64
Skin: Default (HVGA)
```

This tells Eclipse to set up a generic device called "em22," which has the Android 2.2 (FroYo) firmware installed. A 64MB virtual Secure Digital (SD) card will be allocated, along with a half-VGA (320×480) display.

When you are done, you should see something like Figure 1.6, on page 13. Because of updates in the SDK tools since this was written, your screen may look slightly different.

Click Create AVD to create the virtual device. A few seconds later you should see a message that the device has been created. Click OK, select the AVD, and then click Start... and then Launch to bring it up. Close the AVD Manager window when you're done.

Cupcake vs. Donut vs. Eclair vs. FroYo

The version of Android running on your emulator (or real phone) must be compatible with your program's build target. For example, if you try to run an Android 2.2 (FroYo) program on an Android 1.5 (Cupcake) phone, it won't work because Android 1.5 phones can only run 1.5 or earlier programs. Android 2.2 phones, on the other hand, can run programs built for 2.2, 2.1, 2.0.1, 2.0, 1.6, 1.5, and earlier. But it may be a while before most phones have been upgraded (if ever).

So, why not just target Android 1.5? Unfortunately, applications built for 1.5 don't always display correctly on the larger and smaller screens found on 1.6 phones. Luckily, there's an easy way to make your programs compatible with all versions of Android. See Chapter 13, *Write Once, Test Everywhere*, on page 253 for instructions.

Figure 1.5: RUNNING THE "HELLO, ANDROID" PROGRAM

Figure 1.6: Creating an AVD in Eclipse

> **Shortening the Turnaround**
>
> Starting the emulator is expensive. Think about it this way—when you first turn on your phone, it needs to boot up just like any computer system. Closing the emulator is just like turning off the phone or pulling the batteries out. So, don't turn it off!
>
> Leave the emulator window running as long as Eclipse is running. The next time you start an Android program, Eclipse will notice the emulator is already there and will just send it the new program to run.

Let's Try That Again

Once you have a valid AVD, the Android emulator window will start up and boot the Android operating system. The first time you do this, it may take a minute or two, so be patient. You may need to right-click the project and select Run As > Android Application again. If you see an error message saying that the application is not responding, select the option to continue waiting. If you see a key guard screen, swipe it as directed to unlock.

Eclipse will send a copy of your program to the emulator to execute. The application screen comes up, and your "Hello, Android" program is now running (see Figure 1.5, on page 12). That's it! Congratulations on your first Android program.

1.4 Running on a Real Phone

Running an Android program on a physical device such as the Droid or Nexus One during development is almost identical to running it on the emulator. You need to enable USB debugging on the phone itself (by starting the Settings application and selecting Applications > Development > USB Debugging), install the Android USB device driver if you haven't already (Windows only), and then plug the phone into your computer using the USB cable that came with the phone.[7]

---

7. See http://d.android.com/guide/developing/device.html for the latest device driver and installation instructions.

Close the emulator window if it's already open. As long as the phone is plugged in, Eclipse should load and run applications on the phone instead. Alternatively, you can switch between the emulator and the phone by editing your run configuration (Run > Run Configurations...), selecting the Target tab, and changing the Target selection mode to suit your preferences. Setting it to Manual will cause Eclipse to prompt you to select the device each time you run the program. If your phone does not appear in the list, it usually indicates a problem with your USB driver or with your target and minimum SDK levels. You may need to make a change to your AndroidManifest.xml file if your phone does not have the latest version of Android (see Section 13.2, *Building for Multiple Versions*, on page 254).

When you're ready to publish your application for others to use, there are a few more steps you'll need to take. Chapter 14, *Publishing to the Android Market*, on page 269 will cover that in more detail.

1.5 Fast-Forward >>

Thanks to the Eclipse plug-in, creating a skeletal Android program takes only a few seconds. In Chapter 3, *Designing the User Interface*, on page 31, we'll begin to flesh out that skeleton with a real application—a Sudoku game. This sample will be used in several chapters to demonstrate Android's API.

But before delving into that, you should take a few minutes to read Chapter 2, *Key Concepts*, on page 17. Once you grasp the basic concepts such as activities and life cycles, the rest will be much easier to understand.

Although the use of Eclipse to develop Android programs is optional, I highly recommend it. If you've never used Eclipse before, you may want to invest in a quick reference such as the *Eclipse IDE Pocket Guide* [Bur05].

Key Concepts

Now that you have an idea of what Android is, let's take a look at how it works. Some parts of Android may be familiar, such as the Linux kernel, OpenGL, and the SQL database. Others will be completely foreign, such as Android's idea of the application life cycle.

You'll need a good understanding of these key concepts in order to write well-behaved Android applications, so if you read only one chapter in this book, read this one.

2.1 The Big Picture

Let's start by taking a look at the overall system architecture—the key layers and components that make up the Android open source software stack. In Figure 2.1, on the following page, you can see the "20,000-foot" view of Android. Study it closely—there will be a test tomorrow.

Each layer uses the services provided by the layers below it. Starting from the bottom, the following sections highlight the layers provided by Android.

Linux Kernel

Android is built on top of a solid and proven foundation: the Linux kernel. Created by Linus Torvalds in 1991, Linux can be found today in everything from wristwatches to supercomputers. Linux provides the hardware abstraction layer for Android, allowing Android to be ported to a wide variety of platforms in the future.

Internally, Android uses Linux for its memory management, process management, networking, and other operating system services. The Android phone user will never see Linux, and your programs will not

Figure 2.1: ANDROID SYSTEM ARCHITECTURE

make Linux calls directly. As a developer, though, you'll need to be aware it's there.

Some utilities you need during development interact with Linux. For example, the adb shell command[1] will open a Linux shell in which you can enter other commands to run on the device. From there you can examine the Linux file system, view active processes, and so forth, subject to security restrictions.

Native Libraries

The next layer above the kernel contains the Android native libraries. These shared libraries are all written in C or C++, compiled for the particular hardware architecture used by the phone, and preinstalled by the phone vendor.

Some of the most important native libraries include the following:

- *Surface Manager*: Android uses a compositing window manager similar to Vista or Compiz, but it's much simpler. Instead of draw-

---

1. http://d.android.com/guide/developing/tools/adb.html

ing directly to the screen buffer, your drawing commands go into off-screen bitmaps that are then combined with other bitmaps to form the display the user sees. This lets the system create all sorts of interesting effects such as see-through windows and fancy transitions.

- *2D and 3D graphics*: Two- and three-dimensional elements can be combined in a single user interface with Android. The library will use 3D hardware if the device has it or a fast software renderer if it doesn't. See Chapter 4, *Exploring 2D Graphics*, on page 61 and Chapter 10, *3D Graphics in OpenGL*, on page 191.

- *Media codecs*: Android can play video and record and play back audio in a variety of formats including AAC, AVC (H.264), H.263, MP3, and MPEG-4. See Chapter 5, *Multimedia*, on page 93 for an example.

- *SQL database*: Android includes the lightweight SQLite database engine,[2] the same database used in Firefox and the Apple iPhone.[3] You can use this for persistent storage in your application. See Chapter 9, *Putting SQL to Work*, on page 171 for an example.

- *Browser engine*: For the fast display of HTML content, Android uses the WebKit library.[4] This is the same engine used in the Google Chrome browser, Apple's Safari browser, the Apple iPhone, and Nokia's S60 platform. See Chapter 7, *The Connected World*, on page 121 for an example.

These libraries are not applications that stand by themselves. They exist only to be called by higher-level programs. Starting in Android 1.5, you can write and deploy your own native libraries using the Native Development Toolkit (NDK). Native development is beyond the scope of this book, but if you're interested, you can read all about it online.[5]

Android Runtime

Also sitting on top of the kernel is the Android runtime, including the Dalvik virtual machine and the core Java libraries.

---

2. http://www.sqlite.org
3. See http://www.zdnet.com/blog/burnette/iphone-vs-android-development-day-1/682 for a comparison of iPhone and Android development.
4. http://webkit.org
5. http://d.android.com/sdk/ndk

> \\//
> `}{̆´ **Joe Asks...**
> ‿
> ### What's a Dalvik?
>
> Dalvik is a virtual machine (VM) designed and written by Dan Bornstein at Google. Your code gets compiled into machine-independent instructions called *bytecodes*, which are then executed by the Dalvik VM on the mobile device.
>
> Although the bytecode formats are a little different, Dalvik is essentially a Java virtual machine optimized for low memory requirements. It allows multiple VM instances to run at once and takes advantage of the underlying operating system (Linux) for security and process isolation.
>
> Bornstein named Dalvik after a fishing village in Iceland where some of his ancestors lived.

The Dalvik VM is Google's implementation of Java, optimized for mobile devices. All the code you write for Android will be written in Java and run within the VM. Dalvik differs from traditional Java in two important ways:

- The Dalvik VM runs .dex files, which are converted at compile time from standard .class and .jar files. .dex files are more compact and efficient than class files, an important consideration for the limited memory and battery-powered devices that Android targets.
- The core Java libraries that come with Android are different from both the Java Standard Edition (Java SE) libraries and the Java Mobile Edition (Java ME) libraries. There is a substantial amount of overlap, however. In Appendix A, on page 277, you'll find a comparison of Android and standard Java libraries.

Application Framework

Sitting above the native libraries and runtime, you'll find the Application Framework layer. This layer provides the high-level building blocks you will use to create your applications. The framework comes pre-installed with Android, but you can also extend it with your own components as needed.

The most important parts of the framework are as follows:

- *Activity Manager*: This controls the life cycle of applications (see Section 2.2, *It's Alive!*, on page 22) and maintains a common "backstack" for user navigation.

> **Embrace and Extend**
>
> One of the unique and powerful qualities of Android is that all applications have a level playing field. What I mean is that the system applications have to go through the same public API that you use. You can even tell Android to make your application replace the standard applications if you want.

- *Content providers*: These objects encapsulate data that needs to be shared between applications, such as contacts. See Section 2.3, *Content Providers*, on page 27.
- *Resource manager*: Resources are anything that goes with your program that is not code. See Section 2.4, *Using Resources*, on page 27.
- *Location manager*: An Android phone always knows where it is. See Chapter 8, *Locating and Sensing*, on page 153.
- *Notification manager*: Events such as arriving messages, appointments, proximity alerts, alien invasions, and more can be presented in an unobtrusive fashion to the user.

Applications and Widgets

The highest layer in the Android architecture diagram is the Applications and Widgets layer. Think of this as the tip of the Android iceberg. End users will see only these programs, blissfully unaware of all the action going on below the waterline. As an Android developer, however, you know better.

Applications are programs that can take over the whole screen and interact with the user. On the other hand, widgets (which are sometimes called *gadgets*), operate only in a small rectangle of the Home screen application.

The majority of this book will cover application development, because that's what most of you will be writing. Widget development is covered in Chapter 12, *There's No Place Like Home*, on page 229.

When someone buys an Android phone, it will come prepackaged with a number of standard system applications, including the following:

- Phone dialer
- Email

- Contacts
- Web browser
- Android Market

Using the Android Market, the user will be able to download new programs to run on their phone. That's where you come in. By the time you finish this book, you'll be able to write your own killer applications for Android.

Now let's take a closer look at the life cycle of an Android application. It's a little different from what you're used to seeing.

2.2 It's Alive!

On your standard Linux or Windows desktop, you can have many applications running and visible at once in different windows. One of the windows has keyboard focus, but otherwise all the programs are equal. You can easily switch between them, but it's your responsibility as the user to move the windows around so you can see what you're doing and close programs you don't need.

Android doesn't work that way.

In Android, there is one foreground application, which typically takes over the whole display except for the status line. When the user turns on their phone, the first application they see is the Home application (see Figure 2.2, on the facing page).

When the user runs an application, Android starts it and brings it to the foreground. From that application, the user might invoke another application, or another screen in the same application, and then another and another. All these programs and screens are recorded on the *application stack* by the system's Activity Manager. At any time, the user can press the Back button to return to the previous screen on the stack. From the user's point of view, it works a lot like the history in a web browser. Pressing Back returns them to the previous page.

Process != Application

Internally, each user interface screen is represented by an Activity class (see Section 2.3, *Activities*, on page 26). Each activity has its own life cycle. An application is one or more activities plus a Linux process to contain them. That sounds pretty straightforward, doesn't it? But don't get comfortable yet; I'm about to throw you a curve ball.

Figure 2.2: THE HOME APPLICATION

In Android, an application can be "alive" even if its process has been killed. Put another way, the activity life cycle is not tied to the process life cycle. Processes are just disposable containers for activities. This is probably different from every other system you're familiar with, so let's take a closer look before moving on.

Life Cycles of the Rich and Famous

During its lifetime, each activity of an Android program can be in one of several states, as shown in Figure 2.3, on the following page. You, the developer, do not have control over what state your program is in. That's all managed by the system. However, you do get notified when the state is about to change through the on*XX*() method calls.

You override these methods in your Activity class, and Android will call them at the appropriate time:

- onCreate(Bundle): This is called when the activity first starts up. You can use it to perform one-time initialization such as creating

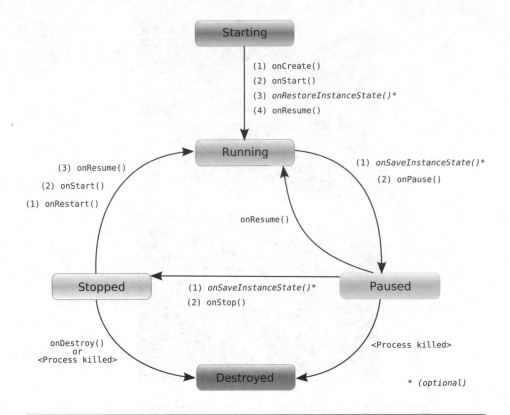

Figure 2.3: LIFE CYCLE OF AN ANDROID ACTIVITY

the user interface. onCreate() takes one parameter that is either **null** or some state information previously saved by the onSaveInstanceState() method.

- onStart(): This indicates the activity is about to be displayed to the user.

- onResume(): This is called when your activity can start interacting with the user. This is a good place to start animations and music.

- onPause(): This runs when the activity is about to go into the background, usually because another activity has been launched in front of it. This is where you should save your program's persistent state, such as a database record being edited.

- onStop(): This is called when your activity is no longer visible to the user and it won't be needed for a while. If memory is tight, onStop() may never be called (the system may simply terminate your process).

> ## Flipping the Lid
>
> Here's a quick way to test that your state-saving code is working correctly. In current versions of Android, an orientation change (between portrait and landscape modes) will cause the system to go through the process of saving instance state, pausing, stopping, destroying, and then creating a new instance of the activity with the saved state. On the T-Mobile G1 phone, for example, flipping the lid on the keyboard will trigger this, and on the Android emulator, pressing `Ctrl+F11` or the `7` or `9` key on the keypad will do it.

- onRestart(): If this method is called, it indicates your activity is being redisplayed to the user from a stopped state.
- onDestroy(): This is called right before your activity is destroyed. If memory is tight, onDestroy() may never be called (the system may simply terminate your process).
- onSaveInstanceState(Bundle): Android will call this method to allow the activity to save per-instance state, such as a cursor position within a text field. Usually you won't need to override it because the default implementation saves the state for all your user interface controls automatically.
- onRestoreInstanceState(Bundle): This is called when the activity is being reinitialized from a state previously saved by the onSave-InstanceState() method. The default implementation restores the state of your user interface.

Activities that are not running in the foreground may be stopped, or the Linux process that houses them may be killed at any time in order to make room for new activities. This will be a common occurrence, so it's important that your application be designed from the beginning with this in mind. In some cases, the onPause() method may be the last method called in your activity, so that's where you should save any data you want to keep around for next time.

In addition to managing your program's life cycle, the Android framework provides a number of building blocks that you use to create your applications. Let's take a look at those next.

2.3 Building Blocks

A few objects are defined in the Android SDK that every developer needs to be familiar with. The most important ones are activities, intents, services, and content providers. You'll see several examples of them in the rest of the book, so I'd like to briefly introduce them now.

Activities

An *activity* is a user interface screen. Applications can define one or more activities to handle different phases of the program. As discussed in Section 2.2, *It's Alive!*, on page 22, each activity is responsible for saving its own state so that it can be restored later as part of the application life cycle. See Section 3.3, *Creating the Opening Screen*, on page 33 for an example. Activities extend the Context class, so you can use them to get global information about your application.

Intents

An *intent* is a mechanism for describing a specific action, such as "pick a photo," "phone home," or "open the pod bay doors." In Android, just about everything goes through intents, so you have plenty of opportunities to replace or reuse components. See Section 3.5, *Implementing an About Box*, on page 46 for an example of an intent.

For example, there is an intent for "send an email." If your application needs to send mail, you can invoke that intent. Or if you're writing a new email application, you can register an activity to handle that intent and replace the standard mail program. The next time somebody tries to send an email, they'll get the option to use your program instead of the standard one.

Services

A *service* is a task that runs in the background without the user's direct interaction, similar to a Unix daemon. For example, consider a music player. The music may be started by an activity, but you want it to keep playing even when the user has moved on to a different program. So, the code that does the actual playing should be in a service. Later, another activity may bind to that service and tell it to switch tracks or stop playing. Android comes with many services built in, along with convenient APIs to access them. Section 12.2, *Live Wallpaper*, on page 238 uses a service to draw an animated picture behind the Home screen.

Content Providers

A *content provider* is a set of data wrapped up in a custom API to read and write it. This is the best way to share global data *between applications*. For example, Google provides a content provider for contacts. All the information there—names, addresses, phone numbers, and so forth—can be shared by any application that wants to use it. See Section 9.5, *Using a ContentProvider*, on page 185 for an example.

2.4 Using Resources

A *resource* is a localized text string, bitmap, or other small piece of noncode information that your program needs. At build time all your resources get compiled into your application. This is useful for internationalization and for supporting multiple device types (see Section 3.4, *Using Alternate Resources*, on page 42).

You will create and store your resources in the res directory inside your project. The Android resource compiler (aapt)[6] processes resources according to which subfolder they are in and the format of the file. For example, PNG and JPG format bitmaps should go in a directory starting with res/drawable, and XML files that describe screen layouts should go in a directory starting with res/layout. You can add suffixes for particular languages, screen orientations, pixel densities, and more (see Section 13.5, *All Screens Great and Small*, on page 264).

The resource compiler compresses and packs your resources and then generates a class named R that contains identifiers you use to reference those resources in your program. This is a little different from standard Java resources, which are referenced by key strings. Doing it this way allows Android to make sure all your references are valid and saves space by not having to store all those resource keys. Eclipse uses a similar method to store and reference the resources in Eclipse plug-ins.

We'll see an example of the code to access a resource in Chapter 3, *Designing the User Interface*, on page 31.

2.5 Safe and Secure

As mentioned earlier, every application runs in its own Linux process. The hardware forbids one process from accessing another process's

---

6. http://d.android.com/guide/developing/tools/aapt.html

memory. Furthermore, every application is assigned a specific user ID. Any files it creates cannot be read or written by other applications.

In addition, access to certain critical operations is restricted, and you must specifically ask for permission to use them in a file named Android-Manifest.xml. When the application is installed, the Package Manager either grants or doesn't grant the permissions based on certificates and, if necessary, user prompts. Here are some of the most common permissions you will need:

- INTERNET: Access the Internet.
- READ_CONTACTS: Read (but don't write) the user's contacts data.
- WRITE_CONTACTS: Write (but don't read) the user's contacts data.
- RECEIVE_SMS: Monitor incoming SMS (text) messages.
- ACCESS_COARSE_LOCATION: Use a coarse location provider such as cell towers or wifi.
- ACCESS_FINE_LOCATION: Use a more accurate location provider such as GPS.

For example, to monitor incoming SMS messages, you would specify this in the manifest file:

```
<manifest xmlns:android="http://schemas.android.com/apk/res/android"
    package="com.google.android.app.myapp" >
    <uses-permission android:name="android.permission.RECEIVE_SMS" />
</manifest>
```

Android can even restrict access to entire parts of the system. Using XML tags in AndroidManifest.xml, you can restrict who can start an activity, start or bind to a service, broadcast intents to a receiver, or access the data in a content provider. This kind of control is beyond the scope of this book, but if you want to learn more, read the online help for the Android security model.[7]

2.6 Fast-Forward >>

The rest of this book will use all the concepts introduced in this chapter. In Chapter 3, *Designing the User Interface*, on page 31, we'll use activities and life-cycle methods to define a sample application. Chapter 4, *Exploring 2D Graphics*, on page 61 will use some of the graphics classes in the Android native libraries. Media codecs will be explored in Chapter 5, *Multimedia*, on page 93, and content providers will be covered in Chapter 9, *Putting SQL to Work*, on page 171.

---

7. http://d.android.com/guide/topics/security/security.html

Part II

Android Basics

Chapter 3

Designing the User Interface

In Chapter 1, *Quick Start*, on page 3, we used the Android Eclipse plug-in to put together a simple "Hello, Android" program in a few minutes. In Part II, we'll create a more substantial example: a Sudoku game. By gradually adding features to the game, you'll learn about many aspects of Android programming. We'll start with the user interface.

You can find all the sample code used in this book at http://pragprog. com/titles/eband3. If you're reading the PDF version of this book, you can click the little gray rectangle before the code listings to download that file directly.

3.1 Introducing the Sudoku Example

Sudoku makes a great sample program for Android because the game itself is so simple. You have a grid of eighty-one tiles (nine across and nine down), and you try to fill them in with numbers so that each column, each row, and each of the three-by-three boxes contains the numbers 1 through 9 only once. When the game starts, some of the numbers (the *givens*) are already filled in. All the player has to do is supply the rest. A true Sudoku puzzle has only one unique solution.

Sudoku is usually played with pencil and paper, but computerized versions are quite popular too. With the paper version, it's easy to make a mistake early on, and when that happens, you have to go back and erase most of your work. In the Android version, you can change the tiles as often as you like without having to brush away all those pesky eraser shavings.

<hr />

Sudoku Trivia

Most people think Sudoku is some kind of ancient Japanese game, but it's not. Although similar puzzles can be traced to 19th-century French magazines, most experts credit retired American architect Howard Garns with the invention of modern Sudoku. Number Place, as it was known at the time, was first published in the United States in 1979 by Dell Magazines.

<hr />

Android Sudoku (see Figure 3.1, on the facing page) will also offer a few hints to take some of the grunt work out of puzzle solving. At one extreme, it could just solve the puzzle for you, but that wouldn't be any fun, would it? So, we have to balance the hints against the challenge and not make it too easy.

3.2 Designing by Declaration

User interfaces can be designed using one of two methods: procedural and declarative. *Procedural* simply means in code. For example, when you're programming a Swing application, you write Java code to create and manipulate all the user interface objects such as JFrame and JButton. Thus, Swing is procedural.

Declarative design, on the other hand, does not involve any code. When you're designing a simple web page, you use HTML, a markup language similar to XML that describes what you want to see on the page, not how you want to do it. HTML is declarative.

Android tries to straddle the gap between the procedural and declarative worlds by letting you create user interfaces in either style. You can stay almost entirely in Java code, or you can stay almost entirely in XML descriptors. If you look up the documentation for any Android user interface component, you'll see both the Java APIs and the corresponding declarative XML attributes that do the same thing.

Which should you use? Either way is valid, but Google's advice is to use declarative XML as much as possible. The XML code is often shorter and easier to understand than the corresponding Java code, and it's less likely to change in future versions.

Figure 3.1: THE SUDOKU EXAMPLE PROGRAM FOR ANDROID

Now let's see how we can use this information to create the Sudoku opening screen.

3.3 Creating the Opening Screen

We'll start with a skeleton Android program created by the Eclipse plug-in. Just as you did in Section 1.2, *Creating Your First Program*, on page 9, create a new "Hello, Android" project, but this time use the following values:

```
Project name: Sudoku
Build Target: Android 2.2
Application name: Sudoku
Package name: org.example.sudoku
Create Activity: Sudoku
Min SDK Version: 8
```

In a real program, of course, you would use your own names here. The package name is particularly important. Each application in the system must have a unique package name. Once you choose a package name, it's a little tricky to change it because it's used in so many places.

I like to keep the Android emulator window up all the time and run the program after every change, since it takes only a few seconds. If you do that and run the program now, you'll see a blank screen that just contains the words "Hello World, Sudoku." The first order of business is to change that into an opening screen for the game, with buttons to let the player start a new game, continue a previous one, get information about the game, and exit. So, what do we have to change to do that?

As discussed in Chapter 2, *Key Concepts*, on page 17, Android applications are a loose collection of activities, each of which define a user interface screen. When you create the Sudoku project, the Android plug-in makes a single activity for you in Sudoku.java:

Sudokuv0/src/org/example/sudoku/Sudoku.java

```
package org.example.sudoku;

import android.app.Activity;
import android.os.Bundle;

public class Sudoku extends Activity {
    /** Called when the activity is first created. */
    @Override
    public void onCreate(Bundle savedInstanceState) {
        super.onCreate(savedInstanceState);
        setContentView(R.layout.main);
    }
}
```

Android calls the onCreate() method of your activity to initialize it. The call to setContentView() fills in the contents of the activity's screen with an Android view widget.

We could have used several lines of Java code, and possibly another class or two, to define the user interface procedurally. But instead, the plug-in chose the declarative route, and we'll continue along those lines. In the previous code, R.layout.main is a resource identifier that refers to the main.xml file in the res/layout directory (see Figure 3.2, on the next page). main.xml declares the user interface in XML, so that's the file we need to modify. At runtime, Android parses and instantiates (*inflates*) the resource defined there and sets it as the view for the current activity.

Figure 3.2: INITIAL RESOURCES IN THE SUDOKU PROJECT

It's important to note that the R class is managed automatically by the Android Eclipse plug-in. When you put a file anywhere in the res directory, the plug-in notices the change and adds resource IDs in R.java in the gen directory for you. If you remove or change a resource file, R.java is kept in sync. If you bring up the file in the editor, it will look something like this:

Sudokuv0/gen/org/example/sudoku/R.java

```
/* AUTO-GENERATED FILE.  DO NOT MODIFY.
 *
 * This class was automatically generated by the
 * aapt tool from the resource data it found.  It
 * should not be modified by hand.
 */
```

```
package org.example.sudoku;

public final class R {
    public static final class attr {
    }
    public static final class drawable {
        public static final int icon=0x7f020000;
    }
    public static final class layout {
        public static final int main=0x7f030000;
    }
    public static final class string {
        public static final int app_name=0x7f040001;
        public static final int hello=0x7f040000;
    }
}
```

The hex numbers are just integers that the Android resource manager uses to load the real data, the strings, and the other assets that are compiled into your package. You don't need to worry about their values. Just keep in mind that they are handles that refer to the data, not the objects that contain the data. Those objects won't be inflated until they are needed. Note that almost every Android program, including the base Android framework itself, has an R class. See the online documentation on android.R for all the built-in resources you can use.[1]

So, now we know we have to modify main.xml. Let's dissect the original definition to see what we have to change. Double-click main.xml in Eclipse to open it. Depending on how you have Eclipse set up, you may see either a visual layout editor or an XML editor. In current versions of ADT, the visual layout editor isn't that useful, so click main.xml or the Source tab at the bottom to see the XML. The first line of main.xml is as follows:

```
<?xml version="1.0" encoding="utf-8"?>
```

All Android XML files start with this line. It just tells the compiler that the file is XML format, in UTF-8 encoding. UTF-8 is almost exactly like regular ASCII text, except it has escape codes for non-ASCII characters such as Japanese glyphs.

---

1. http://d.android.com/reference/android/R.html

Joe Asks...

Why Does Android Use XML? Isn't That Inefficient?

Android is optimized for mobile devices with limited memory and horsepower, so you may find it strange that it uses XML so pervasively. After all, XML is a verbose, human-readable format not known for its brevity or efficiency, right?

Although you see XML when writing your program, the Eclipse plug-in invokes the Android resource compiler, aapt, to preprocess the XML into a compressed binary format. It is this format, not the original XML text, that is stored on the device.

Next we see a reference to *<LinearLayout>*:

```
<LinearLayout
    xmlns:android="http://schemas.android.com/apk/res/android"
    android:orientation="vertical"
    android:layout_width="fill_parent"
    android:layout_height="fill_parent">
    <!-- ... -->
</LinearLayout>
```

A layout is a container for one or more child objects and a behavior to position them on the screen within the rectangle of the parent object. Here is a list of the most common layouts provided by Android:

- FrameLayout: Arranges its children so they all start at the top left of the screen. This is used for tabbed views and image switchers.
- LinearLayout: Arranges its children in a single column or row. This is the most common layout you will use.
- RelativeLayout: Arranges its children in relation to each other or to the parent. This is often used in forms.
- TableLayout: Arranges its children in rows and columns, similar to an HTML table.

Some parameters are common to all layouts:

xmlns:android="http://schemas.android.com/apk/res/android"
    Defines the XML namespace for Android. You should define this once, on the first XML tag in the file.

android:layout_width="fill_parent", android:layout_height="fill_parent"

> Takes up the entire width and height of the parent (in this case, the window). Possible values are fill_parent and wrap_content.

Inside the <*LinearLayout*> tag you'll find one child widget:

```
<TextView
    android:layout_width="fill_parent"
    android:layout_height="wrap_content"
    android:text="@string/hello" />
```

This defines a simple text label. Let's replace that with some different text and a few buttons. Here's our first attempt:

Sudokuv1/res/layout/main1.xml

```
<?xml version="1.0" encoding="utf-8"?>
<LinearLayout
    xmlns:android="http://schemas.android.com/apk/res/android"
    android:orientation="vertical"
    android:layout_width="fill_parent"
    android:layout_height="fill_parent">
    <TextView
        android:layout_width="fill_parent"
        android:layout_height="wrap_content"
        android:text="@string/main_title" />
    <Button
        android:id="@+id/continue_button"
        android:layout_width="fill_parent"
        android:layout_height="wrap_content"
        android:text="@string/continue_label" />
    <Button
        android:id="@+id/new_button"
        android:layout_width="fill_parent"
        android:layout_height="wrap_content"
        android:text="@string/new_game_label" />
    <Button
        android:id="@+id/about_button"
        android:layout_width="fill_parent"
        android:layout_height="wrap_content"
        android:text="@string/about_label" />
    <Button
        android:id="@+id/exit_button"
        android:layout_width="fill_parent"
        android:layout_height="wrap_content"
        android:text="@string/exit_label" />
</LinearLayout>
```

Note: If you see warnings in the editor about missing grammar constraints (DTD or XML schema), just ignore them or turn them off by opening the the Window > Preferences dialog and setting the XML > XML Files > Validation > Indicate when no grammar is specified option to Ignore. You may need to close all editor windows and do a Project > Clean command to completely get rid of the warnings.

In this example, we introduce a new syntax, @+id/*resid*. Instead of referring to a resource ID defined somewhere else, this is how you create a new resource ID to which others can refer. For example, @+id/about_button defines the ID for the About button, which we'll use later to make something happen when the user presses that button.

Also, instead of hard-coding English text into the layout file, we use the @string/*resid* syntax to refer to strings in the res/values/strings.xml file. You can have different versions of this and other resource files based on the locale or other parameters such as screen resolution and orientation.

Open the strings.xml file now, switch to the strings.xml tab at the bottom if necessary, and enter this:

Sudokuv1/res/values/strings.xml

```xml
<?xml version="1.0" encoding="utf-8"?>
<resources>
    <string name="app_name">Sudoku</string>
    <string name="main_title">Android Sudoku</string>
    <string name="continue_label">Continue</string>
    <string name="new_game_label">New Game</string>
    <string name="about_label">About</string>
    <string name="exit_label">Exit</string>
</resources>
```

Save strings.xml so Eclipse will rebuild the project. When you run the program now, you should see something like Figure 3.3, on the following page.

Note: Because this is the third edition of the book, I have a pretty good idea where most people run into trouble. This is it, right here. You've made a lot of changes, so do not be surprised if you get an error message instead of the opening screen. Don't panic; just skip ahead to Section 3.10, *Debugging*, on page 58 for advice on how to diagnose the problem. Usually a clue to the problem is waiting for you in the LogCat view. Sometimes selecting Project > Clean will fix things. If you're still stuck, drop by the book's web forum, and somebody would be happy to help you there.[2]

The current screen is readable, but it could use some cosmetic changes. Let's make the title text larger and centered, make the buttons smaller,

---

2. http://forums.pragprog.com/forums/152

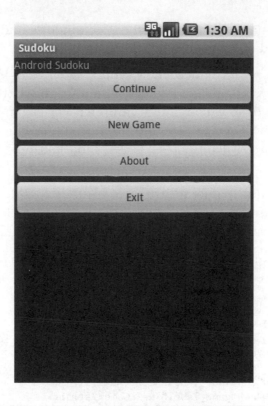

Figure 3.3: First version of the opening screen

and use a different background color. Here's the color definition, which you should put in res/values/colors.xml:

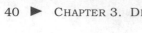

Sudokuv1/res/values/colors.xml

```xml
<?xml version="1.0" encoding="utf-8"?>
<resources>
    <color name="background">#3500ffff</color>
</resources>
```

And here's the new layout:

Sudokuv1/res/layout/main.xml

```xml
<?xml version="1.0" encoding="utf-8"?>
<LinearLayout
    xmlns:android="http://schemas.android.com/apk/res/android"
    android:background="@color/background"
    android:layout_height="fill_parent"
    android:layout_width="fill_parent"
    android:padding="30dip"
```

Figure 3.4: OPENING SCREEN WITH NEW LAYOUT

```
android:orientation="horizontal">
<LinearLayout
    android:orientation="vertical"
    android:layout_height="wrap_content"
    android:layout_width="fill_parent"
    android:layout_gravity="center">
    <TextView
        android:text="@string/main_title"
        android:layout_height="wrap_content"
        android:layout_width="wrap_content"
        android:layout_gravity="center"
        android:layout_marginBottom="25dip"
        android:textSize="24.5sp" />
    <Button
        android:id="@+id/continue_button"
        android:layout_width="fill_parent"
        android:layout_height="wrap_content"
        android:text="@string/continue_label" />
    <Button
        android:id="@+id/new_button"
```

```
                android:layout_width="fill_parent"
                android:layout_height="wrap_content"
                android:text="@string/new_game_label" />
            <Button
                android:id="@+id/about_button"
                android:layout_width="fill_parent"
                android:layout_height="wrap_content"
                android:text="@string/about_label" />
            <Button
                android:id="@+id/exit_button"
                android:layout_width="fill_parent"
                android:layout_height="wrap_content"
                android:text="@string/exit_label" />
    </LinearLayout>
</LinearLayout>
```

The result is shown in Figure 3.4, on the preceding page. This new screen looks good in portrait mode (when the screen is taller than it is wide), but how about landscape mode (wide-screen)? The user can switch modes at any time, for example, by flipping out the keyboard or turning the phone on its side, so you need to handle that.

3.4 Using Alternate Resources

As a test, try switching the emulator to landscape mode (Ctrl+F11 or the 7 or 9 key on the keypad, or Fn+Ctrl+F11 on the Mac). Oops! The Exit button runs off the bottom of the screen (see Figure 3.5, on the next page). How do we fix that?

You could try to adjust the layout so that it works with all orientations. Unfortunately, that's often not possible or leads to odd-looking screens. When that happens, you'll need to create a different layout for landscape mode. That's the approach we'll take here.

Create a file called res/layout-land/main.xml (note the -land suffix) that contains the following layout:

Sudokuv1/res/layout-land/main.xml

```xml
<?xml version="1.0" encoding="utf-8"?>
<LinearLayout
    xmlns:android="http://schemas.android.com/apk/res/android"
    android:background="@color/background"
    android:layout_height="fill_parent"
    android:layout_width="fill_parent"
    android:padding="15dip"
    android:orientation="horizontal">
```

Figure 3.5: IN LANDSCAPE MODE, WE CAN'T SEE THE EXIT BUTTON.

```
<LinearLayout
    android:orientation="vertical"
    android:layout_height="wrap_content"
    android:layout_width="fill_parent"
    android:layout_gravity="center"
    android:paddingLeft="20dip"
    android:paddingRight="20dip">
    <TextView
        android:text="@string/main_title"
        android:layout_height="wrap_content"
        android;layout_width="wrap_content"
        android:layout_gravity="center"
        android:layout_marginBottom="20dip"
        android:textSize="24.5sp" />
    <TableLayout
        android:layout_height="wrap_content"
        android:layout_width="wrap_content"
        android:layout_gravity="center"
        android:stretchColumns="*">
        <TableRow>
            <Button
                android:id="@+id/continue_button"
                android:text="@string/continue_label" />
            <Button
                android:id="@+id/new_button"
                android:text="@string/new_game_label" />
        </TableRow>
```

Figure 3.6: USING A LANDSCAPE-SPECIFIC LAYOUT LETS US SEE ALL THE BUTTONS.

```
    <TableRow>
        <Button
            android:id="@+id/about_button"
            android:text="@string/about_label" />
        <Button
            android:id="@+id/exit_button"
            android:text="@string/exit_label" />
    </TableRow>
    </TableLayout>
  </LinearLayout>
</LinearLayout>
```

This uses a TableLayout to create two columns of buttons. Now run the program again (see Figure 3.6). Even in landscape mode, all the buttons are visible.

You can use resource suffixes to specify alternate versions of any resources, not just the layout. For example, you can use them to provide localized text strings in different languages. Android's screen density support depends heavily on these resource suffixes (see Section 13.5, *All Screens Great and Small*, on page 264).

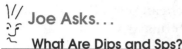

Joe Asks...

What Are Dips and Sps?

Historically, programmers always designed computer interfaces in terms of pixels. For example, you might make a field 300 pixels wide, allow 5 pixels of spacing between columns, and define icons 16-by-16 pixels in size. The problem is that if you run that program on new displays with more and more dots per inch (dpi), the user interface appears smaller and smaller. At some point, it becomes too hard to read.

Resolution-independent measurements help solve this problem. Android supports all the following units:

- **px** (pixels): Dots on the screen.

- **in** (inches): Size as measured by a ruler.

- **mm** (millimeters): Size as measured by a ruler.

- **pt** (points): 1/72 of an inch.

- **dp** (density-independent pixels): An abstract unit based on the density of the screen. On a display with 160 dots per inch, 1dp = 1px.

- **dip**: Synonym for dp, used more often in Google examples.

- **sp** (scale-independent pixels): Similar to **dp** but also scaled by the user's font size preference.

To make your interface scalable to any current and future type of display, I recommend you always use the **sp** unit for text sizes and the **dip** unit for everything else. You should also consider using vector graphics instead of bitmaps (see Chapter 4, *Exploring 2D Graphics*, on page 61).

3.5 Implementing an About Box

When the user selects the About button, meaning that either they touch it (if they have a touch screen) or they navigate to it with the D-pad (directional pad) or trackball and press the selection button, we want to pop up a window with some information about Sudoku.

After scrolling through the text, the user can press the Back button to dismiss the window. We can accomplish this in several ways:

- Define a new Activity, and start it.
- Use the AlertDialog class, and show it.
- Subclass Android's Dialog class, and show that.

For this example, let's define a new activity. Like the main Sudoku activity, the About activity will need a layout file. We will name it res/layout/about.xml:

Sudokuv1/res/layout/about.xml

```xml
<?xml version="1.0" encoding="utf-8"?>
<ScrollView
    xmlns:android="http://schemas.android.com/apk/res/android"
    android:layout_width="fill_parent"
    android:layout_height="fill_parent"
    android:padding="10dip">
    <TextView
        android:id="@+id/about_content"
        android:layout_width="wrap_content"
        android:layout_height="wrap_content"
        android:text="@string/about_text" />
</ScrollView>
```

We need only one version of this layout because it will look fine in both portrait and landscape modes.

Now add strings for the title of the About dialog box and the text it contains to res/values/strings.xml:

Sudokuv1/res/values/strings.xml

```xml
    <string name="about_title">About Android Sudoku</string>
    <string name="about_text">\
Sudoku is a logic-based number placement puzzle.
Starting with a partially completed 9x9 grid, the
objective is to fill the grid so that each
row, each column, and each of the 3x3 boxes
(also called <i>blocks</i>) contains the digits
1 to 9 exactly once.
</string>
```

Note how a string resource can contain simple HTML formatting and can span multiple lines. In case you're wondering, the backslash character (\) in about_text prevents an extra blank from appearing before the first word.

The About activity should be defined in About.java. All it needs to do is override onCreate() and call setContentView(). To create a new class in Eclipse, use File > New > Class. Specify the following:

```
Source folder: Sudoku/src
Package: org.example.sudoku
Name: About
```

Edit the class so it looks like this:

```
Sudokuv1/src/org/example/sudoku/About.java
```

```java
package org.example.sudoku;

import android.app.Activity;
import android.os.Bundle;

public class About extends Activity {
    @Override
    protected void onCreate(Bundle savedInstanceState) {
        super.onCreate(savedInstanceState);
        setContentView(R.layout.about);
    }
}
```

Next we need to wire all this up to the About button in the Sudoku class. Start by adding a few imports that we'll need to Sudoku.java:

```
Sudokuv1/src/org/example/sudoku/Sudoku.java
```

```java
import android.content.Intent;
import android.view.View;
import android.view.View.OnClickListener;
```

In the onCreate() method, add code to call findViewById() to look up an Android view given its resource ID, and add code to call setOnClickListener() to tell Android which object to tickle when the user touches or clicks the view:

```
Sudokuv1/src/org/example/sudoku/Sudoku.java
```

```java
@Override
public void onCreate(Bundle savedInstanceState) {
    super.onCreate(savedInstanceState);
    setContentView(R.layout.main);

    // Set up click listeners for all the buttons
    View continueButton = findViewById(R.id.continue_button);
```

```
continueButton.setOnClickListener(this);
View newButton = findViewById(R.id.new_button);
newButton.setOnClickListener(this);
View aboutButton = findViewById(R.id.about_button);
aboutButton.setOnClickListener(this);
View exitButton = findViewById(R.id.exit_button);
exitButton.setOnClickListener(this);
}
```

While we're in here, we do the same for all the buttons. Recall that constants like R.id.about_button are created by the Eclipse plug-in in R.java when it sees @+id/about_button in res/layout/main.xml.

The setOnClickListener() method needs to be passed an object that implements the OnClickListener Java interface. We're passing it the this variable, so we had better make the current class (Sudoku) implements that interface, or we'll get a compiler error. OnClickListener has one method in it called onClick(), so we have to add that method to our class as well:[3]

`Sudokuv1/src/org/example/sudoku/Sudoku.java`

```
public class Sudoku extends Activity implements OnClickListener {
    // ...
    public void onClick(View v) {
        switch (v.getId()) {
        case R.id.about_button:
            Intent i = new Intent(this, About.class);
            startActivity(i);
            break;
        // More buttons go here (if any) ...
        }
    }
}
```

To start an activity in Android, we first need to create an instance of the Intent class. There are two kinds of intents: *public* (named) intents that are registered with the system and can be called from any application and *private* (anonymous) intents that are used within a single application. For this example, we just need the latter kind. If you run the program and select the About button now, you will get an error (see Figure 3.7, on the next page). What happened?

We forgot one important step: every activity needs to be declared in AndroidManifest.xml. To do that, double-click the file to open it, switch

---

3. If you're a Java expert, you may be wondering why we didn't use an anonymous inner class to handle the clicks. You could, but according to the Android developers, every new inner class takes up an extra 1KB of memory.

Figure 3.7: MOUNTAIN VIEW, WE HAVE A PROBLEM

to XML mode if necessary by selecting the AndroidManifest.xml tab at the bottom, and add a new <activity> tag after the closing tag of the first one:

```
<activity android:name=".About"
      android:label="@string/about_title">
</activity>
```

Now if you save the manifest, run the program again, and select the About button, you should see something like Figure 3.8, on the following page. Press the Back button (Esc on the emulator) when you're done.

That looks OK, but wouldn't it be nice if we could see the initial screen behind the About text?

3.6 Applying a Theme

A *theme* is a collection of styles that override the look and feel of Android widgets. Themes were inspired by Cascading Style Sheets (CSS) used for web pages—they separate the content of a screen and its presentation or style. Android is packaged with several themes that you can

Figure 3.8: FIRST VERSION OF THE ABOUT SCREEN

reference by name,[4] or you can make up your own theme by subclassing existing ones and overriding their default values.

We could define our own custom theme in res/values/styles.xml, but for this example we'll just take advantage of a predefined one. To use it, open the AndroidManifest.xml editor again, and change the definition of the About activity so it has a theme property.

Sudokuv1/AndroidManifest.xml

```
<activity android:name=".About"
    android:label="@string/about_title"
    android:theme="@android:style/Theme.Dialog">
</activity>
```

---

4. See http://d.android.com/reference/android/R.style.html for symbols beginning with "Theme_."

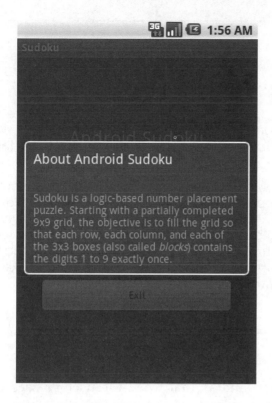

Figure 3.9: ABOUT SCREEN AFTER APPLYING THE DIALOG BOX THEME

The @android: prefix in front of the style name means this is a reference to a resource defined by Android, not one that is defined in your program.

Running the program again, the About box now looks like Figure 3.9.

Many programs need menus and options, so the next two sections will show you how to define them.

3.7 Adding a Menu

Android supports two kinds of menus. First, there is the menu you get when you press the physical Menu button. Second, there is a context menu that pops up when you press and hold your finger on the screen (or press and hold the trackball or the D-pad center button).

> \|/
> ⁻⁞⁻ **Joe Asks...**
> ⁻ <u>**Why Not Use an HTML View?**</u>
>
> Android supports embedding a web browser directly into a view through the WebView class (see Section 7.2, *Web with a View*, on page 126). So, why didn't we just use that for the About box?
>
> Actually, you could do it either way. A WebView would support far more sophisticated formatting than a simple TextView, but it does have some limitations (such as the inability to use a transparent background). Also, WebView is a heavyweight widget that will be slower and take more memory than TextView. For your own applications, use whichever one makes the most sense for your needs.

Let's do the first kind so that when the user presses the Menu key, they'll open a menu like the one in Figure 3.10, on the next page. First we need to define a few strings that we'll use later:

`Sudokuv1/res/values/strings.xml`

```
<string name="settings_label">Settings...</string>
<string name="settings_title">Sudoku settings</string>
<string name="settings_shortcut">s</string>
<string name="music_title">Music</string>
<string name="music_summary">Play background music</string>
<string name="hints_title">Hints</string>
<string name="hints_summary">Show hints during play</string>
```

Then we define the menu using XML in res/menu/menu.xml:

`Sudokuv1/res/menu/menu.xml`

```
<?xml version="1.0" encoding="utf-8"?>
<menu xmlns:android="http://schemas.android.com/apk/res/android">
   <item android:id="@+id/settings"
      android:title="@string/settings_label"
      android:alphabeticShortcut="@string/settings_shortcut" />
</menu>
```

Next we need to modify the Sudoku class to bring up the menu we just defined. To do that, we'll need a few more imports.

Figure 3.10: THE OPTIONS MENU CONTAINS ONE ITEM FOR CHANGING THE SETTINGS

Sudokuv1/src/org/example/sudoku/Sudoku.java

```java
import android.view.Menu;
import android.view.MenuInflater;
import android.view.MenuItem;
```

Then we override the Sudoku.onCreateOptionsMenu() method:

Sudokuv1/src/org/example/sudoku/Sudoku.java

```java
@Override
public boolean onCreateOptionsMenu(Menu menu) {
   super.onCreateOptionsMenu(menu);
   MenuInflater inflater = getMenuInflater();
   inflater.inflate(R.menu.menu, menu);
   return true;
}
```

getMenuInflater() returns an instance of MenuInflater that we use to read the menu definition from XML and turns it into a real view. When the user selects any menu item, onOptionsItemSelected() will be called. Here's the definition for that method:

Sudokuv1/src/org/example/sudoku/Sudoku.java

```java
@Override
public boolean onOptionsItemSelected(MenuItem item) {
   switch (item.getItemId()) {
   case R.id.settings:
      startActivity(new Intent(this, Prefs.class));
      return true;
   // More items go here (if any) ...
   }
   return false;
}
```

Prefs is a class that we're going to define that displays all our preferences and allows the user to change them.

3.8 Adding Settings

Android provides a nice facility for defining what all your program preferences are and how to display them using almost no code. You define the preferences in a resource file called res/xml/settings.xml:

Sudokuv1/res/xml/settings.xml

```xml
<?xml version="1.0" encoding="utf-8"?>
<PreferenceScreen
   xmlns:android="http://schemas.android.com/apk/res/android">
   <CheckBoxPreference
      android:key="music"
      android:title="@string/music_title"
      android:summary="@string/music_summary"
      android:defaultValue="true" />
   <CheckBoxPreference
      android:key="hints"
      android:title="@string/hints_title"
      android:summary="@string/hints_summary"
      android:defaultValue="true" />
</PreferenceScreen>
```

The Sudoku program has two settings: one for background music and one for displaying hints. The keys are constant strings that will be used under the covers in Android's preferences database.

Next define the Prefs class, and make it extend PreferenceActivity:

Sudokuv1/src/org/example/sudoku/Prefs.java

```java
package org.example.sudoku;

import android.os.Bundle;
import android.preference.PreferenceActivity;

public class Prefs extends PreferenceActivity {
   @Override
   protected void onCreate(Bundle savedInstanceState) {
      super.onCreate(savedInstanceState);
      addPreferencesFromResource(R.xml.settings);
   }
}
```

The addPreferencesFromResource() method reads the settings definition from XML and inflates it into views in the current activity. All the heavy lifting takes place in the PreferenceActivity class.

Figure 3.11: IT'S NOT MUCH TO LOOK AT, BUT WE GOT IT FOR FREE.

Don't forget to register the Prefs activity in AndroidManifest.xml:

Sudokuv1/AndroidManifest.xml
```
<activity android:name=".Prefs"
    android:label="@string/settings_title">
</activity>
```

Now rerun Sudoku, press the Menu key, select the Settings... item, and watch with amazement as the Sudoku settings page appears (see Figure 3.11). Try changing the values there and exiting the program, and then come back in and make sure they're all still set.

Code that reads the settings and does something with them will be discussed in a different chapter (Chapter 6, *Storing Local Data*, on page 109). For now let's move on to the New Game button.

3.9 Starting a New Game

If you've played any Sudoku games, you know that some are easy and some are maddeningly hard. So when the user selects New Game, we want to pop up a dialog box asking them to select between three difficulty levels. Selecting from a list of things is easy to do in Android.

First we'll need a few more strings in res/values/strings.xml:

Sudokuv1/res/values/strings.xml

```
<string name="new_game_title">Difficulty</string>
<string name="easy_label">Easy</string>
<string name="medium_label">Medium</string>
<string name="hard_label">Hard</string>
```

Create the list of difficulties as an array resource in res/values/arrays.xml:

Sudokuv1/res/values/arrays.xml

```
<?xml version="1.0" encoding="utf-8"?>
<resources>
   <array name="difficulty">
      <item>@string/easy_label</item>
      <item>@string/medium_label</item>
      <item>@string/hard_label</item>
   </array>
</resources>
```

We'll need a few more imports in the Sudoku class:

Sudokuv1/src/org/example/sudoku/Sudoku.java

```
import android.app.AlertDialog;
import android.content.DialogInterface;
import android.util.Log;
```

Add code in the switch statement of the onClick() method to handle clicking the New Game button:

Sudokuv1/src/org/example/sudoku/Sudoku.java

```
case R.id.new_button:
   openNewGameDialog();
   break;
```

The openNewGameDialog() method takes care of creating the user interface for the difficulty list.

Sudokuv1/src/org/example/sudoku/Sudoku.java

```
private static final String TAG = "Sudoku";

private void openNewGameDialog() {
   new AlertDialog.Builder(this)
```

Figure 3.12: DIFFICULTY SELECTION DIALOG BOX

```
        .setTitle(R.string.new_game_title)
        .setItems(R.array.difficulty,
         new DialogInterface.OnClickListener() {
             public void onClick(DialogInterface dialoginterface,
                   int i) {
                startGame(i);
             }
        })
        .show();
}

private void startGame(int i) {
    Log.d(TAG, "clicked on " + i);
    // Start game here...
}
```

The setItems() method takes two parameters: the resource ID of the item list and a listener that will be called when one of the items is selected.

When you run the program now and press New Game, you'll get the dialog box in Figure 3.12.

We're not actually going to start the game yet, so instead when you select a difficulty level, we just print a debug message using the Log.d() method, passing it a tag string and a message to print.

3.10 Debugging

The same techniques you use to debug programs on other platforms can be applied to Android. These include printing messages to the log and stepping through your program in a debugger.

Debugging with Log Messages

The Log class provides several static methods to print messages of various severity levels to the Android system log:

- Log.e(): Errors
- Log.w(): Warnings
- Log.i(): Information
- Log.d(): Debugging
- Log.v(): Verbose
- Log.wtf(): What a Terrible Failure[5]

Users will never see this log, but as a developer you can view it in a couple of ways. In Eclipse, open the LogCat view by selecting Window > Show View > Other... > Android > LogCat (see Figure 3.13, on the next page). The view can be filtered by severity or by the tag you specified on the method call.

If you're not using Eclipse, you can see the same output by running the adb logcat command.[6] I recommend you start this command in a separate window and leave it running all the time that the emulator is running. It won't interfere with any other monitors.

I can't stress enough how useful the Android log will be during development. Remember that error we saw earlier with the About box (Figure 3.7, on page 49)? If you had opened the LogCat view at that point, you would have seen this message: "ActivityNotFoundException: Unable to find explicit activity class...have you declared this activity in your AndroidManifest.xml?" It doesn't get any plainer than that.

---

5. Since Android 2.2.
6. http://d.android.com/guide/developing/tools/adb.html

Figure 3.13: DEBUGGING OUTPUT IN THE LOGCAT VIEW

Debugging with the Debugger

In addition to log messages, you can use the Eclipse debugger to set breakpoints, single step, and view the state of your program. First, enable your project for debugging by adding the android:debuggable="true" option in your AndroidManifest.xml file:[7]

`Sudokuv1/AndroidManifest.xml`

```
<application android:icon="@drawable/icon"
      android:label="@string/app_name"
      android:debuggable="true">
```

Then, simply right-click the project, and select Debug As > Android Application.

3.11 Exiting the Game

This game doesn't really need an Exit button, because the user can just press the Back key or the Home key to do something else. But I wanted to add one to show you how to terminate an activity.

---

7. This is optional if you're using the emulator but is required on a real device. Just remember to remove the option before releasing your code to the public.

Add this to the switch statement in the onClick() method:

Sudokuv1/src/org/example/sudoku/Sudoku.java

```
case R.id.exit_button:
    finish();
    break;
```

When the Exit button is selected, we call the finish() method. This shuts down the activity and returns control to the next activity on the Android application stack (usually the Home screen).

3.12 Fast-Forward >>

Whew, that was a lot to cover in one chapter! Starting from scratch, you learned how to use layout files to organize your user interface and how to use Android resources for text, colors, and more. You added controls such as buttons and text fields, applied themes to change the program's appearance, and even added menus and preferences for good measure.

Android is a complex system, but you don't have to know all of it to get started. When you need help, the hundreds of pages of reference material online go into more depth on all the classes and methods used here.[8] Another great source for tips and tricks is Planet Android.[9] And of course, if you get stuck, you can always drop by the discussion forum for this book.[10] The other readers and I will be happy to help you out.

In Chapter 4, *Exploring 2D Graphics*, on the next page, we will use Android's graphics API to draw the tiles for the Sudoku game.

---

8. To view the online documentation, open the docs subdirectory of your Android SDK install directory, or point your browser to http://d.android.com/guide.

9. http://www.planetandroid.com

10. http://forums.pragprog.com/forums/152

Chapter 4

Exploring 2D Graphics

So far, we've covered the basic concepts and philosophy of Android and how to create a simple user interface with a few buttons and a dialog box. You're really starting to get the hang of this Android thing. But something is missing...what is it? Oh yeah, the fun!

Good graphics can add a bit of fun and excitement to any application. Android puts one of the most powerful graphics libraries available on a mobile device at your fingertips. Actually, it puts two of them there: one for two-dimensional graphics and one for three-dimensional graphics.[1]

In this chapter, we will cover 2D graphics and apply that knowledge to implement the game part of our Sudoku example. Chapter 10, *3D Graphics in OpenGL*, on page 191 will cover 3D graphics using the OpenGL ES library.

4.1 Learning the Basics

Android provides a complete native two-dimensional graphics library in its android.graphics package. With a basic understanding of classes such as Color and Canvas, you'll be up and drawing in no time.

Color

Android colors are represented with four numbers, one each for alpha, red, green, and blue (ARGB). Each component can have 256 possible values, or 8 bits, so a color is typically packed into a 32-bit integer. For efficiency, Android code uses an integer instead of an instance of the Color class.

---

1. Functionality for four-dimensional graphics was considered for Android, but it was dropped because of a lack of time.

Red, green, and blue are self-explanatory, but alpha might not be. *Alpha* is a measure of transparency. The lowest value, 0, indicates the color is completely transparent. It doesn't really matter what the values for RGB are, if A is 0. The highest value, 255, indicates the color is completely opaque. Values in the middle are used for translucent, or semitransparent, colors. They let you see some of what is underneath the object being drawn in the foreground.

To create a color, you can use one of the static constants on the Color class, like this:

```
int color = Color.BLUE; // solid blue
```

or if you know the alpha, red, green, and blue numbers, you can use one of the static factory methods such as the following:

```
// Translucent purple
color = Color.argb(127, 255, 0, 255);
```

If possible, though, you're usually better off defining all your colors in an XML resource file. This lets you change them easily in one place later:

```
<?xml version="1.0" encoding="utf-8"?>
<resources>
   <color name="mycolor">#7fff00ff</color>
</resources>
```

You can reference colors by name in other XML files, as we did in Chapter 3, or you can use them in Java code like this:

```
color = getResources().getColor(R.color.mycolor);
```

The getResources() method returns the ResourceManager class for the current activity, and getColor() asks the manager to look up a color given a resource ID.

Paint

One of the Android native graphics library's most important classes is the Paint class. It holds the style, color, and other information needed to draw any graphics including bitmaps, text, and geometric shapes.

Normally when you paint something on the screen, you want to draw it in a solid color. You set that color with the Paint.setColor() method.

For example:

```
cPaint.setColor(Color.LTGRAY);
```

This uses the predefined color value for light gray.

Canvas

The Canvas class represents a surface on which you draw. Initially canvases start off devoid of any content, like blank transparencies for an overhead projector. Methods on the Canvas class let you draw lines, rectangles, circles, or other arbitrary graphics on the surface.

In Android, the display screen is taken up by an Activity, which hosts a View, which in turn hosts a Canvas. You get an opportunity to draw on that canvas by overriding the View.onDraw() method. The only parameter to onDraw() is a canvas on which you can draw.

Here's an example activity called Graphics, which contains a view called GraphicsView:

```java
public class Graphics extends Activity {
    @Override
    public void onCreate(Bundle savedInstanceState) {
        super.onCreate(savedInstanceState);
        setContentView(new GraphicsView(this));
    }

    static public class GraphicsView extends View {
        public GraphicsView(Context context) {
            super(context);
        }
        @Override
        protected void onDraw(Canvas canvas) {
            // Drawing commands go here
        }
    }
}
```

We're going to put some drawing commands into the onDraw() method in the next section.

Path

The Path class holds a set of vector-drawing commands such as lines, rectangles, and curves. Here's an example that defines a circular path:

```java
circle = new Path();
circle.addCircle(150, 150, 100, Direction.CW);
```

This defines a circle at position x=150, y=150, with a radius of 100 pixels. Now that we've defined the path, let's use it to draw the circle's outline plus some text around the inside:

```java
private static final String QUOTE = "Now is the time for all " +
        "good men to come to the aid of their country.";
    canvas.drawPath(circle, cPaint);
    canvas.drawTextOnPath(QUOTE, circle, 0, 20, tPaint);
```

Figure 4.1: DRAWING TEXT AROUND A CIRCLE

You can see the result in Figure 4.1. Since the circle was drawn in the clockwise direction (Direction.CW), the text is also drawn that way.

If you want to get really fancy, Android provides a number of PathEffect classes that let you do things such as apply a random permutation to a path, cause all the line segments along a path to be smoothed out with curves or broken up into segments, and create other effects.

Drawable

In Android, a Drawable class is used for a visual element like a bitmap or solid color that is intended for display only. You can combine drawables with other graphics, or you can use them in user interface widgets (for example, as the background for a button or view).

Drawables can take a variety of forms:

- *Bitmap*: A PNG or JPEG image.

- *NinePatch*: A stretchable PNG image, so named because originally it divided the image into nine sections. These are used for the background of resizable bitmap buttons.
- *Shape*: Vector-drawing commands, based on Path. This is sort of a poor man's SVG.
- *Layers*: A container for child drawables that draw on top of each other in a certain z-order.
- *States*: A container that shows one of its child drawables based on its state (a bit mask). One use is to set various selection and focus states for buttons.
- *Levels*: A container that shows only one of its child drawables based on its level (a range of integers). This could be used for a battery or signal strength gauge.
- *Scale*: A container for one child drawable that modifies its size based on the current level. One use might be a zoomable picture viewer.

Drawables are often defined in XML. Here's a common example where a drawable is defined to be a gradient from one color to another (in this case, white to gray). The angle specifies the direction of the gradient (270 degrees means top to bottom). This will be used for the background of a view:

```
<?xml version="1.0" encoding="utf-8"?>
<shape xmlns:android="http://schemas.android.com/apk/res/android">
    <gradient
        android:startColor="#FFFFFF"
        android:endColor="#808080"
        android:angle="270" />
</shape>
```

To use it, we could either refer to it in XML with the android:background= attribute or call the setBackgroundResource() method in the view's onCreate() method like this:

```
setBackgroundResource(R.drawable.background);
```

This gives our GraphicsView example a nice gradient background, as shown in Figure 4.2, on the following page.

Drawables should be placed in different directories depending on the screen density for which they are designed (see Section 3.4, *Using Alternate Resources*, on page 42).

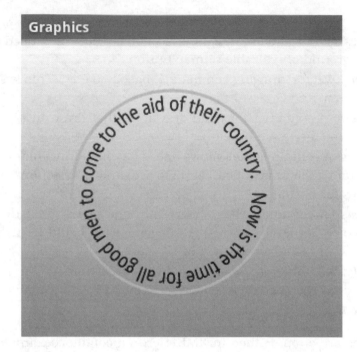

Figure 4.2: USING A GRADIENT BACKGROUND DEFINED IN XML

4.2 Adding Graphics to Sudoku

It's time to apply what we've learned to our Sudoku example. When we left it at the end of Chapter 3, the Sudoku game had an opening screen, an About dialog box, and a way to start a new game. But it was missing one very important part: the game! We'll use the native 2D graphics library to implement that part.

Starting the Game

First we need to fill in the code that starts the game. startGame() takes one parameter, the index of the difficulty name selected from the list.

Here's the new definition:

```
Sudokuv2/src/org/example/sudoku/Sudoku.java
private void startGame(int i) {
    Log.d(TAG, "clicked on " + i);
    Intent intent = new Intent(this, Game.class);
    intent.putExtra(Game.KEY_DIFFICULTY, i);
    startActivity(intent);
}
```

> **Sudoku Trivia**
>
> A few years after it was published in the United States, Number Place was picked up by the Japanese publisher Nikoli, who gave it the much cooler-sounding name Sudoku (which means "single number" in Japanese). From there it was exported around the world, and the rest is history. Sadly, Garns died in 1989 before getting a chance to see his creation become a worldwide sensation.

The game part of Sudoku will be another activity called Game, so we create a new intent to kick it off. We place the difficulty number in an extraData area provided in the intent, and then we call the startActivity() method to launch the new activity.

The extraData area is a map of key/value pairs that will be passed along to the intent. The keys are strings, and the values can be any primitive type, array of primitives, Bundle, or a subclass of Serializable or Parcelable.

Defining the Game Class

Here's the outline of the Game activity:

Sudokuv2/src/org/example/sudoku/Game.java

```
package org.example.sudoku;

import android.app.Activity;
import android.app.Dialog;
import android.os.Bundle;
import android.util.Log;
import android.view.Gravity;
import android.widget.Toast;

public class Game extends Activity {
    private static final String TAG = "Sudoku";

    public static final String KEY_DIFFICULTY =
        "org.example.sudoku.difficulty";
    public static final int DIFFICULTY_EASY = 0;
    public static final int DIFFICULTY_MEDIUM = 1;
    public static final int DIFFICULTY_HARD = 2;

    private int puzzle[];

    private PuzzleView puzzleView;
```

```
    @Override
    protected void onCreate(Bundle savedInstanceState) {
        super.onCreate(savedInstanceState);
        Log.d(TAG, "onCreate");

        int diff = getIntent().getIntExtra(KEY_DIFFICULTY,
                DIFFICULTY_EASY);
        puzzle = getPuzzle(diff);
        calculateUsedTiles();

        puzzleView = new PuzzleView(this);
        setContentView(puzzleView);
        puzzleView.requestFocus();
    }
    // ...
}
```

The onCreate() method fetches the difficulty number from the intent and selects a puzzle to play. Then it creates an instance of the PuzzleView class, setting the PuzzleView as the new contents of the view. Since this is a fully customized view, it was easier to do this in code than in XML.

The calculateUsedTiles() method, which is defined in Section 4.4, *The Rest of the Story*, on page 81, uses the rules of Sudoku to figure out, for each tile in the nine-by-nine grid, which numbers are not valid for the tile because they appear elsewhere in the horizontal or vertical direction or in the three-by-three subgrid.

This is an activity, so we need to register it in AndroidManifest.xml:

Sudokuv2/AndroidManifest.xml

```
<activity android:name=".Game"
        android:label="@string/game_title"/>
```

We also need to add a few more string resources to res/values/strings.xml:

Sudokuv2/res/values/strings.xml

```
<string name="game_title">Game</string>
<string name="no_moves_label">No moves</string>
<string name="keypad_title">Keypad</string>
```

Defining the PuzzleView Class

Next we need to define the PuzzleView class. Instead of using an XML layout, this time let's do it entirely in Java.

> ### What Size Is It Anyway?
>
> A common mistake made by new Android developers is to use the width and height of a view inside its constructor. When a view's constructor is called, Android doesn't know yet how big the view will be, so the sizes are set to zero. The real sizes are calculated during the layout stage, which occurs after construction but before anything is drawn. You can use the onSizeChanged() method to be notified of the values when they are known, or you can use the getWidth() and getHeight() methods later, such as in the onDraw() method.

Here's the outline:

`Sudokuv2/src/org/example/sudoku/PuzzleView.java`

```java
package org.example.sudoku;

import android.content.Context;
import android.graphics.Canvas;
import android.graphics.Paint;
import android.graphics.Rect;
import android.graphics.Paint.FontMetrics;
import android.graphics.Paint.Style;
import android.util.Log;
import android.view.KeyEvent;
import android.view.MotionEvent;
import android.view.View;
import android.view.animation.AnimationUtils;

public class PuzzleView extends View {
    private static final String TAG = "Sudoku";
    private final Game game;
    public PuzzleView(Context context) {
        super(context);
        this.game = (Game) context;
        setFocusable(true);
        setFocusableInTouchMode(true);
    }
    // ...
}
```

In the constructor we keep a reference to the Game class and set the option to allow user input in the view. Inside PuzzleView, we need to implement the onSizeChanged() method. This is called after the view is created and Android knows how big everything is.

> **Other Ways to Do It**
>
> When I was writing this example, I tried several different approaches such as using a button for each tile or declaring a grid of ImageView classes in XML. After many false starts, I found that the approach of having one view for the entire puzzle and drawing lines and numbers inside that proved to be the fastest and easiest way for this application.
>
> It does have its drawbacks, though, such as the need to draw the selection and explicitly handle keyboard and touch events. When designing your own program, I recommend trying standard widgets and views first and then falling back to custom drawing only if that doesn't work for you.

Sudokuv2/src/org/example/sudoku/PuzzleView.java

```java
private float width;     // width of one tile
private float height;    // height of one tile
private int selX;        // X index of selection
private int selY;        // Y index of selection
private final Rect selRect = new Rect();

@Override
protected void onSizeChanged(int w, int h, int oldw, int oldh) {
    width = w / 9f;
    height = h / 9f;
    getRect(selX, selY, selRect);
    Log.d(TAG, "onSizeChanged: width " + width + ", height "
        + height);
    super.onSizeChanged(w, h, oldw, oldh);
}
private void getRect(int x, int y, Rect rect) {
    rect.set((int) (x * width), (int) (y * height), (int) (x
        * width + width), (int) (y * height + height));
}
```

We use onSizeChanged() to calculate the size of each tile on the screen (1/9th of the total view width and height). Note this is a floating-point number, so it's possible that we could end up with a fractional number of pixels. selRect is a rectangle we'll use later to keep track of the selection cursor.

At this point we've created a view for the puzzle, and we know how big it is. The next step is to draw the grid lines that separate the tiles on the board.

Drawing the Board

Android calls a view's onDraw() method every time any part of the view needs to be updated. To simplify things, onDraw() pretends that you're re-creating the entire screen from scratch. In reality, you may be drawing only a small portion of the view as defined by the canvas's clip rectangle. Android takes care of doing the clipping for you.

Start by defining a few new colors to play with in res/values/colors.xml:

Sudokuv2/res/values/colors.xml

```
<color name="puzzle_background">#ffe6f0ff</color>
<color name="puzzle_hilite">#ffffffff</color>
<color name="puzzle_light">#64c6d4ef</color>
<color name="puzzle_dark">#6456648f</color>
<color name="puzzle_foreground">#ff000000</color>
<color name="puzzle_hint_0">#64ff0000</color>
<color name="puzzle_hint_1">#6400ff80</color>
<color name="puzzle_hint_2">#2000ff80</color>
<color name="puzzle_selected">#64ff8000</color>
```

Here's the basic outline for onDraw():

Sudokuv2/src/org/example/sudoku/PuzzleView.java

```
@Override
protected void onDraw(Canvas canvas) {
    // Draw the background...
    Paint background = new Paint();
    background.setColor(getResources().getColor(
        R.color.puzzle_background));
    canvas.drawRect(0, 0, getWidth(), getHeight(), background);

    // Draw the board...
    // Draw the numbers...
    // Draw the hints...
    // Draw the selection...
}
```

The first parameter is the Canvas on which to draw. In this code, we're just drawing a background for the puzzle using the puzzle_background color.

Now let's add the code to draw the grid lines for the board:

```
// Draw the board...
// Define colors for the grid lines
Paint dark = new Paint();
dark.setColor(getResources().getColor(R.color.puzzle_dark));

Paint hilite = new Paint();
hilite.setColor(getResources().getColor(R.color.puzzle_hilite));

Paint light = new Paint();
light.setColor(getResources().getColor(R.color.puzzle_light));

// Draw the minor grid lines
for (int i = 0; i < 9; i++) {
   canvas.drawLine(0, i * height, getWidth(), i * height,
        light);
   canvas.drawLine(0, i * height + 1, getWidth(), i * height
        + 1, hilite);
   canvas.drawLine(i * width, 0, i * width, getHeight(),
        light);
   canvas.drawLine(i * width + 1, 0, i * width + 1,
        getHeight(), hilite);
}

// Draw the major grid lines
for (int i = 0; i < 9; i++) {
   if (i % 3 != 0)
      continue;
   canvas.drawLine(0, i * height, getWidth(), i * height,
        dark);
   canvas.drawLine(0, i * height + 1, getWidth(), i * height
        + 1, hilite);
   canvas.drawLine(i * width, 0, i * width, getHeight(), dark);
   canvas.drawLine(i * width + 1, 0, i * width + 1,
        getHeight(), hilite);
}
```

The code uses three different colors for the grid lines: a light color between each tile, a dark color between the three-by-three blocks, and a highlight color drawn on the edge of each tile to make them look like they have a little depth. The order in which the lines are drawn is important, since lines drawn later will be drawn over the top of earlier lines. You can see what this will look like in Figure 4.3, on the next page. Next, we need some numbers to go inside those lines.

Figure 4.3: DRAWING THE GRID LINES WITH THREE SHADES OF GRAY FOR AN EMBOSSED EFFECT

Drawing the Numbers

The following code draws the puzzle numbers on top of the tiles. The tricky part here is getting each number positioned and sized so it goes in the exact center of its tile.

Sudokuv2/src/org/example/sudoku/PuzzleView.java

```java
// Draw the numbers...
// Define color and style for numbers
Paint foreground = new Paint(Paint.ANTI_ALIAS_FLAG);
foreground.setColor(getResources().getColor(
    R.color.puzzle_foreground));
foreground.setStyle(Style.FILL);
foreground.setTextSize(height * 0.75f);
foreground.setTextScaleX(width / height);
foreground.setTextAlign(Paint.Align.CENTER);
```

Figure 4.4: CENTERING THE NUMBERS INSIDE THE TILES

```
// Draw the number in the center of the tile
FontMetrics fm = foreground.getFontMetrics();
// Centering in X: use alignment (and X at midpoint)
float x = width / 2;
// Centering in Y: measure ascent/descent first
float y = height / 2 - (fm.ascent + fm.descent) / 2;
for (int i = 0; i < 9; i++) {
   for (int j = 0; j < 9; j++) {
      canvas.drawText(this.game.getTileString(i, j), i
            * width + x, j * height + y, foreground);
   }
}
```

We call the getTileString() method (defined in Section 4.4, *The Rest of the Story*, on page 81) to find out what numbers to display. To calculate the size of the numbers, we set the font height to three-fourths the height of the tile, and we set the aspect ratio to be the same as the tile's aspect ratio. We can't use absolute pixel or point sizes because we want the program to work at any resolution.

To determine the position of each number, we center it in both the x and y dimensions. The x direction is easy—just divide the tile width by 2. But for the y direction, we have to adjust the starting position downward a little so that the midpoint of the tile will be the midpoint of the number instead of its baseline. We use the graphics library's FontMetrics class to tell how much vertical space the letter will take in total, and then we divide that in half to get the adjustment. You can see the results in Figure 4.4, on the preceding page.

That takes care of displaying the puzzle's starting numbers (the givens). The next step is to allow the player to enter their guesses for all the blank spaces.

4.3 Handling Input

One difference in Android programming—as opposed to, say, iPhone programming—is that Android phones come in many shapes and sizes and have a variety of input methods. They might have a keyboard, a D-pad, a touch screen, a trackball, or some combination of these.

A good Android program, therefore, needs to be ready to support whatever input hardware is available, just like it needs to be ready to support any screen resolution.

Defining and Updating the Selection

First we're going to implement a little cursor that shows the player which tile is currently selected. The selected tile is the one that will be modified when the player enters a number. This code will draw the selection in onDraw():

Sudokuv2/src/org/example/sudoku/PuzzleView.java

```
// Draw the selection...
Log.d(TAG, "selRect=" + selRect);
Paint selected = new Paint();
selected.setColor(getResources().getColor(
     R.color.puzzle_selected));
canvas.drawRect(selRect, selected);
```

We use the selection rectangle calculated earlier in onSizeChanged() to draw an alpha-blended color on top of the selected tile.

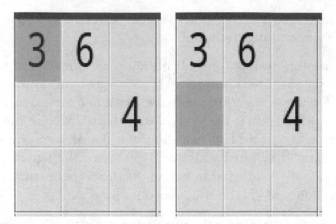

Figure 4.5: DRAWING AND MOVING THE SELECTION

Next we provide a way to move the selection by overriding the onKey-Down() method:

Sudokuv2/src/org/example/sudoku/PuzzleView.java

```java
@Override
public boolean onKeyDown(int keyCode, KeyEvent event) {
    Log.d(TAG, "onKeyDown: keycode=" + keyCode + ", event="
            + event);
    switch (keyCode) {
    case KeyEvent.KEYCODE_DPAD_UP:
        select(selX, selY - 1);
        break;
    case KeyEvent.KEYCODE_DPAD_DOWN:
        select(selX, selY + 1);
        break;
    case KeyEvent.KEYCODE_DPAD_LEFT:
        select(selX - 1, selY);
        break;
    case KeyEvent.KEYCODE_DPAD_RIGHT:
        select(selX + 1, selY);
        break;
    default:
        return super.onKeyDown(keyCode, event);
    }
    return true;
}
```

If the user has a directional pad (D-pad) and they press the up, down, left, or right button, we call select() to move the selection cursor in that direction.

How about a trackball? We could override the onTrackballEvent() method, but it turns out that if you don't handle trackball events, Android will translate them into D-pad events automatically. Therefore, we can leave it out for this example.

Inside the select() method, we calculate the new x and y coordinates of the selection and then use getRect() again to calculate the new selection rectangle.

Sudokuv2/src/org/example/sudoku/PuzzleView.java

```java
private void select(int x, int y) {
    invalidate(selRect);
    selX = Math.min(Math.max(x, 0), 8);
    selY = Math.min(Math.max(y, 0), 8);
    getRect(selX, selY, selRect);
    invalidate(selRect);
}
```

Notice the two calls to invalidate(). The first one tells Android that the area covered by the old selection rectangle (on the left of Figure 4.5, on the facing page) needs to be redrawn. The second invalidate() call says that the new selection area (on the right of the figure) needs to be redrawn too. We don't actually draw anything here.

This is an important point: never call any drawing functions except in the onDraw() method. Instead, you use the invalidate() method to mark rectangles as *dirty*. The window manager will combine all the dirty rectangles at some point in the future and call onDraw() again for you. The dirty rectangles become the clip region, so screen updates are optimized to only those areas that change.

Now let's provide a way for the player to enter a new number on the selected tile.

Entering Numbers

To handle keyboard input, we just add a few more cases to the onKeyDown() method for the numbers 0 through 9 (0 or space means erase the number).

> **Optimizing Refreshes**
>
> In an earlier version of this example, I invalidated the entire screen whenever the cursor was moved. Thus, on every key press, the whole puzzle had to be redrawn. This caused it to lag noticeably. Switching the code to invalidate only the smallest rectangles that changed made it run much faster.

Sudokuv2/src/org/example/sudoku/PuzzleView.java

```java
case KeyEvent.KEYCODE_0:
case KeyEvent.KEYCODE_SPACE: setSelectedTile(0); break;
case KeyEvent.KEYCODE_1:      setSelectedTile(1); break;
case KeyEvent.KEYCODE_2:      setSelectedTile(2); break;
case KeyEvent.KEYCODE_3:      setSelectedTile(3); break;
case KeyEvent.KEYCODE_4:      setSelectedTile(4); break;
case KeyEvent.KEYCODE_5:      setSelectedTile(5); break;
case KeyEvent.KEYCODE_6:      setSelectedTile(6); break;
case KeyEvent.KEYCODE_7:      setSelectedTile(7); break;
case KeyEvent.KEYCODE_8:      setSelectedTile(8); break;
case KeyEvent.KEYCODE_9:      setSelectedTile(9); break;
case KeyEvent.KEYCODE_ENTER:
case KeyEvent.KEYCODE_DPAD_CENTER:
    game.showKeypadOrError(selX, selY);
    break;
```

To support the D-pad, we check for the Enter or center D-pad button in onKeyDown() and have it pop up a keypad that lets the user select which number to place.

For touch, we override the onTouchEvent() method and show the same keypad, which will be defined later:

Sudokuv2/src/org/example/sudoku/PuzzleView.java

```java
@Override
public boolean onTouchEvent(MotionEvent event) {
    if (event.getAction() != MotionEvent.ACTION_DOWN)
        return super.onTouchEvent(event);

    select((int) (event.getX() / width),
        (int) (event.getY() / height));
    game.showKeypadOrError(selX, selY);
    Log.d(TAG, "onTouchEvent: x " + selX + ", y " + selY);
    return true;
}
```

Ultimately, all roads will lead back to a call to setSelectedTile() to change the number on a tile:

Sudokuv2/src/org/example/sudoku/PuzzleView.java

```
public void setSelectedTile(int tile) {
   if (game.setTileIfValid(selX, selY, tile)) {
      invalidate();// may change hints
   } else {
      // Number is not valid for this tile
      Log.d(TAG, "setSelectedTile: invalid: " + tile);
   }
}
```

The showKeypadOrError() and setTileIfValid() methods will be defined in Section 4.4, *The Rest of the Story*, on page 81.

Note the call to invalidate() with no parameters. That marks the whole screen as dirty, which violates my own advice earlier! However, in this case, it's necessary because any new numbers added or removed might change the hints that we are about to implement in the next section.

Adding Hints

How can we help the player out a little without solving the whole puzzle for them? How about if we draw the background of each tile differently depending on how many possible moves it has. Add this to onDraw() before drawing the selection:

Sudokuv2/src/org/example/sudoku/PuzzleView.java

```
// Draw the hints...
// Pick a hint color based on #moves left
Paint hint = new Paint();
int c[] = { getResources().getColor(R.color.puzzle_hint_0),
      getResources().getColor(R.color.puzzle_hint_1),
      getResources().getColor(R.color.puzzle_hint_2), };
Rect r = new Rect();
for (int i = 0; i < 9; i++) {
   for (int j = 0; j < 9; j++) {
      int movesleft = 9 - game.getUsedTiles(i, j).length;
      if (movesleft < c.length) {
         getRect(i, j, r);
         hint.setColor(c[movesleft]);
         canvas.drawRect(r, hint);
      }
   }
}
```

Figure 4.6: Tiles are highlighted based on how many possible values the tile can have.

We use three states for zero, one, and two possible moves. If there are zero moves, that means the player has done something wrong and needs to backtrack.

The result will look like Figure 4.6. Can you spot the mistake(s) made by the player?[2]

Shaking Things Up

What if the user tries to enter an obviously invalid number, such as a number that already appears in the three-by-three block? Just for fun, let's make the screen wiggle back and forth when they do that. First we add a call to the invalid number case in setSelectedTile().

---

2. The two numbers on the bottom row's middle block are wrong.

Sudokuv2/src/org/example/sudoku/PuzzleView.java

```
Log.d(TAG, "setSelectedTile: invalid: " + tile);
startAnimation(AnimationUtils.loadAnimation(game,
    R.anim.shake));
```

This loads and runs a resource called R.anim.shake, defined in res/anim/shake.xml, that shakes the screen for 1,000 milliseconds (1 second) by 10 pixels from side to side.

Sudokuv2/res/anim/shake.xml

```
<?xml version="1.0" encoding="utf-8"?>
<translate
    xmlns:android="http://schemas.android.com/apk/res/android"
    android:fromXDelta="0"
    android:toXDelta="10"
    android:duration="1000"
    android:interpolator="@anim/cycle_7" />
```

The number of times to run the animation and the velocity and acceleration of the animation are controlled by an animation interpolator defined in XML.

Sudokuv2/res/anim/cycle_7.xml

```
<?xml version="1.0" encoding="utf-8"?>
<cycleInterpolator
    xmlns:android="http://schemas.android.com/apk/res/android"
    android:cycles="7" />
```

This particular one will cause the animation to be repeated seven times.

4.4 The Rest of the Story

Now let's go back and tie up a few loose ends, starting with the Keypad class. These pieces are necessary for the program to compile and operate but have nothing to do with graphics. Feel free to skip ahead to Section 4.5, *Making More Improvements*, on page 91 if you like.

Creating the Keypad

The keypad is handy for phones that don't have keyboards. It displays a grid of the numbers 1 through 9 in an activity that appears on top of the puzzle. The whole purpose of the keypad dialog box is to return a number selected by the player.

Here's the user interface layout from res/layout/keypad.xml:

Sudokuv2/res/layout/keypad.xml

```xml
<?xml version="1.0" encoding="utf-8"?>
<TableLayout
    xmlns:android="http://schemas.android.com/apk/res/android"
    android:id="@+id/keypad"
    android:orientation="vertical"
    android:layout_width="wrap_content"
    android:layout_height="wrap_content"
    android:stretchColumns="*">
    <TableRow>
        <Button android:id="@+id/keypad_1"
            android:text="1">
        </Button>
        <Button android:id="@+id/keypad_2"
            android:text="2">
        </Button>
        <Button android:id="@+id/keypad_3"
            android:text="3">
        </Button>
    </TableRow>
    <TableRow>
        <Button android:id="@+id/keypad_4"
            android:text="4">
        </Button>
        <Button android:id="@+id/keypad_5"
            android:text="5">
        </Button>
        <Button android:id="@+id/keypad_6"
            android:text="6">
        </Button>
    </TableRow>
    <TableRow>
        <Button android:id="@+id/keypad_7"
            android:text="7">
        </Button>
        <Button android:id="@+id/keypad_8"
            android:text="8">
        </Button>
        <Button android:id="@+id/keypad_9"
            android:text="9">
        </Button>
    </TableRow>
</TableLayout>
```

Next let's define the Keypad class.

Here's the outline:

Sudokuv2/src/org/example/sudoku/Keypad.java

```java
package org.example.sudoku;

import android.app.Dialog;
import android.content.Context;
import android.os.Bundle;
import android.view.KeyEvent;
import android.view.View;

public class Keypad extends Dialog {

    protected static final String TAG = "Sudoku";

    private final View keys[] = new View[9];
    private View keypad;

    private final int useds[];
    private final PuzzleView puzzleView;

    public Keypad(Context context, int useds[], PuzzleView puzzleView) {
        super(context);
        this.useds = useds;
        this.puzzleView = puzzleView;
    }

    @Override
    protected void onCreate(Bundle savedInstanceState) {
        super.onCreate(savedInstanceState);

        setTitle(R.string.keypad_title);
        setContentView(R.layout.keypad);
        findViews();
        for (int element : useds) {
            if (element != 0)
                keys[element - 1].setVisibility(View.INVISIBLE);
        }
        setListeners();
    }

    // ...
}
```

If a particular number is not valid (for example, the same number already appears in that row), then we make the number invisible in the grid so the player can't select it (see Figure 4.7, on the following page).

Figure 4.7: INVALID VALUES ARE HIDDEN IN THE KEYPAD VIEW.

The findViews() method fetches and saves the views for all the keypad keys and the main keypad window:

`Sudokuv2/src/org/example/sudoku/Keypad.java`

```java
private void findViews() {
    keypad = findViewById(R.id.keypad);
    keys[0] = findViewById(R.id.keypad_1);
    keys[1] = findViewById(R.id.keypad_2);
    keys[2] = findViewById(R.id.keypad_3);
    keys[3] = findViewById(R.id.keypad_4);
    keys[4] = findViewById(R.id.keypad_5);
    keys[5] = findViewById(R.id.keypad_6);
    keys[6] = findViewById(R.id.keypad_7);
    keys[7] = findViewById(R.id.keypad_8);
    keys[8] = findViewById(R.id.keypad_9);
}
```

setListeners() loops through all the keypad keys and sets a listener for each one. It also sets a listener for the main keypad window.

Sudokuv2/src/org/example/sudoku/Keypad.java

```java
private void setListeners() {
    for (int i = 0; i < keys.length; i++) {
        final int t = i + 1;
        keys[i].setOnClickListener(new View.OnClickListener(){
            public void onClick(View v) {
                returnResult(t);
            }});
    }
    keypad.setOnClickListener(new View.OnClickListener(){
        public void onClick(View v) {
            returnResult(0);
        }});
}
```

When the player selects one of the buttons on the keypad, it calls the returnResult() method with the number for that button. If the player selects a place that doesn't have a button, then returnResult() is called with a zero, indicating the tile should be erased.

onKeyDown() is called when the player uses the keyboard to enter a number:

Sudokuv2/src/org/example/sudoku/Keypad.java

```java
@Override
public boolean onKeyDown(int keyCode, KeyEvent event) {
    int tile = 0;
    switch (keyCode) {
    case KeyEvent.KEYCODE_0:
    case KeyEvent.KEYCODE_SPACE: tile = 0; break;
    case KeyEvent.KEYCODE_1:     tile = 1; break;
    case KeyEvent.KEYCODE_2:     tile = 2; break;
    case KeyEvent.KEYCODE_3:     tile = 3; break;
    case KeyEvent.KEYCODE_4:     tile = 4; break;
    case KeyEvent.KEYCODE_5:     tile = 5; break;
    case KeyEvent.KEYCODE_6:     tile = 6; break;
    case KeyEvent.KEYCODE_7:     tile = 7; break;
    case KeyEvent.KEYCODE_8:     tile = 8; break;
    case KeyEvent.KEYCODE_9:     tile = 9; break;
    default:
        return super.onKeyDown(keyCode, event);
    }
    if (isValid(tile)) {
        returnResult(tile);
    }
    return true;

}
```

If the number is valid for the current tile, then it calls returnResult();
otherwise, the keystroke is ignored.

The isValid() method checks to see whether the given number is valid for
the current position:

Sudokuv2/src/org/example/sudoku/Keypad.java

```java
private boolean isValid(int tile) {
    for (int t : useds) {
        if (tile == t)
            return false;
    }
    return true;
}
```

If it appears in the useds array, then it's not valid because the same
number is already used in the current row, column, or block.

The returnResult() method is called to return the number selected to the
calling activity:

Sudokuv2/src/org/example/sudoku/Keypad.java

```java
private void returnResult(int tile) {
    puzzleView.setSelectedTile(tile);
    dismiss();
}
```

We call the PuzzleView.setSelectedTile() method to change the puzzle's current tile. The dismiss call terminates the Keypad dialog box. Now that we
have the activity, let's call it in the Game class and retrieve the result:

Sudokuv2/src/org/example/sudoku/Game.java

```java
protected void showKeypadOrError(int x, int y) {
    int tiles[] = getUsedTiles(x, y);
    if (tiles.length == 9) {
        Toast toast = Toast.makeText(this,
                R.string.no_moves_label, Toast.LENGTH_SHORT);
        toast.setGravity(Gravity.CENTER, 0, 0);
        toast.show();
    } else {
        Log.d(TAG, "showKeypad: used=" + toPuzzleString(tiles));
        Dialog v = new Keypad(this, tiles, puzzleView);
        v.show();
    }
}
```

To decide which numbers are possible, we pass the Keypad a string in
the extraData area containing all the numbers that have already been
used.

Implementing the Game Logic

The rest of the code in Game.java concerns itself with the logic of the game, in particular with determining which are and aren't valid moves according to the rules. The setTileIfValid() method is a key part of that. Given an x and y position and the new value of a tile, it changes the tile only if the value provided is valid.

Sudokuv2/src/org/example/sudoku/Game.java

```java
protected boolean setTileIfValid(int x, int y, int value) {
    int tiles[] = getUsedTiles(x, y);
    if (value != 0) {
        for (int tile : tiles) {
            if (tile == value)
                return false;
        }
    }
    setTile(x, y, value);
    calculateUsedTiles();
    return true;
}
```

To detect valid moves, we create an array for every tile in the grid. For each position, it keeps a list of filled-in tiles that are currently visible from that position. If a number appears on the list, then it won't be valid for the current tile. The getUsedTiles() method retrieves that list for a given tile position:

Sudokuv2/src/org/example/sudoku/Game.java

```java
private final int used[][][] = new int[9][9][];

protected int[] getUsedTiles(int x, int y) {
    return used[x][y];
}
```

The array of used tiles is somewhat expensive to compute, so we cache the array and recalculate it only when necessary by calling calculateUsedTiles():

Sudokuv2/src/org/example/sudoku/Game.java

```java
private void calculateUsedTiles() {
    for (int x = 0; x < 9; x++) {
        for (int y = 0; y < 9; y++) {
            used[x][y] = calculateUsedTiles(x, y);
            // Log.d(TAG, "used[" + x + "][" + y + "] = "
            // + toPuzzleString(used[x][y]));
        }
    }
}
```

calculateUsedTiles() simply calls calculateUsedTiles(x, y) on every position in the nine-by-nine grid:

Sudokuv2/src/org/example/sudoku/Game.java

```
Line 1    private int[] calculateUsedTiles(int x, int y) {
            int c[] = new int[9];
            // horizontal
            for (int i = 0; i < 9; i++) {
    5           if (i == x)
                    continue;
                int t = getTile(i, y);
                if (t != 0)
                    c[t - 1] = t;
    10      }
            // vertical
            for (int i = 0; i < 9; i++) {
                if (i == y)
                    continue;
    15          int t = getTile(x, i);
                if (t != 0)
                    c[t - 1] = t;
            }
            // same cell block
    20      int startx = (x / 3) * 3;
            int starty = (y / 3) * 3;
            for (int i = startx; i < startx + 3; i++) {
                for (int j = starty; j < starty + 3; j++) {
                    if (i == x && j == y)
    25                  continue;
                    int t = getTile(i, j);
                    if (t != 0)
                        c[t - 1] = t;
                }
    30      }
            // compress
            int nused = 0;
            for (int t : c) {
                if (t != 0)
    35              nused++;
            }
            int c1[] = new int[nused];
            nused = 0;
            for (int t : c) {
    40          if (t != 0)
                    c1[nused++] = t;
            }
            return c1;
        }
```

We start with an array of nine zeros. On line 4, we check all the tiles on the same horizontal row as the current tile, and if a tile is occupied, we stuff its number into the array.

On line 12, we do the same thing for all the tiles on the same vertical column, and on line 20, we do the same for tiles in the three-by-three block.

The last step, starting at line 32, is to compress the zeros out of the array before we return it. We do this so that array.length can be used to quickly tell how many used tiles are visible from the current position.

Miscellaneous

Here are a few other utility functions and variables that round out the implementation. easyPuzzle, mediumPuzzle, and hardPuzzle are our hard-coded Sudoku puzzles for easy, medium, and hard difficulty levels, respectively.

Sudokuv2/src/org/example/sudoku/Game.java

```
private final String easyPuzzle =
    "360000000004230800000004200" +
    "070460003820000014500013020" +
    "001900000070483000000000045";
private final String mediumPuzzle =
    "650000070000506000014000005" +
    "007009000002314700000700800" +
    "500000630000201000030000097";
private final String hardPuzzle =
    "009000000080605020501078000" +
    "000000700706040102004000000" +
    "000720903090301080000000600";
```

getPuzzle() simply takes a difficulty level and returns a puzzle:

Sudokuv2/src/org/example/sudoku/Game.java

```
private int[] getPuzzle(int diff) {
    String puz;
    // TODO: Continue last game
    switch (diff) {
    case DIFFICULTY_HARD:
        puz = hardPuzzle;
        break;
    case DIFFICULTY_MEDIUM:
        puz = mediumPuzzle;
        break;
    case DIFFICULTY_EASY:
    default:
        puz = easyPuzzle;
        break;
    }
    return fromPuzzleString(puz);
}
```

Later we'll change getPuzzle() to implement a continue function.

toPuzzleString() converts a puzzle from an array of integers to a string. fromPuzzleString() does the opposite.

Sudokuv2/src/org/example/sudoku/Game.java

```java
static private String toPuzzleString(int[] puz) {
    StringBuilder buf = new StringBuilder();
    for (int element : puz) {
        buf.append(element);
    }
    return buf.toString();
}

static protected int[] fromPuzzleString(String string) {
    int[] puz = new int[string.length()];
    for (int i = 0; i < puz.length; i++) {
        puz[i] = string.charAt(i) - '0';
    }
    return puz;
}
```

The getTile() method takes x and y positions and returns the number currently occupying that tile. If it's zero, that means the tile is blank.

Sudokuv2/src/org/example/sudoku/Game.java

```java
private int getTile(int x, int y) {
    return puzzle[y * 9 + x];
}

private void setTile(int x, int y, int value) {
    puzzle[y * 9 + x] = value;
}
```

getTileString() is used when displaying a tile. It will return either a string with the value of the tile or an empty string if the tile is blank.

Sudokuv2/src/org/example/sudoku/Game.java

```java
protected String getTileString(int x, int y) {
    int v = getTile(x, y);
    if (v == 0)
        return "";
    else
        return String.valueOf(v);
}
```

Once all these pieces are in place, you should have a playable Sudoku game. Give it a try to verify it works. As with any code, though, there is room for improvement.

4.5 Making More Improvements

Although the code presented in this chapter performs acceptably for a Sudoku game, more complex programs will likely need to be more carefully written in order to squeeze the last drop of performance out of the device. In particular, the onDraw() method is a very performance-critical piece of code, so it's best to do as little as possible there.

Here are some ideas for speeding up this method:

- If possible, avoid doing any object allocations in the method onDraw().
- Prefetch things such as color constants elsewhere (for example, in the view's constructor).
- Create your Paint objects up front, and just use existing instances in onDraw().
- For values used multiple times, such as the width returned by getWidth(), retrieve the value at the beginning of the method and then access it from your local copy.

As a further exercise for the reader, I encourage you to think about how you could make the Sudoku game graphically richer. For example, you could add some fireworks when the player solves the puzzle or make the tiles spin around like Vanna White does. A moving background behind the puzzle might be interesting. Let your imagination go wild. If you want to make a top-notch product, touches like this can add pizzazz to an otherwise ordinary offering.

In Chapter 5, *Multimedia*, on page 93, we'll enhance the program with a little mood music, and in Chapter 6, *Storing Local Data*, on page 109, we'll see how to remember the puzzle state and finally implement that Continue button.

4.6 Fast-Forward >>

In this chapter, we just scratched the surface of Android's graphics capabilities. The native 2D library is quite large, so as you're actually writing your programs, be sure to take advantage of the tooltips, auto-completion, and Javadoc provided by the Android Eclipse plug-in. The online documentation for the android.graphics[3] package goes into much more detail if you need it.

---

3. http://d.android.com/reference/android/graphics/package-summary.html

If your program needs more advanced graphics, you may want to look ahead a bit and read Chapter 10, *3D Graphics in OpenGL*, on page 191. There you'll find information on how to use Android's 3D graphics library, which is based on the OpenGL ES standard. Otherwise, turn to the next chapter for an introduction to the wonderful world of Android audio and video.

Chapter 5

Multimedia

Remember those Apple television ads with the silhouette people dancing wildly to the beat of their iPods? That's the kind of excitement you want your products to generate.[1] Music, sound effects, and video can make your programs more immersive and engaging than text and graphics alone.

This chapter will show you how to add multimedia to your Android application. You may not have your users cavorting in the aisles, but if you do it properly, you can at least put smiles on their faces.

5.1 Playing Audio

It was a dark and stormy night.... There goes the starting shot, and they're off.... The crowd goes wild as State sinks a three-pointer with one second remaining....

Audio cues permeate the environment and set the tempo for our emotions. Think of sound as another way to get into your user's head. Just like you use graphics on the display to convey some information to the user, you can use audio to back that up and reinforce it.

Android supports sound and music output through the MediaPlayer class in the android.media package.[2] Let's try it with a simple example that plays sounds when you press a key on the keyboard or D-pad.

---

1. Of course, normal people older than the age of 8 can't dance like that...except perhaps that time when my kids put a lizard in my...well, I digress.
2. http://d.android.com/guide/topics/media

Figure 5.1: SAVE SOUND EFFECTS IN A COMPRESSED FORMAT THAT ANDROID CAN PLAY.

We'll start by creating a "Hello, Android" project, using the following parameters in the New Android Project dialog box:

```
Project name: Audio
Build Target: Android 2.2
Application name: Audio
Package name: org.example.audio
Create Activity: Audio
Min SDK Version: 8
```

Next we'll need a few sounds to play. For this example, I created my own with the Windows Sound Recorder program (Start > Programs > Accessories > Entertainment > Sound Recorder on Windows XP) and an inexpensive headset. After getting the sound levels right, I recorded each sound, selected File > Save As... from the menu, clicked the Change... button, and selected a format Android can recognize (see Figure 5.1). You can find all the sound files and source code for these examples on the book's website.

Copy the sound files into the res/raw directory of your project. As you recall from Section 2.4, *Using Resources*, on page 27, simply copying a file into the res directory causes the Android Eclipse plug-in to define a Java symbol for you in the R class. When you're done, the project should look like Figure 5.2, on the following page.

Now it's time to fill out the Audio activity. First we declare a field called mp to hold an instance of the MediaPlayer class. In this program we're just going to have one MediaPlayer active at any given time.

Audio/src/org/example/audio/Audio.java
```java
package org.example.audio;

import android.app.Activity;
import android.media.AudioManager;
import android.media.MediaPlayer;
import android.os.Bundle;
import android.view.KeyEvent;

public class Audio extends Activity {
    private MediaPlayer mp;

    @Override
    public void onCreate(Bundle savedInstanceState) {
        super.onCreate(savedInstanceState);
        setContentView(R.layout.main);
        setVolumeControlStream(AudioManager.STREAM_MUSIC);
    }
}
```

The setVolumeControlStream() method tells Android that when the user presses the volume up or down key while this application is running, it should adjust the volume for music and other media instead of the ringer.

Next, we need to intercept the key presses and play the right sounds. We do that by overriding the Activity.onKeyDown() method.

Audio/src/org/example/audio/Audio.java
```java
@Override
public boolean onKeyDown(int keyCode, KeyEvent event) {
    int resId;
    switch (keyCode) {
    case KeyEvent.KEYCODE_DPAD_UP:
        resId = R.raw.up;
        break;
    case KeyEvent.KEYCODE_DPAD_DOWN:
        resId = R.raw.down;
        break;
```

Figure 5.2: Copy audio files into the res/raw directory of your project.

```
     case KeyEvent.KEYCODE_DPAD_LEFT:
         resId = R.raw.left;
         break;
     case KeyEvent.KEYCODE_DPAD_RIGHT:
15       resId = R.raw.right;
         break;
     case KeyEvent.KEYCODE_DPAD_CENTER:
     case KeyEvent.KEYCODE_ENTER:
         resId = R.raw.enter;
20       break;
     case KeyEvent.KEYCODE_A:
         resId = R.raw.a;
         break;
     case KeyEvent.KEYCODE_S:
25       resId = R.raw.s;
         break;
     case KeyEvent.KEYCODE_D:
         resId = R.raw.d;
         break;
30   case KeyEvent.KEYCODE_F:
         resId = R.raw.f;
         break;
     default:
         return super.onKeyDown(keyCode, event);
35   }

     // Release any resources from previous MediaPlayer
     if (mp != null) {
         mp.release();
40   }

     // Create a new MediaPlayer to play this sound
     mp = MediaPlayer.create(this, resId);
     mp.start();
45
     // Indicate this key was handled
     return true;
 }
```

The first part of the method selects a resource based on which key you pressed. Then on line 39, we call the release() method to stop any sounds already playing and free up any resources associated with the old MediaPlayer. If you forget to do that, the program will crash (see the sidebar on the following page).

On line 43, we use the create() method to create a new MediaPlayer using the selected sound resource and call the start() method to begin playing it. The start() method is asynchronous, so it returns immediately regardless of how long the sound lasts. If you like, you can use setOnCompletionListener() to be notified when the clip is finished.

When Things Go Wrong

If you do much multimedia programming, you'll soon discover that Android's MediaPlayer can be a fickle beast. The version in newer versions of Android is much improved over its predecessors, but it can still crash at the slightest provocation. One reason this happens is that MediaPlayer is mostly a native application with a thin layer of Java on top of it. The native player code is optimized for performance, and it doesn't seem to do much error checking.

Fortunately, Android's strong Linux process protections prevent any harm from being done if a crash occurs. The emulator (or the phone if you're running on a real device) and other applications will continue to run normally. The user would just see the application go away, possibly with a dialog box containing an error message.

During development, though, you can get considerably more diagnostic information to help you determine what went wrong. Messages and tracebacks will be printed to the Android system log, which you can view with the LogCat view in Eclipse or the adb logcat command (see Section 3.10, *Debugging with Log Messages*, on page 58).

If you run the program now and then press one of the keys (for example, the Enter key or the center D-pad key), you should hear a sound. If you don't hear anything, check your volume control (don't laugh), or look at the debugging messages in the LogCat view. If you run this on a phone with no keyboard, D-pad, or trackball, press and hold the Menu key to get the soft keyboard to appear.

Note that audio output may be choppy or delayed in some cases. Try different formats (such as OGG instead of MP3) and lower bit rates. You may also want to investigate using the SoundPool class, which explicitly supports simultaneous streams. It was buggy and poorly documented in the 1.0 release, but as of 1.5 it appears to be stable.

For our next trick, we'll play a movie using only one line of code.

Joe Asks...

What Audio Formats Does Android Support?

Well, there's support on paper, there's support in the emulator, and there's support on the actual devices. On paper, Android supports the following file types (this is subject to change with new releases):

- WAV (PCM uncompressed)
- AAC (Apple iPod format, unprotected)
- MP3 (MPEG-3)
- WMA (Windows media audio)
- AMR (Speech codec)
- OGG (Ogg Vorbis)*
- MIDI (Instruments)

In reality, I've found that only the OGG, WAV, and MP3 formats work well in the emulator, and thus those are the only ones that I can recommend for application development. Android's native audio format appears to be 44.1kHz 16-bit stereo. However, since WAV files at that rate are huge, you should just stick to OGG or MP3 files (mono for voice or stereo for music). OGG files seem to work best for short clips like game sound effects.

Stay away from unusual rates like 8kHz because the resampling artifacts make those rates sound terrible. Use 11kHz, 22kHz, or 44.1kHz sampling rates for the best results. Remember that although the phone may have a tiny speaker, many of your users are going to be plugging in headphones (like an iPod), so you want your audio to be high quality.

---

*. http://www.vorbis.com

Joe Asks...

What Kind of Video Can You Watch on Android?

Here's what is officially supported:

- MP4 (MPEG-4 low bit rate)
- H.263 (3GP)
- H.264 (AVC)

As of Android 1.5, H.263 is the recommended video format because every hardware platform supports it and it's relatively efficient to encode and decode. It is also compatible with other devices such as the iPhone. You can use a program like QuickTime Pro* to convert video from one format to another. Use the lowest resolution and bit rate that you can in order to save space, but don't set it so low that you sacrifice quality.

---
*. http://www.apple.com/quicktime/pro

5.2 Playing Video

Video is more than just a bunch of pictures shown one right after another. It's sound as well, and the sound has to be closely synchronized with the images.

Android's MediaPlayer class works with video the same way it does with plain audio. The only difference is that you need to create a Surface for the player to use to draw the images. You can use the start() and stop() methods to control playback.

I'm not going to show you another MediaPlayer example, however, because there is a simpler way to embed videos in your application: the VideoView class. To demonstrate it, create a new Android project called Video using these parameters:

```
Project name: Video
Build Target: Android 2.2
Application name: Video
Package name: org.example.video
Create Activity: Video
Min SDK Version: 8
```

Change the layout (res/layout/main.xml) to this:

Videov1/res/layout/main.xml

```xml
<?xml version="1.0" encoding="utf-8"?>
<FrameLayout
    xmlns:android="http://schemas.android.com/apk/res/android"
    android:layout_width="fill_parent"
    android:layout_height="fill_parent">
    <VideoView
        android:id="@+id/video"
        android:layout_height="wrap_content"
        android:layout_width="wrap_content"
        android:layout_gravity="center" />
</FrameLayout>
```

Open Video.java, and change the onCreate() method as follows:

Videov1/src/org/example/video/Video.java

```java
package org.example.video;

import android.app.Activity;
import android.os.Bundle;
import android.widget.VideoView;

public class Video extends Activity {
    @Override
    public void onCreate(Bundle savedInstanceState) {
        super.onCreate(savedInstanceState);

        // Fill view from resource
        setContentView(R.layout.main);
        VideoView video = (VideoView) findViewById(R.id.video);

        // Load and start the movie
        video.setVideoPath("/data/samplevideo.3gp");
        video.start();
    }
}
```

The setVideoPath() method opens the file, sizes it to its container while preserving the aspect ratio, and begins playing it.

Now you need to upload something to play. To do that, run the following command:

```
C:\> adb push c:\code\samplevideo.3gp /data/samplevideo.3gp
1649 KB/s (369870 bytes in 0.219s)
```

You can find samplevideo.3gp in the download package for this book, or you can create one of your own. The directory used here (/data) is just for illustrative purposes and should not really be used for media files.

Figure 5.3: EMBEDDING A VIDEO IS EASY WITH VIDEOVIEW.

It will work only on the emulator because that directory is protected on real devices.

Note that Android doesn't seem to care what extension you give the file. You can also upload and download files in Eclipse with the File Explorer view in the Android perspective, but I find the command line to be easier for simple things like this.

There's one more thing: we'd like the video to take over the whole screen including the title bar and status bar. To do that, all you need to do is specify the right theme in AndroidManifest.xml:

```
Videov1/AndroidManifest.xml
<?xml version="1.0" encoding="utf-8"?>
<manifest xmlns:android="http://schemas.android.com/apk/res/android"
    package="org.example.video"
    android:versionCode="1"
    android:versionName="1.0">
  <application android:icon="@drawable/icon"
      android:label="@string/app_name">
```

```
    <activity android:name=".Video"
        android:label="@string/app_name"
        android:theme="@android:style/Theme.NoTitleBar.Fullscreen">
      <intent-filter>
         <action android:name="android.intent.action.MAIN" />
         <category android:name="android.intent.category.LAUNCHER" />
      </intent-filter>
    </activity>
  </application>
    <uses-sdk android:minSdkVersion="3" android:targetSdkVersion="8" />
</manifest>
```

Once all that is done, when you run the program, you should see and hear the movie clip (see Figure 5.3, on the preceding page). Try rotating the display to verify it works in both portrait and landscape modes. *Voila!* Instant video goodness.

Now let's polish up the Sudoku sample with a little mood music.

5.3 Adding Sounds to Sudoku

In this section, we're going to take what we've learned and add background music to the Sudoku game we've been building. One song will play during the opening screen, and another will play during the actual game. This will demonstrate not just how to play music but also some important life-cycle considerations.

To add music to the main screen, we just need to override these two methods in the Sudoku class:

`Sudokuv3/src/org/example/sudoku/Sudoku.java`

```
@Override
protected void onResume() {
    super.onResume();
    Music.play(this, R.raw.main);
}

@Override
protected void onPause() {
    super.onPause();
    Music.stop(this);
}
```

If you recall from Section 2.2, *It's Alive!*, on page 22, the onResume() method is called when the activity is ready to begin interacting with the user. This is a good place to start up the music, so we put a Music.play() call there. The Music class will be defined shortly.

\\// Joe Asks...
;·{
~ __Why Does It Restart the Video When I Rotate the Display?__

Android assumes by default that your program knows nothing about screen rotations. To pick up possible resource changes, Android destroys and re-creates your activity from scratch. That means onCreate( ) is called again, which means the video is started again (as this example is currently written).

This behavior will be fine for 90 percent of all applications, so most developers will not have to worry about it. It's even a useful way to test your application life-cycle and state-saving/restoring code (see Section 2.2, *It's Alive!*, on page 22). However, there are a couple of ways to be smarter and optimize the transition.

The simplest way is to implement onRetainNonConfigurationInstance( ) in your activity to save some data that will be kept across the calls to onDestroy( ) and onCreate( ). When you come back, you use getLastNonConfigurationInstance( ) in the new instance of your activity to recover that information. You can keep anything, even references to your current intent and running threads.

The more complicated way is to use the android:configChanges= property in AndroidManifest.xml to inform Android which changes you can handle. For example, if you set it to *keyboardHidden|orientation*, then Android will not destroy and re-create your activity when the user flips the keyboard. Instead, it will call onConfigurationChanged(Configuration) and assume you know what you're doing.*

---

*. See http://d.android.com/reference/android/app/Activity.html#Configuration-Changes for more details.

Joe Asks...

Shouldn't We Use a Background Service for Music?

We haven't said much about the Android Service class, but you may have seen it used in some music-playing examples on the Web. Basically, a Service is a way to start a background process that can run even after your current activity finishes. Services are similar to, but not quite the same as, Linux daemons. If you're writing a general-purpose music player and want the music to continue while you're reading mail or browsing the Web, then, yes, a Service would be appropriate. In most cases, though, you want the music to end when your program ends, so you don't need to use the Service class.

R.raw.main refers to res/raw/main.mp3. You can find these sound files in the Sudokuv3 project of the downloadable samples on the book's website.

The onPause() method is the paired bookend for onResume(). Android pauses the current activity prior to resuming a new one, so in Sudoku, when you start a new game, the Sudoku activity will be paused, and then the Game activity will be started. onPause() will also be called when the user presses the Back or Home key. These are all places where we want our title music to stop, so we call Music.stop() in onPause().

Now let's do something similar for the music on the Game activity:

`Sudokuv3/src/org/example/sudoku/Game.java`

```java
@Override
protected void onResume() {
    super.onResume();
    Music.play(this, R.raw.game);
}

@Override
protected void onPause() {
    super.onPause();
    Music.stop(this);
}
```

> ### Sudoku Trivia
>
> Dozens of Sudoku variants exist, although none has gained the popularity of the original. One uses a sixteen-by-sixteen grid, with hexadecimal numbers. Another, called Gattai 5 or Samurai Sudoku, uses five nine-by-nine grids that overlap at the corner regions.

If you compare this to what we did to the Sudoku class, you'll notice that we're referencing a different sound resource, R.raw.game (res/raw/game.mp3).

The final piece of the musical puzzle is the Music class, which will manage the MediaPlayer class used to play the current music:

Sudokuv3/src/org/example/sudoku/Music.java

```
Line 1   package org.example.sudoku;

   -     import android.content.Context;
   -     import android.media.MediaPlayer;
   5
   -     public class Music {
   -         private static MediaPlayer mp = null;
   -
   -         /** Stop old song and start new one */
   10        public static void play(Context context, int resource) {
   -             stop(context);
   -             mp = MediaPlayer.create(context, resource);
   -             mp.setLooping(true);
   -             mp.start();
   15        }
   -
   -         /** Stop the music */
   -         public static void stop(Context context) {
   -             if (mp != null) {
   20                mp.stop();
   -                 mp.release();
   -                 mp = null;
   -             }
   -         }
   25    }
```

The play() method first calls the stop() method to halt whatever music is currently playing. Next, it creates a new MediaPlayer instance using MediaPlayer.create(), passing it a context and a resource ID.

After we have a player, we then set an option to make it repeat the music in a loop and then start it playing. The start() method comes back immediately.

The stop() method that begins on line 18 is simple. After a little defensive check to make sure we actually have a MediaPlayer to work with, we call its stop() and release() methods. The MediaPlayer.stop() method, strangely enough, stops the music. The release() method frees system resources associated with the player. Since those are native resources, we can't wait until normal Java garbage collection reclaims them. Leaving out release() is a good way to make your program fail unexpectedly (not that this has ever happened to me, of course; I'm just saying *you* should keep that in mind).

Now comes the fun part—try playing Sudoku with these changes in place. Stress test it in every way you can imagine, such as switching to different activities, pressing the Back button and the Home button from different points in the game, starting the program when it's already running at different points, rotating the display, and so forth. Proper life-cycle management is a pain sometimes, but your users will appreciate the effort.

5.4 Fast-Forward >>

In this chapter, we covered playing audio and video clips using the Android SDK. We didn't discuss recording because most programs will not need to do that, but if you happen to be the exception, then look up the MediaRecorder class in the online documentation.[3]

In Chapter 6, *Storing Local Data*, on page 109, you'll learn about some simple ways Android programs can store data between invocations. If you don't need to do that, then you can skip ahead to Chapter 7, *The Connected World*, on page 121 and learn about network access.

---

3. http://d.android.com/reference/android/media/MediaRecorder.html

Storing Local Data

So far, we've concentrated on writing applications that don't need to keep data around when they exit. They start up, run, and go away, leaving no trace that they were ever there. However, most real programs need persistent state, whether it's a simple font size setting, an embarrassing photo from your last office party, or next week's meal plan. Whatever it is, Android lets you permanently store it on your mobile device for later use and protects it from accidental or malicious access by other programs.

Your application can store data using several different techniques depending on the size of the data, its structure, its lifetime, and whether it will be shared with other programs. In this chapter, we'll take a look at three simple methods to keep local data: the preferences API, instance state bundles, and flash memory files. In Chapter 9, *Putting SQL to Work*, on page 171, we'll delve into more advanced techniques using the built-in SQLite database engine.

6.1 Adding Options to Sudoku

In Section 3.7, *Adding a Menu*, on page 51, we used the onCreateOptionsMenu() method to add a menu containing one item to the main Sudoku screen. When the user presses the Menu key and selects the Settings... item, the code starts the Prefs activity, which lets the user change the options for the game. Because Prefs extends PreferenceActivity, the values for the settings are stored in the program's preferences area, but originally we didn't do anything with them. Now we're going to implement them.

> **Sudoku Trivia**
>
> There are 6,670,903,752,021,072,936,960 possible classic Sudoku solution grids. If you eliminate duplicates that are just rotations, reflections, or relabelings of each other, you're left with "only" 5,472,730,538 solutions.

First let's modify the Prefs class to add a couple of getter methods that retrieve the current values of our two options. Here's the new definition:

Sudokuv4/src/org/example/sudoku/Prefs.java

```java
package org.example.sudoku;

import android.content.Context;
import android.os.Bundle;
import android.preference.PreferenceActivity;
import android.preference.PreferenceManager;

public class Prefs extends PreferenceActivity {
    // Option names and default values
    private static final String OPT_MUSIC = "music";
    private static final boolean OPT_MUSIC_DEF = true;
    private static final String OPT_HINTS = "hints";
    private static final boolean OPT_HINTS_DEF = true;

    @Override
    protected void onCreate(Bundle savedInstanceState) {
        super.onCreate(savedInstanceState);
        addPreferencesFromResource(R.xml.settings);
    }

    /** Get the current value of the music option */
    public static boolean getMusic(Context context) {
        return PreferenceManager.getDefaultSharedPreferences(context)
                .getBoolean(OPT_MUSIC, OPT_MUSIC_DEF);
    }

    /** Get the current value of the hints option */
    public static boolean getHints(Context context) {
        return PreferenceManager.getDefaultSharedPreferences(context)
                .getBoolean(OPT_HINTS, OPT_HINTS_DEF);
    }
}
```

Be careful that the option keys (music and hints) match the keys used in res/xml/settings.xml.

Music.play() has to be modified to check for the music preference:

Sudokuv4/src/org/example/sudoku/Music.java

```
public static void play(Context context, int resource) {
    stop(context);

    // Start music only if not disabled in preferences
    if (Prefs.getMusic(context)) {
        mp = MediaPlayer.create(context, resource);
        mp.setLooping(true);
        mp.start();
    }
}
```

And PuzzleView.onDraw() also needs to be modified to check for the hints preference:

Sudokuv4/src/org/example/sudoku/PuzzleView.java

```
if (Prefs.getHints(getContext())) {
    // Draw the hints...
}
```

If getHints() returns true, we draw the highlights for the hints, as shown in Figure 4.6, on page 80. Otherwise, we just skip that part.

Next I'll show you how to use the preferences API to store things other than just options.

6.2 Continuing an Old Game

At any time the player can decide to quit playing our Sudoku game and go do something else. Maybe their boss walked in, or they got a phone call or a notification of an important appointment. Whatever the reason, we want to allow the player to come back later and continue where they left off.

First we need to save the current state of the puzzle somewhere. The preferences API can be used for more than just options; it can store any small stand-alone bits of information that go with your program. In this case, the state of the puzzle can be saved as a string of eighty-one characters, one for each tile.

In the Game class, we'll start by defining a couple of constants—one for the puzzle data key and one for a flag to tell us to continue the previous game rather than start a new one.

Sudokuv4/src/org/example/sudoku/Game.java

```
private static final String PREF_PUZZLE = "puzzle" ;
protected static final int DIFFICULTY_CONTINUE = -1;
```

Next we need to save the current puzzle whenever the game is paused. See Section 2.2, *It's Alive!*, on page 22 for a description of onPause() and the other life-cycle methods.

Sudokuv4/src/org/example/sudoku/Game.java

```
@Override
protected void onPause() {
    super.onPause();
    Log.d(TAG, "onPause");
    Music.stop(this);

    // Save the current puzzle
    getPreferences(MODE_PRIVATE).edit().putString(PREF_PUZZLE,
            toPuzzleString(puzzle)).commit();
}
```

Now the puzzle is saved, but how do we read the saved data? Remember that when the game is started, the getPuzzle() method is called, and the difficulty level is passed in. We'll use that for continuing as well.

Sudokuv4/src/org/example/sudoku/Game.java

```
private int[] getPuzzle(int diff) {
    String puz;
    switch (diff) {
    case DIFFICULTY_CONTINUE:
        puz = getPreferences(MODE_PRIVATE).getString(PREF_PUZZLE,
                easyPuzzle);
        break;
        // ...
    }
    return fromPuzzleString(puz);
}
```

All we need to do is add a check for DIFFICULTY_CONTINUE. If that is set, then instead of starting with a fresh puzzle, we read the one we stuffed into the preferences.

Next, we need to make the Continue button on the main screen (see Figure 3.4, on page 41) actually do something. Here is where we set that up.

Sudokuv4/src/org/example/sudoku/Sudoku.java

```java
public void onClick(View v) {
    switch (v.getId()) {
    case R.id.continue_button:
        startGame(Game.DIFFICULTY_CONTINUE);
        break;
        // ...
    }
}
```

We added a case in Sudoku.onClick() to call startGame() when the Continue button is pressed, passing it DIFFICULTY_CONTINUE. startGame() passes the difficulty to the Game activity, and Game.onCreate() calls Intent.getIntExtra() to read the difficulty and passes that to getPuzzle() (you can see the code for that in Section 4.2, *Starting the Game*, on page 66).

There's one more thing to do: restore from our saved game when our activity goes away and comes back on its own (such as if another activity is started and then the user comes back to the Game activity). This modification to the Game.onCreate() method will take care of that:

Sudokuv4/src/org/example/sudoku/Game.java

```java
@Override
protected void onCreate(Bundle savedInstanceState) {
    // ...
    // If the activity is restarted, do a continue next time
    getIntent().putExtra(KEY_DIFFICULTY, DIFFICULTY_CONTINUE);
}
```

That pretty much covers it for preferences. Next let's look at saving instance state.

6.3 Remembering the Current Position

If you change the screen orientation while Sudoku is running, you'll notice that it forgets where its cursor is. That's because we use a custom PuzzleView view. Normal Android views save their view state automatically, but since we made our own, we don't get that for free.

Unlike persistent state, instance state is not permanent. It lives in a Bundle class on Android's application stack. Instance state is intended to be used for small bits of information such as cursor positions.

Here's what we have to do to implement it:

Sudokuv4/src/org/example/sudoku/PuzzleView.java

```
Line 1  import android.os.Bundle;
    -   import android.os.Parcelable;
    -
    -   public class PuzzleView extends View {
    5       private static final String SELX = "selX";
    -       private static final String SELY = "selY";
    -       private static final String VIEW_STATE = "viewState";
    -       private static final int ID = 42;
    -
   10       public PuzzleView(Context context) {
    -           // ...
    -           setId(ID);
    -       }
    -
   15       @Override
    -       protected Parcelable onSaveInstanceState() {
    -           Parcelable p = super.onSaveInstanceState();
    -           Log.d(TAG, "onSaveInstanceState");
    -           Bundle bundle = new Bundle();
   20           bundle.putInt(SELX, selX);
    -           bundle.putInt(SELY, selY);
    -           bundle.putParcelable(VIEW_STATE, p);
    -           return bundle;
    -       }
   25       @Override
    -       protected void onRestoreInstanceState(Parcelable state) {
    -           Log.d(TAG, "onRestoreInstanceState");
    -           Bundle bundle = (Bundle) state;
    -           select(bundle.getInt(SELX), bundle.getInt(SELY));
   30           super.onRestoreInstanceState(bundle.getParcelable(VIEW_STATE));
    -       }
    -       // ...
    -   }
```

On line 5, we define some constants for keys to save and restore the cursor position. We need to save both our own x and y positions, plus any state needed by the underlying View class.

As part of Activity.onSaveInstanceState() processing, Android will walk down the view hierarchy and call View.onSaveInstanceState() on every view it finds that has an ID. The same thing happens for onRestoreInstanceState(). Normally, this ID would come from XML, but since Puzzle-View was created in code, we need to set it ourselves. We make up an arbitrary number on line 8 (any value will do as long as it's positive) and then use the setId() method to assign it on line 12.

The onSaveInstanceState() method is defined on line 16. We call the superclass to get its state, and then we save ours and theirs in a Bundle. Failing to call the superclass will result in a runtime error.

Later, onRestoreInstanceState() (line 26) will be called to tease out the information we saved. We get our own x and y positions from the Bundle, and then we call the superclass to let it get whatever it needs. After making these changes, the cursor will be remembered by PuzzleView, just like any other Android view.

Next let's look at keeping data in plain old files.

6.4 Accessing the Internal File System

Android runs Linux under the covers, so there's a real file system mounted in there with a root directory and everything. The files are stored on nonvolatile flash memory built into the device, so they are not lost when the phone is turned off.

All of the usual Java file I/O routines from the java.io package are available for your program to use, with the caveat that your process has limited permissions so it can't mess up any other application's data. In fact, the main thing it can access is a package private directory created at install time (/data/data/*packagename*).

A few helper methods are provided on the Context class (and thus on the Activity class extended by each of your activities) to let you read and write data there. Here are the ones you're most likely to need:

deleteFile()	Delete a private file. Returns true if it worked, false otherwise.
fileList()	Return a list of all files in the application's private area in a String array.
openFileInput()	Open a private file for reading. Returns a java.io.FileInputStream.
openFileOutput()	Open a private file for writing. Returns a java.io.FileOutputStream.

However, since this internal memory is limited, I recommend you keep the size of any data you put there low, say a megabyte or two at the most, and carefully handle I/O errors when writing in case the space runs out.

Luckily, internal memory isn't the only storage that you have to work with.

All in the Family

If you recall from Section 2.5, *Safe and Secure*, on page 27, each application normally gets its own user ID at install time. That user ID is the only one that is allowed to read and write from the application's private directory. However, if two applications are signed* by the same digital certificate, then Android assumes they are from the same developer and gives them the same user ID.

On the one hand, that allows them to share all sorts of data with each other if they so choose. But on the other, it also means they'll need to take special care to stay out of each other's way.

---

*. http://d.android.com/guide/topics/security/security.html#signing

---

6.5 Accessing SD Cards

Some Android devices will include a slot for additional flash memory to be plugged in, typically a Secure Digital (SD) card. These memory cards, if present, are much larger than the built-in memory, and thus they're ideal for storing multimegabyte music and video files. They cannot be used for code, and every application can read and write files there.

In Section 5.2, *Playing Video*, on page 100, we uploaded a sample video file to the /data directory of the emulated device. This is the wrong place for it, since we're not supposed to put large files on the internal file system. So, now I'm going to show you a better way.

The first step is to create and format a virtual SD card that we can "plug in" to the emulator. Luckily we've already done this—if you recall, in Section 1.3, *Creating an AVD*, on page 9 when we created the "em22" virtual device, we gave it a 64MB virtual SD card as well. You can make it any size you like, but if you make it too small, it may cause the emulator to crash; if you make it too big, you'll just waste space on your computer's disk drive.

Next, let's copy the sample video to the SD card:

```
C:\> adb push c:\code\samplevideo.3gp /sdcard/samplevideo.3gp
1468 KB/s (369870 bytes in 0.246s)
```

Then we need to modify the onCreate() method of the Video class to play the movie from the SD card instead of the /data directory:

Videov2/src/org/example/video/Video.java

```
// Load and start the movie
video.setVideoPath("/sdcard/samplevideo.3gp");
video.start();
```

Now try to run the program. The video should play normally.

Note: Starting with Android 1.6, you will need to request the WRITE_EXTERNAL_STORAGE permission in your manifest file if you want to write to the SD card from your application. Reading from the card doesn't require any special permissions.

Starting with Android 2.2, your application can use the Context.getExternalFilesDir() method to get the directory on the external file system where it can place persistent files it owns. Android will delete the files when the application is uninstalled.

6.6 Fast-Forward >>

In this chapter, we covered a couple of basic ways to store local data on the Android platform. That should be enough to get you started, but for structured data such as phone lists and recipes, you'll need something more advanced. See Chapter 9, *Putting SQL to Work*, on page 171 for directions on how to use Android's built-in SQLite database and how to share information between applications using content providers. For instructions on installing applications on external storage, see Section 13.6, *Installing on the SD Card*, on page 265

This brings us to the end of Part II. With the help of the Sudoku example, you've learned all the basics of Android programming, including user interfaces, 2D graphics, audio, video, and simple data storage.

Now it's time to leave Sudoku behind and move beyond the basics.

Part III

Beyond the Basics

Chapter 7

The Connected World

Over the next few chapters, we'll cover more advanced topics such as network access and location-based services. You can write many useful applications without these features, but going beyond the basic features of Android will really help you add value to your programs, giving them much more functionality with a minimum of effort.

What do you use your mobile phone for? Aside from making calls, more and more people are using their phones as mobile Internet devices. Analysts predict that in a few years mobile phones will surpass desktop computers as the number-one way to connect to the Internet.[1] This point has already been reached in some parts of the world.[2]

Android phones are well equipped for the new connected world of the mobile Internet. First, Android provides a full-featured web browser based on the WebKit open source project.[3] This is the same engine you will find in Google Chrome, the Apple iPhone, and the Safari desktop browser but with a twist. Android lets you use the browser as a component right inside your application.

Second, Android gives your programs access to standard network services like TCP/IP sockets. This lets you consume web services from Google, Yahoo, Amazon, and many other sources on the Internet.

---

1. http://archive.mobilecomputingnews.com/2010/0205.html
2. http://www.comscore.com/press/release.asp?press=1742
3. http://webkit.org

Figure 7.1: OPENING A BROWSER USING AN ANDROID INTENT

In this chapter, you'll learn how to take advantage of all these features and more through four example programs:

- *BrowserIntent*: Demonstrates opening an external web browser using an Android intent
- *BrowserView*: Shows you how to embed a browser directly into your application
- *LocalBrowser*: Explains how JavaScript in an embedded WebView and Java code in your Android program can talk to each other
- *Translate*: Uses data binding, threading, and web services for an amusing purpose

7.1 Browsing by Intent

The simplest thing you can do with Android's networking API is to open a browser on a web page of your choice. You might want to do this to provide a link to your home page from your program or to access some server-based application such as an ordering system. In Android all it takes is three lines of code.

To demonstrate, let's write a new example called BrowserIntent, which will have an edit field where you can enter a URL and a Go button you press to open the browser on that URL (see Figure 7.1). Start by creating a new "Hello, Android" project with the following values in the New Project wizard:

```
Project name: BrowserIntent
Build Target: Android 2.2
Application name: BrowserIntent
Package name: org.example.browserintent
Create Activity: BrowserIntent
Min SDK Version: 8
```

Once you have the basic program, change the layout file (res/layout/main.xml) so it looks like this:

`BrowserIntent/res/layout/main.xml`

```xml
<?xml version="1.0" encoding="utf-8"?>
<LinearLayout
    xmlns:android="http://schemas.android.com/apk/res/android"
    android:orientation="horizontal"
    android:layout_width="fill_parent"
    android:layout_height="fill_parent">
    <EditText
        android:id="@+id/url_field"
        android:layout_width="wrap_content"
        android:layout_height="wrap_content"
        android:layout_weight="1.0"
        android:lines="1"
        android:inputType="textUri"
        android:imeOptions="actionGo" />
    <Button
        android:id="@+id/go_button"
        android:layout_width="wrap_content"
        android:layout_height="wrap_content"
        android:text="@string/go_button" />
</LinearLayout>
```

This defines our two controls, an EditText control and a Button.

On EditText, we set android:layout_weight="1.0" to make the text area fill up all the horizontal space to the left of the button, and we also set android:lines="1" to limit the height of the control to one vertical line. Note that this has no effect on the amount of text the user can enter here, just the way it is displayed.

Android 1.5 introduced support for soft keyboards and other alternate input methods. The options for android:inputType="textUri" and android:imeOptions="actionGo" are hints for how the soft keyboard should appear. They tell Android to replace the standard keyboard with one that has convenient buttons for ".com" and "/" to enter web addresses and has a Go button that opens the web page.[4]

As always, human-readable text should be put in a resource file, res/values/strings.xml.

---

4. See http://d.android.com/reference/android/widget/TextView.html and http://android-developers.blogspot.com/2009/04/updating-applications-for-on-screen.html for more information on input options.

BrowserIntent/res/values/strings.xml

```xml
<?xml version="1.0" encoding="utf-8"?>
<resources>
    <string name="app_name">BrowserIntent</string>
    <string name="go_button">Go</string>
</resources>
```

Next we need to fill in the onCreate() method in the BrowserIntent class. This is where we'll build the user interface and hook up all the behavior. If you don't feel like typing all this in, the complete source code is available online at the book's website.[5]

BrowserIntent/src/org/example/browserintent/BrowserIntent.java

```java
Line 1  package org.example.browserintent;

        import android.app.Activity;
        import android.content.Intent;
     5  import android.net.Uri;
        import android.os.Bundle;
        import android.view.KeyEvent;
        import android.view.View;
        import android.view.View.OnClickListener;
    10  import android.view.View.OnKeyListener;
        import android.widget.Button;
        import android.widget.EditText;

        public class BrowserIntent extends Activity {
    15      private EditText urlText;
            private Button goButton;

            @Override
            public void onCreate(Bundle savedInstanceState) {
    20          super.onCreate(savedInstanceState);
                setContentView(R.layout.main);

                // Get a handle to all user interface elements
                urlText = (EditText) findViewById(R.id.url_field);
    25          goButton = (Button) findViewById(R.id.go_button);

                // Setup event handlers
                goButton.setOnClickListener(new OnClickListener() {
                    public void onClick(View view) {
    30                  openBrowser();
                    }
                });
                urlText.setOnKeyListener(new OnKeyListener() {
                    public boolean onKey(View view, int keyCode, KeyEvent event) {
```

---

5. http://pragprog.com/titles/eband3

```
35          if (keyCode == KeyEvent.KEYCODE_ENTER) {
                openBrowser();
                return true;
            }
            return false;
40        }
        });
    }
}
```

Inside onCreate(), we call setContentView() on line 21 to load the view from its definition in the layout resource, and then we call findViewById() on line 24 to get a handle to our two user interface controls.

Line 28 tells Android to run some code when the user selects the Go button, either by touching it or by navigating to it and pressing the center D-pad button. When that happens, we call the openBrowser() method, which will be defined in a moment.

As a convenience, if the user types an address and hits the Enter key (if their phone has one), we want the browser to open just like they had clicked Go. To do this, we define a listener starting on line 33 that will be called every time the user types a keystroke into the edit field. If it's the Enter key, then we call the openBrowser() method to open the browser; otherwise, we return false to let the text control handle the key normally.

Now comes the part you've been waiting for: the openBrowser() method. As promised, it's three lines long:

BrowserIntent/src/org/example/browserintent/BrowserIntent.java

```
/** Open a browser on the URL specified in the text box */
private void openBrowser() {
    Uri uri = Uri.parse(urlText.getText().toString());
    Intent intent = new Intent(Intent.ACTION_VIEW, uri);
    startActivity(intent);
}
```

The first line retrieves the address of the web page as a string (for example, "http://www.android.com") and converts it to a uniform resource identifier (URI).

Note: Don't leave off the "http://" part of the URL when you try this. If you do, the program will crash because Android won't know how to handle the address. In a real program you could add that if the user omitted it.

Figure 7.2: VIEWING A WEB PAGE WITH THE DEFAULT BROWSER

The next line creates a new Intent class with an action of ACTION_VIEW, passing it the Uri class just created as the object we want to view. Finally, we call the startActivity() method to request that this action be performed.

When the Browser activity starts, it will create its own view (see Figure 7.2), and your program will be paused. If the user presses the Back key at that point, the browser window will go away, and your application will continue. But what if you want to see some of your user interface and a web page at the same time? Android allows you to do that by using the WebView class.

7.2 Web with a View

On your desktop computer, a web browser is a large, complicated, memory-gobbling program with all sorts of features like bookmarks, plug-ins, Flash animations, tabs, scroll bars, printing, and so forth.

When I was working on the Eclipse project and someone suggested replacing some common text views with embedded web browsers, I thought they were crazy. Wouldn't it make more sense, I argued, to simply enhance the text viewer to do italics or tables or whatever it was that was missing?

It turns out they weren't crazy because:

- A web browser can be (relatively) lean and mean if you strip out everything but the basic rendering engine.
- If you enhance a text view to add more and more things that a browser engine can do, you end up with either an overly complicated, bloated text viewer or an underpowered browser.

Android provides a wrapper around the WebKit browser engine called WebView that you can use to get the real power of a browser with as little as 1MB of overhead. Although 1MB is still significant on an embedded device, there are many cases where using a WebView is appropriate.

WebView works pretty much like any other Android view except that it has a few extra methods specific to the browser. I'm going to show you how it works by doing an embedded version of the previous example. This one will be called BrowserView instead of BrowserIntent, since it uses an embedded View instead of an Intent. Start by creating a new "Hello, Android" project using these settings:

```
Project name: BrowserView
Build Target: Android 2.2
Application name: BrowserView
Package name: org.example.browserview
Create Activity: BrowserView
Min SDK Version: 8
```

The layout file for BrowserView is similar to the one in BrowserIntent, except we've added a WebView at the bottom:

`BrowserView/res/layout/main.xml`

```xml
<?xml version="1.0" encoding="utf-8"?>
<LinearLayout
    xmlns:android="http://schemas.android.com/apk/res/android"
    android:orientation="vertical"
    android:layout_width="fill_parent"
    android:layout_height="fill_parent">
    <LinearLayout
        android:orientation="horizontal"
        android:layout_width="fill_parent"
        android:layout_height="wrap_content">
        <EditText
            android:id="@+id/url_field"
            android:layout_width="wrap_content"
            android:layout_height="wrap_content"
            android:layout_weight="1.0"
            android:lines="1"
            android:inputType="textUri"
            android:imeOptions="actionGo" />
```

```
        <Button
            android:id="@+id/go_button"
            android:layout_width="wrap_content"
            android:layout_height="wrap_content"
            android:text="@string/go_button" />
    </LinearLayout>
    <WebView
        android:id="@+id/web_view"
        android:layout_width="fill_parent"
        android:layout_height="wrap_content"
        android:layout_weight="1.0" />
</LinearLayout>
```

We use two LinearLayout controls to make everything appear in the right place. The outermost control divides the screen into top and bottom regions; the top has the text area and button, and the bottom has the WebView. The innermost LinearLayout is the same as before; it just makes the text area go on the left and the button on the right.

The onCreate() method for BrowserView is exactly the same as before, except that now there is one extra view to look up:

BrowserView/src/org/example/browserview/BrowserView.java

```
import android.webkit.WebView;
// ...

public class BrowserView extends Activity {
    private WebView webView;
    // ...
    @Override
    public void onCreate(Bundle savedInstanceState) {
        // ...
        webView = (WebView) findViewById(R.id.web_view);
        // ...
    }
}
```

The openBrowser() method, however, is different:

BrowserView/src/org/example/browserview/BrowserView.java

```
/** Open a browser on the URL specified in the text box */
private void openBrowser() {
    webView.getSettings().setJavaScriptEnabled(true);
    webView.loadUrl(urlText.getText().toString());
}
```

Figure 7.3: EMBEDDING A BROWSER USING WEBVIEW

The loadUrl() method causes the browser engine to begin loading and displaying a web page at the given address. It returns immediately even though the actual loading may take some time (if it finishes at all).

Don't forget to update the string resources:

BrowserView/res/values/strings.xml

```xml
<?xml version="1.0" encoding="utf-8"?>
<resources>
    <string name="app_name">BrowserView</string>
    <string name="go_button">Go</string>
</resources>
```

We need to make one more change to the program. Add this line to AndroidManifest.xml before the <*application*> tag:

BrowserView/AndroidManifest.xml

```xml
<uses-permission android:name="android.permission.INTERNET" />
```

If you leave this out, Android will not give your application access to the Internet, and you'll get a "Web page not available" error.

Try running the program now, and enter a valid web address starting with "http://"; when you press Return or select the Go button, the web page should appear (see Figure 7.3).

Joe Asks...

Why Didn't BrowserIntent Need <uses-permission>?

The previous example, BrowserIntent, simply fired off an intent to request that some other application view the web page. That other application (the browser) is the one that needs to ask for Internet permissions in its own AndroidManifest.xml.

WebView has dozens of other methods you can use to control what is being displayed or get notifications on state changes.

You can find a complete list in the online documentation for WebView, but here are the methods you are most likely to need:

- addJavascriptInterface(): Allows a Java object to be accessed from JavaScript (more on this one in the next section)
- createSnapshot(): Creates a screenshot of the current page
- getSettings(): Returns a WebSettings object used to control the settings
- loadData(): Loads the given string data into the browser
- loadDataWithBaseURL(): Loads the given data using a base URL
- loadUrl(): Loads a web page from the given URL
- setDownloadListener(): Registers callbacks for download events, such as when the user downloads a .zip or .apk file
- setWebChromeClient(): Registers callbacks for events that need to be done outside the WebView rectangle, such as updating the title or progress bar or opening a JavaScript dialog box
- setWebViewClient(): Lets the application set hooks in the browser to intercept events such as resource loads, key presses, and authorization requests
- stopLoading(): Stops the current page from loading

One of the most powerful things you can do with the WebView control is to talk back and forth between it and the Android application that contains it. Let's take a closer look at this feature now.

> ## Joe Asks...
>
> ### Is Allowing JavaScript to Call Java Dangerous?
>
> Whenever you allow a web page to access local resources or call functions outside the browser sandbox, you need to consider the security implications very carefully. For example, you wouldn't want to create a method to allow JavaScript to read data from any arbitrary path name because that might expose some private data to a malicious site that knew about your method and your filenames.
>
> Here are a few things to keep in mind. First, don't rely on security by obscurity. Enforce limits on the pages that can use your methods and on the things those methods can do. And remember the golden rule of security: *don't rule things out; rule them in.* In other words, don't try to check for all the bad things that someone can ask you to do (for example, invalid characters in a query). You're bound to miss something. Instead, disallow everything, and pass only the good things you know are safe.

7.3 From JavaScript to Java and Back

Your Android device can do a number of cool things such as store local data, draw graphics, play music, make calls, and determine its location. Wouldn't it be nice if you could access that functionality from a web page? With an embedded WebView control, you can.

The key is the addJavascriptInterface() method in the WebView class. You can use it to extend the Document Object Model (DOM) inside the embedded browser and to define new object that JavaScript code can access. When the JavaScript code invokes methods on that object, it will actually be invoking methods in your Android program.

You can call JavaScript methods from your Android program too. All you have to do is call the loadUrl() method, passing it a URL of the form **javascript:***code-to-execute*. Instead of going to a new page, the browser will execute the given JavaScript expression inside the current page. You can call a method, change JavaScript variables, modify the browser document—anything you need.

Figure 7.4: Communicating between Android and an embedded WebView

To demonstrate calls between JavaScript in the WebView and Java in the Android program, let us now build a program that is half HTML/ JavaScript and half Android (see Figure 7.4). The top part of the application window is a WebView control, and the bottom part is a TextView and Button from the Android user interface. When you click the buttons and links, it makes calls between the two environments.

Start by creating a "Hello, Android" program using these parameters:

```
Project name: LocalBrowser
Build Target: Android 2.2
Application name: LocalBrowser
Package name: org.example.localbrowser
Create Activity: LocalBrowser
Min SDK Version: 8
```

The user interface for this program will be split into two parts. The first part is defined in the Android layout file, res/layout/main.xml:

LocalBrowser/res/layout/main.xml

```xml
<?xml version="1.0" encoding="utf-8"?>
<LinearLayout
    xmlns:android="http://schemas.android.com/apk/res/android"
    android:orientation="vertical"
    android:layout_width="fill_parent"
    android:layout_height="fill_parent">
    <WebView
        android:id="@+id/web_view"
        android:layout_width="fill_parent"
        android:layout_height="fill_parent"
        android:layout_weight="1.0" />
    <LinearLayout
        android:orientation="vertical"
        android:layout_width="fill_parent"
        android:layout_height="fill_parent"
        android:layout_weight="1.0"
        android:padding="5sp">
        <TextView
            android:layout_width="fill_parent"
            android:layout_height="wrap_content"
            android:textSize="24sp"
            android:text="@string/textview" />
        <Button
            android:id="@+id/button"
            android:text="@string/call_javascript_from_android"
            android:layout_width="wrap_content"
            android:layout_height="wrap_content"
            android:textSize="18sp" />
        <TextView
            android:id="@+id/text_view"
            android:layout_width="fill_parent"
            android:layout_height="wrap_content"
            android:textSize="18sp" />
    </LinearLayout>
</LinearLayout>
```

The second part is the index.html file that will be loaded into the Web-View. This file goes in the assets directory, not the res directory, because it's not a compiled resource. Anything in the assets directory is copied verbatim onto local storage when your program is installed. The directory is intended to be used for local copies of HTML, images, and scripts that the browser can view without being connected to the network.

```
LocalBrowser/assets/index.html
```

```
Line 1   <html>
    -    <head>
    -    <script language="JavaScript">
    -      function callJS(arg) {
    5        document.getElementById('replaceme').innerHTML = arg;
    -      }
    -    </script>
    -    </head>
    -    <body>
   10    <h1>WebView</h1>
    -    <p>
    -    <a href="#" onclick="window.alert('Alert from JavaScript')">
    -      Display JavaScript alert</a>
    -    </p>
   15    <p>
    -    <a href="#" onclick="window.android.callAndroid('Hello from Browser')">
    -      Call Android from JavaScript</a>
    -    </p>
    -    <p id="replaceme">
   20    </p>
    -    </body>
    -    </html>
```

Line 4 of index.html defines the callJS() function that our Android program will be calling later. It takes a string argument and inserts it at the *replaceme* tag, which is at line 19.

In Figure 7.4, on page 132, you see two HTML links that are defined starting at line 12. The first one just calls a standard window.alert() function to open a window displaying a short message. The second link, at line 16, calls the callAndroid() method on the window.android object. If you loaded this page into a normal web browser, window.android would be undefined. But since we're embedding a browser into an Android application, we can define the object ourselves so the page can use it.

Next we turn to the Android code in the LocalBrowser class. Here's the basic outline, including all the imports we'll need later:

```
LocalBrowser/src/org/example/localbrowser/LocalBrowser.java
```

```
Line 1   package org.example.localbrowser;

    -    import android.app.Activity;
    -    import android.os.Bundle;
    5    import android.os.Handler;
    -    import android.util.Log;
```

```
 -     import android.view.View;
 -     import android.view.View.OnClickListener;
 -     import android.webkit.JsResult;
10     import android.webkit.WebChromeClient;
 -     import android.webkit.WebView;
 -     import android.widget.Button;
 -     import android.widget.TextView;
 -     import android.widget.Toast;
15
 -     public class LocalBrowser extends Activity {
 -         private static final String TAG = "LocalBrowser";
 -         private final Handler handler = new Handler();
 -         private WebView webView;
20         private TextView textView;
 -         private Button button;
 -
 -         @Override
 -         public void onCreate(Bundle savedInstanceState) {
25             super.onCreate(savedInstanceState);
 -             setContentView(R.layout.main);
 -
 -             // Find the Android controls on the screen
 -             webView = (WebView) findViewById(R.id.web_view);
30             textView = (TextView) findViewById(R.id.text_view);
 -             button = (Button) findViewById(R.id.button);
 -             // Rest of onCreate follows...
 -         }
 -     }
```

Note the initialization of a Handler object at line 18. JavaScript calls
come in on a special thread dedicated to the browser, but Android user
interface calls can be made only from the main (GUI) thread. We'll use
the Handler class to make the transition.

To call Android Java code from JavaScript, you need to define a plain
old Java object with one or more methods, like this:

LocalBrowser/src/org/example/localbrowser/LocalBrowser.java

```
/** Object exposed to JavaScript */
private class AndroidBridge {
    public void callAndroid(final String arg) { // must be final
        handler.post(new Runnable() {
            public void run() {
                Log.d(TAG, "callAndroid(" + arg + ")");
                textView.setText(arg);
            }
        });
    }
}
```

When JavaScript calls the callAndroid() method, the application creates a new Runnable object and posts it on the running queue of the main thread using Handler.post(). As soon as the main thread gets a chance, it will invoke the run() method, which will call setText() to change the text on the TextView object. Now it's time to tie everything together in the onCreate() method. First we turn on JavaScript (it's off by default) and register our bridge to JavaScript:

LocalBrowser/src/org/example/localbrowser/LocalBrowser.java

```
// Turn on JavaScript in the embedded browser
webView.getSettings().setJavaScriptEnabled(true);

// Expose a Java object to JavaScript in the browser
webView.addJavascriptInterface(new AndroidBridge(),
    "android");
```

Then we create an anonymous WebChromeClient object and register it with the setWebChromeClient() method.

LocalBrowser/src/org/example/localbrowser/LocalBrowser.java

```
// Set up a function to be called when JavaScript tries
// to open an alert window
webView.setWebChromeClient(new WebChromeClient() {
    @Override
    public boolean onJsAlert(final WebView view,
            final String url, final String message,
            JsResult result) {
        Log.d(TAG, "onJsAlert(" + view + ", " + url + ", "
                + message + ", " + result + ")");
        Toast.makeText(LocalBrowser.this, message, 3000).show();
        result.confirm();
        return true; // I handled it
    }
});
```

The term *chrome* here refers to all the trimmings around a browser window. If this were a full-blown browser client, we'd need to handle navigation, bookmarks, menus, and so forth. In this case, all we want to do is change what happens with JavaScript code when the browser tries to open a JavaScript alert (using window.alert()). Inside onJsAlert() we use the Android Toast class to create a message window that will appear for a short amount of time (in this case, 3000 milliseconds, or 3 seconds).

Once we finish configuring the WebView, we can use loadUrl() to load the local web page:

LocalBrowser/src/org/example/localbrowser/LocalBrowser.java

```
// Load the web page from a local asset
webView.loadUrl("file:///android_asset/index.html");
```

URLs of the form "file:///android_asset/*filename*" (note the three forward slashes) have a special meaning to Android's browser engine. As you might have guessed, they refer to files in the assets directory. In this case, we're loading the index.html file defined earlier.

Here is the res/values/strings.xml file for the LocalBrowser example:

LocalBrowser/res/values/strings.xml

```
<?xml version="1.0" encoding="utf-8"?>
<resources>
    <string name="app_name">LocalBrowser</string>
    <string name="textview">TextView</string>
    <string name="call_javascript_from_android">
        Call JavaScript from Android
    </string>
</resources>
```

The last thing we have to do is wire up the button at the bottom of the screen so it will make a JavaScript call (a call from Java to JavaScript).

LocalBrowser/src/org/example/localbrowser/LocalBrowser.java

```
// This function will be called when the user presses the
// button on the Android side
button.setOnClickListener(new OnClickListener() {
    public void onClick(View view) {
        Log.d(TAG, "onClick(" + view + ")");
        webView.loadUrl("javascript:callJS('Hello from Android')");
    }
});
```

To do that, we set a listener for button clicks using setOnClickListener(). When the button is pressed, onClick() is called, which turns around and calls WebView.loadUrl(), passing it a JavaScript expression to evaluate in the browser. The expression is a call to the callJS() function defined in index.html.

Run the program now, and try it. When you click "Display JavaScript alert," an Android message window will appear. When you click "Call Android from JavaScript," the string "Hello from Browser" will be displayed in an Android text control. And finally, when you press the "Call JavaScript from Android" button, the string "Hello from Android" is sent to the browser and inserted in the HTML where it will be displayed at the end of the web page.

Sometimes you don't need to display a web page, but you just need to access some kind of web service or other server-side resource. In the next section, I'll show you how to do this.

7.4 Using Web Services

Android provides a full set of Java-standard networking APIs, such as the java.net.HttpURLConnection package, that you can use in your programs. The tricky part is to make the calls asynchronously so that your program's user interface will be responsive at all times.

Consider what would happen if you just make a blocking network call in your main (GUI) thread. Until that call returns (and it might never return), your application cannot respond to any user interface events such as keystrokes or button presses. It will appear hung to the user. Obviously, that's something you'll have to avoid.

The java.util.concurrent package is perfect for this kind of work. First created by Doug Lea as a stand-alone library and later incorporated into Java 5, this package supports concurrent programming at a higher level than the regular Java Thread class. The ExecutorService class manages one or more threads for you, and all you have to do is submit tasks (instances of Runnable or Callable) to the executor to have them run. An instance of the Future class is returned, which is a reference to some as-yet-unknown future value that will be returned by your task (if any). You can limit the number of threads that are created, and you can interrupt running tasks if necessary.

To illustrate these concepts, let's create a fun little program that calls the Google Translation API.[6] Have you ever laughed at strange translations to and from foreign languages, especially computer-generated translations? This program will let the user enter a phrase in one language, ask Google to translate to a second language, and then ask Google to translate it back into the first language. Ideally, you'd end up with the same words you started with, but this is not always the case, as you can see in Figure 7.5, on the facing page.

---

6. http://code.google.com/apis/ajaxlanguage

Figure 7.5: MACHINE TRANSLATION IS STILL A WORK IN PROGRESS.

To use this program, simply select the starting and target languages, and then start typing a phrase. As you type, the program will use the Google Translation web service to translate your text into and out of the target language.

To create this application, start with a "Hello, Android" application using these parameters:

```
Project name: Translate
Build Target: Android 2.2
Application name: Translate
Package name: org.example.translate
Create Activity: Translate
Min SDK Version: 8
```

Since this example will access the Internet to make a web service call, we will need to tell Android to grant us permission.

Lost in Translation

When I first thought of this example, I imagined that it would be easy to get some hilarious results. Unfortunately (or fortunately, depending on your point of view), the Google service does a pretty good job with most languages. If you find any especially funny cases where the translator really flubs up, please post them on the discussion forum at the book's website (http://pragprog.com/titles/eband3) for others to enjoy.

Add this line to AndroidManifest.xml before the *<application>* XML tag:

`Translate/AndroidManifest.xml`

```
<uses-permission android:name="android.permission.INTERNET" />
```

The layout for this example is a little more complicated than usual, so we'll use the TableLayout view. TableLayout lets you arrange your views into rows and columns, taking care of alignment and stretching the columns to fit the content. It's similar to using *<table>* and *<tr>* tags in HTML.

`Translate/res/layout/main.xml`

```xml
<?xml version="1.0" encoding="utf-8"?>
<ScrollView
    xmlns:android="http://schemas.android.com/apk/res/android"
    android:layout_width="fill_parent"
    android:layout_height="fill_parent">
  <TableLayout
      android:layout_width="fill_parent"
      android:layout_height="fill_parent"
      android:stretchColumns="1"
      android:padding="10dip">
    <TableRow>
      <TextView android:text="@string/from_text" />
      <Spinner android:id="@+id/from_language" />
    </TableRow>
    <EditText
        android:id="@+id/original_text"
        android:hint="@string/original_hint"
        android:padding="10dip"
        android:textSize="18sp" />
    <TableRow>
      <TextView android:text="@string/to_text" />
      <Spinner android:id="@+id/to_language" />
    </TableRow>
```

```
    <TextView
        android:id="@+id/translated_text"
        android:padding="10dip"
        android:textSize="18sp" />
    <TextView android:text="@string/back_text" />
    <TextView
        android:id="@+id/retranslated_text"
        android:padding="10dip"
        android:textSize="18sp" />
    </TableLayout>
</ScrollView>
```

In this example, we have six rows, each row containing one or two columns. Note that if there is only one view in a row, you don't have to use a TableRow to contain it. Also, it's not necessary to use android: layout_width= and android:layout_height= on every view like you have to with LinearLayout.

The Spinner class is a new one we haven't seen before. It's similar to a combo box in other user interface toolkits. The user selects the spinner (for example, by touching it), and a list of possible values appears for them to pick. In this example, we're going to use this control for selecting from a list of languages.

The actual list is stored as an Android resource in the file res/values/ arrays.xml:

Translate/res/values/arrays.xml

```xml
<?xml version="1.0" encoding="utf-8"?>
<resources>
    <array name="languages">
        <item>Bulgarian (bg)</item>
        <item>Chinese Simplified (zh-CN)</item>
        <item>Chinese Traditional (zh-TW)</item>
        <item>Catalan (ca)</item>
        <item>Croatian (hr)</item>
        <item>Czech (cs)</item>
        <item>Danish (da)</item>
        <item>Dutch (nl)</item>
        <item>English (en)</item>
        <item>Filipino (tl)</item>
        <item>Finnish (fi)</item>
        <item>French (fr)</item>
        <item>German (de)</item>
        <item>Greek (el)</item>
        <item>Indonesian (id)</item>
        <item>Italian (it)</item>
        <item>Japanese (ja)</item>
        <item>Korean (ko)</item>
```

```
        <item>Latvian (lv)</item>
        <item>Lithuanian (lt)</item>
        <item>Norwegian (no)</item>
        <item>Polish (pl)</item>
        <item>Portuguese (pt-PT)</item>
        <item>Romanian (ro)</item>
        <item>Russian (ru)</item>
        <item>Spanish (es)</item>
        <item>Serbian (sr)</item>
        <item>Slovak (sk)</item>
        <item>Slovenian (sl)</item>
        <item>Swedish (sv)</item>
        <item>Ukrainian (uk)</item>
    </array>
</resources>
```

This defines a list called languages that contains most of the languages recognized by the Google Translation API. Note that each value has a long name (for example, *Spanish*) and a short name (for example, *es*). We'll use the short name when passing the language to the translator.

Now let's start modifying the Translate class. Here's the basic outline:

Translate/src/org/example/translate/Translate.java

```
Line 1  package org.example.translate;

        import java.util.concurrent.ExecutorService;
        import java.util.concurrent.Executors;
     5  import java.util.concurrent.Future;
        import java.util.concurrent.RejectedExecutionException;

        import android.app.Activity;
        import android.os.Bundle;
    10  import android.os.Handler;
        import android.text.Editable;
        import android.text.TextWatcher;
        import android.view.View;
        import android.widget.AdapterView;
    15  import android.widget.ArrayAdapter;
        import android.widget.EditText;
        import android.widget.Spinner;
        import android.widget.TextView;
        import android.widget.AdapterView.OnItemSelectedListener;
    20
        public class Translate extends Activity {
            private Spinner fromSpinner;
            private Spinner toSpinner;
            private EditText origText;
```

```
25    private TextView transText;
 -    private TextView retransText;

 -
 -    private TextWatcher textWatcher;
 -    private OnItemSelectedListener itemListener;
30
 -    private Handler guiThread;
 -    private ExecutorService transThread;
 -    private Runnable updateTask;
 -    private Future transPending;
35
 -    @Override
 -    public void onCreate(Bundle savedInstanceState) {
 -        super.onCreate(savedInstanceState);
 -
40        setContentView(R.layout.main);
 -        initThreading();
 -        findViews();
 -        setAdapters();
 -        setListeners();
45    }
 -  }
```

After declaring a few variables, we define the onCreate() method starting at line 37 to initialize the threading and user interface. Don't worry, we'll fill out all those other methods it calls as we go.

The findViews() method, called from line 42, just gets a handle to all the user interface elements defined in the layout file:

Translate/src/org/example/translate/Translate.java

```
private void findViews() {
    fromSpinner = (Spinner) findViewById(R.id.from_language);
    toSpinner = (Spinner) findViewById(R.id.to_language);
    origText = (EditText) findViewById(R.id.original_text);
    transText = (TextView) findViewById(R.id.translated_text);
    retransText = (TextView) findViewById(R.id.retranslated_text);
}
```

The setAdapters() method, called from onCreate() on line 43, defines a data source for the spinners:

Translate/src/org/example/translate/Translate.java

```
private void setAdapters() {
    // Spinner list comes from a resource,
    // Spinner user interface uses standard layouts
    ArrayAdapter<CharSequence> adapter = ArrayAdapter.createFromResource(
            this, R.array.languages,
            android.R.layout.simple_spinner_item);
```

```
\!/
:·{    Joe Asks...
~       Is All This Delay and Threading Stuff Really Necessary?
```

One reason you need to do it this way is to avoid making too many calls to the external web service. Imagine what happens as the user enters the word *scissors*. The program sees the word typed in a character at a time, first *s*, then *c*, then *i*, and so on, possibly with backspaces because nobody can remember how to spell *scissors*. Do you really want to make a web service request for every character? Not really. Besides putting unnecessary load on the server, it would be wasteful in terms of power. Each request requires the device's radio to transmit and receive several data packets, which uses up a bit of battery power. You want to wait until the user finishes typing before sending the request, but how do you tell they are done?

The algorithm used here is that as soon as the user types a letter, a delayed request is started. If they don't type another letter before the one-second delay is up, then the request goes through. Otherwise, the first request is removed from the request queue before it goes out. If the request is already in progress, we try to interrupt it. The same goes for language changes, except we use a smaller delay. The good news is that now that I've done it once for you, you can use the same pattern in your own asynchronous programs.

```
adapter.setDropDownViewResource(
      android.R.layout.simple_spinner_dropdown_item);
fromSpinner.setAdapter(adapter);
toSpinner.setAdapter(adapter);

// Automatically select two spinner items
fromSpinner.setSelection(8); // English (en)
toSpinner.setSelection(11); // French (fr)
}
```

In Android, an Adapter is a class that binds a data source (in this case, the languages array defined in arrays.xml) to a user interface control (in this case, a spinner). We use the standard layouts provided by Android for individual items in the list and for the drop-down box you see when you select the spinner.

Next we set up the user interface handlers in the setListeners() routine (called from line 44 of onCreate()):

```
Translate/src/org/example/translate/Translate.java
private void setListeners() {
  // Define event listeners
  textWatcher = new TextWatcher() {
    public void beforeTextChanged(CharSequence s, int start,
        int count, int after) {
      /* Do nothing */
    }
    public void onTextChanged(CharSequence s, int start,
        int before, int count) {
      queueUpdate(1000 /* milliseconds */);
    }
    public void afterTextChanged(Editable s) {
      /* Do nothing */
    }
  };
  itemListener = new OnItemSelectedListener() {
    public void onItemSelected(AdapterView parent, View v,
        int position, long id) {
      queueUpdate(200 /* milliseconds */);
    }
    public void onNothingSelected(AdapterView parent) {
      /* Do nothing */
    }
  };

  // Set listeners on graphical user interface widgets
  origText.addTextChangedListener(textWatcher);
  fromSpinner.setOnItemSelectedListener(itemListener);
  toSpinner.setOnItemSelectedListener(itemListener);
}
```

We define two listeners: one that is called when the text to translate is changed and one that is called when the language is changed. queue-Update() puts a delayed update request on the main thread's to-do list using a Handler. We arbitrarily use a 1,000-millisecond delay for text changes and a 200-millisecond delay for language changes.

The update request is defined inside the initThreading() method:

```
Translate/src/org/example/translate/Translate.java
Line 1  private void initThreading() {
   -      guiThread = new Handler();
   -      transThread = Executors.newSingleThreadExecutor();
```

```
 5      // This task does a translation and updates the screen
  -     updateTask = new Runnable() {
  -         public void run() {
  -             // Get text to translate
  -             String original = origText.getText().toString().trim();
10
  -             // Cancel previous translation if there was one
  -             if (transPending != null)
  -                 transPending.cancel(true);

15             // Take care of the easy case
  -             if (original.length() == 0) {
  -                 transText.setText(R.string.empty);
  -                 retransText.setText(R.string.empty);
  -             } else {
20                 // Let user know we're doing something
  -                 transText.setText(R.string.translating);
  -                 retransText.setText(R.string.translating);

  -                 // Begin translation now but don't wait for it
25                 try {
  -                     TranslateTask translateTask = new TranslateTask(
  -                             Translate.this, // reference to activity
  -                             original, // original text
  -                             getLang(fromSpinner), // from language
30                             getLang(toSpinner) // to language
  -                     );
  -                     transPending = transThread.submit(translateTask);
  -                 } catch (RejectedExecutionException e) {
  -                     // Unable to start new task
35                     transText.setText(R.string.translation_error);
  -                     retransText.setText(R.string.translation_error);
  -                 }
  -             }
  -         }
40     };
  - }
```

We have two threads: the main Android thread used for the user interface and a translate thread that we'll create for running the actual translation job. We represent the first one with an Android Handler and the second with Java's ExecutorService.

Line 6 defines the update task, which will be scheduled by the queueUpdate() method. When it gets to run, it first fetches the current text to translate and then prepares to send a translation job to the translate thread. It cancels any translation that is already in progress (on line 13), takes care of the case where there is no text to translate (line 17), and fills in the two text controls where translated text will appear with the string "Translating..." (line 21). That text will be replaced later by the actual translated text.

Finally, on line 26, we create an instance of TranslateTask, giving it a reference to the Translate activity so it can call back to change the text, a string containing the original text, and the short names of the two languages selected in the spinners. Line 32 submits the new task to the translation thread, returning a reference to the Future return value. In this case, we don't really have a return value since TranslateTask changes the GUI directly, but we use the Future reference back on line 13 to cancel the translation if necessary.

To finish up the Translate class, here are a few utility functions used in other places:

Translate/src/org/example/translate/Translate.java

```java
/** Extract the language code from the current spinner item */
private String getLang(Spinner spinner) {
    String result = spinner.getSelectedItem().toString();
    int lparen = result.indexOf('(');
    int rparen = result.indexOf(')');
    result = result.substring(lparen + 1, rparen);
    return result;
}


/** Request an update to start after a short delay */
private void queueUpdate(long delayMillis) {
    // Cancel previous update if it hasn't started yet
    guiThread.removeCallbacks(updateTask);
    // Start an update if nothing happens after a few milliseconds
    guiThread.postDelayed(updateTask, delayMillis);
}


/** Modify text on the screen (called from another thread) */
public void setTranslated(String text) {
    guiSetText(transText, text);
}


/** Modify text on the screen (called from another thread) */
public void setRetranslated(String text) {
    guiSetText(retransText, text);
}


/** All changes to the GUI must be done in the GUI thread */
private void guiSetText(final TextView view, final String text) {
    guiThread.post(new Runnable() {
        public void run() {
            view.setText(text);
        }
    });
}
```

The getLang() method figures out which item is currently selected in a spinner, gets the string for that item, and parses out the short language code needed by the Translation API.

queueUpdate() puts an update request on the main thread's request queue but tells it to wait a little while before actually running it. If there was already a request on the queue, it's removed.

The setTranslated() and setRetranslated() methods will be used by TranslateTask to update the user interface when translated results come back from the web service. They both call a private function called guiSet-Text(), which uses the Handler.post() method to ask the main GUI thread to update the text on a TextView control. This extra step is necessary because you can't call user interface functions from non-user-interface threads, and guiSetText() will be called by the translate thread.

Here is the res/values/strings.xml file for the Translate example:

Translate/res/values/strings.xml

```
<?xml version="1.0" encoding="utf-8"?>
<resources>
    <string name="app_name">Translate</string>
    <string name="from_text">From:</string>
    <string name="to_text">To:</string>
    <string name="back_text">And back again:</string>
    <string name="original_hint">Enter text to translate</string>
    <string name="empty"></string>
    <string name="translating">Translating...</string>
    <string name="translation_error">(Translation error)</string>
    <string name="translation_interrupted">(Translation
        interrupted)</string>
</resources>
```

Finally, here's the definition of the TranslateTask class:

Translate/src/org/example/translate/TranslateTask.java

```
package org.example.translate;

import java.io.BufferedReader;
import java.io.IOException;
import java.io.InputStreamReader;
import java.net.HttpURLConnection;
import java.net.URL;
import java.net.URLEncoder;

import org.json.JSONException;
import org.json.JSONObject;

import android.util.Log;
```

```java
public class TranslateTask implements Runnable {
    private static final String TAG = "TranslateTask";
    private final Translate translate;
    private final String original, from, to;

    TranslateTask(Translate translate, String original, String from,
            String to) {
        this.translate = translate;
        this.original = original;
        this.from = from;
        this.to = to;
    }

    public void run() {
        // Translate the original text to the target language
        String trans = doTranslate(original, from, to);
        translate.setTranslated(trans);

        // Then translate what we got back to the first language.
        // Ideally it would be identical but it usually isn't.
        String retrans = doTranslate(trans, to, from); // swapped
        translate.setRetranslated(retrans);
    }

    /**
     * Call the Google Translation API to translate a string from one
     * language to another. For more info on the API see:
     * http://code.google.com/apis/ajaxlanguage
     */
    private String doTranslate(String original, String from,
            String to) {
        String result = translate.getResources().getString(
                R.string.translation_error);
        HttpURLConnection con = null;
        Log.d(TAG, "doTranslate(" + original + ", " + from + ", "
                + to + ")");

        try {
            // Check if task has been interrupted
            if (Thread.interrupted())
                throw new InterruptedException();

            // Build RESTful query for Google API
            String q = URLEncoder.encode(original, "UTF-8");
            URL url = new URL(
                    "http://ajax.googleapis.com/ajax/services/language/translate"
                        + "?v=1.0" + "&q=" + q + "&langpair=" + from
                        + "%7C" + to);
            con = (HttpURLConnection) url.openConnection();
            con.setReadTimeout(10000 /* milliseconds */);
            con.setConnectTimeout(15000 /* milliseconds */);
```

```java
        con.setRequestMethod("GET");
        con.addRequestProperty("Referer",
            "http://www.pragprog.com/titles/eband3/hello-android");
        con.setDoInput(true);

        // Start the query
        con.connect();

        // Check if task has been interrupted
        if (Thread.interrupted())
            throw new InterruptedException();

        // Read results from the query
        BufferedReader reader = new BufferedReader(
            new InputStreamReader(con.getInputStream(), "UTF-8"));
        String payload = reader.readLine();
        reader.close();

        // Parse to get translated text
        JSONObject jsonObject = new JSONObject(payload);
        result = jsonObject.getJSONObject("responseData")
            .getString("translatedText")
            .replace("&#39;", "'")
            .replace("&amp;", "&");

        // Check if task has been interrupted
        if (Thread.interrupted())
            throw new InterruptedException();

    } catch (IOException e) {
        Log.e(TAG, "IOException", e);
    } catch (JSONException e) {
        Log.e(TAG, "JSONException", e);
    } catch (InterruptedException e) {
        Log.d(TAG, "InterruptedException", e);
        result = translate.getResources().getString(
            R.string.translation_interrupted);
    } finally {
        if (con != null) {
            con.disconnect();
        }
    }

    // All done
    Log.d(TAG, "   -> returned " + result);
    return result;
    }
}
```

This is a nice example of calling a RESTful web service using HttpURL-Connection, parsing results in JavaScript Object Notation (JSON) format, and handling all sorts of network errors and requests for interruptions. I'm not going to explain it in detail here because it contains nothing Android-specific except for a few debugging messages.

7.5 Fast-Forward >>

In this chapter, we covered a lot of ground, from opening a simple web page to using an asynchronous web service. HTML/JavaScript programming is beyond the scope of this book, but several good references are available. If you're going to do much concurrent programming with classes such as ExecutorService, I recommend *Java Concurrency in Practice* [Goe06] by Brian Goetz.

The next chapter will explore a new level of interactivity through location and sensor services. If you're anxious to learn more about data sources and data binding, you can skip ahead to Chapter 9, *Putting SQL to Work*, on page 171.

Chapter 8

Locating and Sensing

The Android platform uses many different technologies. Some of them are new, and some have been seen before in other settings. What's unique about Android is how these technologies work together. In this chapter, we'll consider the following:

- Location awareness, through inexpensive GPS devices
- Handheld accelerometers, such as those found on the Nintendo Wii remote
- Mashups, often combining maps with other information

Several popular Android programs use these concepts to create a more compelling and relevant experience for the user. For example, the Locale application[1] can adapt the settings on your phone based on where you are. Are you always forgetting to set your ringer to vibrate when you're at work or the movies? Locale can take care of that using the Android Location API described here.

8.1 Location, Location, Location

Right now there are thirty-one satellites zipping around the world with nothing better to do than help you find your way to the grocery store. The Global Positioning System (GPS), originally developed by the military but then converted to civilian use, beams highly precise time signals to Earth-based receivers such as the one in your Android phone. With good reception and a little math, the GPS chip can figure out your position to within 50 feet.[2]

---

1. http://www.androidlocale.com
2. You don't have to know how GPS works to use it, but if you're curious, see http://electronics.howstuffworks.com/gadgets/travel/gps.htm.

> ### Joe Asks...
> #### Does GPS Let Anyone Snoop on My Location?
>
> No. GPS receivers are just that—receivers. The GPS chip, and thus any program running in your Android device, knows where it is. But unless one of those programs deliberately transmits that information, nobody can use it to find you.

In addition to GPS, Android also supports calculating your position using information from nearby cell phone towers, and if you're connected to a wifi hotspot, it can use that too. Keep in mind that all these location providers are unreliable to some extent. When you walk inside a building, for example, GPS signals can't reach you.

To demonstrate Android's location services, let's write a test program that simply displays your current position and keeps updating it on the screen as you move around. You can see the program in Figure 8.1, on the facing page.

Where Am I?

Start by creating a "Hello, Android" application using these parameters in the New Project wizard:

```
Project name: LocationTest
Build Target: Android 2.2
Application name: LocationTest
Package name: org.example.locationtest
Create Activity: LocationTest
Min SDK Version: 8
```

Access to location information is protected by Android permissions. To gain access, you'll need to add these lines in the AndroidManifest.xml file before the <application> tag:

LocationTest/AndroidManifest.xml

```
<uses-permission
  android:name="android.permission.ACCESS_COARSE_LOCATION" />
<uses-permission
  android:name="android.permission.ACCESS_FINE_LOCATION" />
```

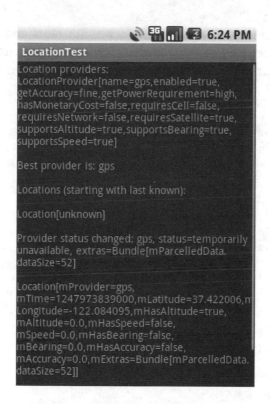

Figure 8.1: TESTING THE LOCATIONMANAGER

In this example, both fine-grained location providers such as GPS and coarse-grained location providers such as cell tower triangulation will be supported.

For the user interface, we're going to print all the location data into a big scrolling TextView, which is defined in res/layout/main.xml:

LocationTest/res/layout/main.xml

```xml
<?xml version="1.0" encoding="utf-8"?>
<ScrollView
    xmlns:android="http://schemas.android.com/apk/res/android"
    android:orientation="vertical"
    android:layout_width="fill_parent"
    android:layout_height="fill_parent">
    <TextView
        android:id="@+id/output"
        android:layout_width="fill_parent"
        android:layout_height="wrap_content" />
</ScrollView>
```

With the preliminaries out of the way, we can start coding. Here's the outline of the LocationTest class and the onCreate() method. (Ignore the reference to LocationListener on line 15 for now; we'll come back to it later.)

LocationTest/src/org/example/locationtest/LocationTest.java

```
Line 1   package org.example.locationtest;

         import java.util.List;

    5    import android.app.Activity;
         import android.location.Criteria;
         import android.location.Location;
         import android.location.LocationListener;
         import android.location.LocationManager;
   10    import android.location.LocationProvider;
         import android.os.Bundle;
         import android.widget.TextView;

         public class LocationTest extends Activity implements
   15        LocationListener {
           private LocationManager mgr;
           private TextView output;
           private String best;

   20      @Override
           public void onCreate(Bundle savedInstanceState) {
             super.onCreate(savedInstanceState);
             setContentView(R.layout.main);

   25        mgr = (LocationManager) getSystemService(LOCATION_SERVICE);
             output = (TextView) findViewById(R.id.output);

             log("Location providers:");
             dumpProviders();
   30
             Criteria criteria = new Criteria();
             best = mgr.getBestProvider(criteria, true);
             log("\nBest provider is: " + best);

   35        log("\nLocations (starting with last known):");
             Location location = mgr.getLastKnownLocation(best);
             dumpLocation(location);
           }
         }
```

The starting point for Android location services is the getSystemService() call on line 25. It returns a LocationManager class that we save into a field for later use.

On line 29, we call our dumpProviders() method to print a list of all the location providers in the system.

Next we need to pick one of the possible providers to use. I've seen some examples that simply pick the first available one, but I recommend using the getBestProvider() method, as shown here. Android will pick the best provider according to a Criteria that you provide (see line 31). If you have any restrictions on cost, power, accuracy, and so on, this is where you put them. In this example, there are no restrictions.

Depending on the provider, it may take some time for the device to figure out your current location. This could be a few seconds, a minute, or more. However, Android remembers the last position it returned, so we can query and print that immediately on line 36. This location could be out of date—for example, if the device was turned off and moved—but it's usually better than nothing.

Knowing where we were is only half the fun. Where are we going next?

Updating the Location

To have Android notify you about location changes, call the requestLocationUpdates() method on the LocationManager object. To save battery power, we want updates only when the program is in the foreground. Therefore, we need to hook into the Android activity life-cycle methods by overriding onResume() and onPause():

LocationTest/src/org/example/locationtest/LocationTest.java

```
@Override
protected void onResume() {
    super.onResume();
    // Start updates (doc recommends delay >= 60000 ms)
    mgr.requestLocationUpdates(best, 15000, 1, this);
}

@Override
protected void onPause() {
    super.onPause();
    // Stop updates to save power while app paused
    mgr.removeUpdates(this);
}
```

When the application resumes, we call requestLocationUpdates() to start the update process. It takes four parameters: the provider name, a delay (so you don't get updates too often), a minimum distance (changes less than this are ignored), and a LocationListener object.

When the application pauses, we call removeUpdates() to stop getting updates. The location provider will be powered down if it's not needed for a while.

Now you know why LocationTest implements LocationListener, so we could just pass a reference to the activity instead of making a new listener object. That will save us about 1KB of memory at runtime.

Here's the definition of the four methods required by that interface:

LocationTest/src/org/example/locationtest/LocationTest.java

```java
public void onLocationChanged(Location location) {
    dumpLocation(location);
}

public void onProviderDisabled(String provider) {
    log("\nProvider disabled: " + provider);
}

public void onProviderEnabled(String provider) {
    log("\nProvider enabled: " + provider);
}

public void onStatusChanged(String provider, int status,
        Bundle extras) {
    log("\nProvider status changed: " + provider + ", status="
        + S[status] + ", extras=" + extras);
}
```

The most important method in the bunch is onLocationChanged().

As the name suggests, it's called every time the provider notices that the device's location has changed. The onProviderDisabled(), onProviderEnabled(), and onStatusChanged() methods can be used to switch to other providers in case your first choice becomes unavailable.

The code for the remaining methods of LocationTest—log(), dumpProviders(), and dumpLocation()—is not very interesting, but here it is for completeness:

LocationTest/src/org/example/locationtest/LocationTest.java

```java
// Define human readable names
private static final String[] A = { "invalid", "n/a", "fine", "coarse" };
private static final String[] P = { "invalid", "n/a", "low", "medium",
        "high" };
private static final String[] S = { "out of service",
        "temporarily unavailable", "available" };
```

```java
/** Write a string to the output window */
private void log(String string) {
    output.append(string + "\n");
}

/** Write information from all location providers */
private void dumpProviders() {
    List<String> providers = mgr.getAllProviders();
    for (String provider : providers) {
        dumpProvider(provider);
    }
}

/** Write information from a single location provider */
private void dumpProvider(String provider) {
    LocationProvider info = mgr.getProvider(provider);
    StringBuilder builder = new StringBuilder();
    builder.append("LocationProvider[")
           .append("name=")
           .append(info.getName())
           .append(",enabled=")
           .append(mgr.isProviderEnabled(provider))
           .append(",getAccuracy=")
           .append(A[info.getAccuracy() + 1])
           .append(",getPowerRequirement=")
           .append(P[info.getPowerRequirement() + 1])
           .append(",hasMonetaryCost=")
           .append(info.hasMonetaryCost())
           .append(",requiresCell=")
           .append(info.requiresCell())
           .append(",requiresNetwork=")
           .append(info.requiresNetwork())
           .append(",requiresSatellite=")
           .append(info.requiresSatellite())
           .append(",supportsAltitude=")
           .append(info.supportsAltitude())
           .append(",supportsBearing=")
           .append(info.supportsBearing())
           .append(",supportsSpeed=")
           .append(info.supportsSpeed())
           .append("]");
    log(builder.toString());
}

/** Describe the given location, which might be null */
private void dumpLocation(Location location) {
    if (location == null)
        log("\nLocation[unknown]");
    else
        log("\n" + location.toString());
}
```

If you don't want to type it all in, you can find it all in the downloadable samples on the book's website.

Emulation Notes

If you run the LocationTest example on a real device, it will show your current position as you walk around. On the emulator, it uses a fake GPS provider that always returns the same position unless you change it. Let's do that now.

In Eclipse you can change your simulated location using the Emulator Control view (Window > Show View > Other... > Android > Emulator Control). Scroll down to the bottom, and you'll find a place to enter the longitude and latitude manually. When you click the Send button, Eclipse will send the new position to the emulated device, and you'll see it displayed in any programs that are watching for it.

You can also run the Dalvik Debug Monitor Service (DDMS) program outside of Eclipse and send fake position changes in that way. In addition to manual, position-at-a-time updates, you can use a recorded path read from an external file. See the DDMS documentation for more information.[3]

With Android location providers, you can find out where you are in a broad, global sense. If you want more local information such as tilt and temperature, you have to use a different API. That's the subject of the next section.

8.2 Set Sensors to Maximum

Let's say you're writing a racing game so you need to give the player a way to steer their car on the screen. One way would be to use buttons, like driving games on a Sony PlayStation or the Nintendo DS. Press right to steer right, press left to steer left, and hold down another button for the gas. It works, but it's not very natural.

Have you ever watched somebody play one of those games? Unconsciously, they sway from side to side when making a hairpin curve, jerk the controller when bumping into another car, lean forward when speeding up, and pull back when putting on the brakes. Wouldn't it be

---

3. http://d.android.com/guide/developing/tools/ddms.html

cool if those motions actually had some effect on the game play? Now they can.

Engaging Sensors

The Android SDK supports many different types of sensor devices:

- TYPE_ACCELEROMETER: Measures acceleration in the x-, y-, and z-axes
- TYPE_LIGHT: Tells you how bright your surrounding area is
- TYPE_MAGNETIC_FIELD: Returns magnetic attraction in the x-, y-, and z-axes
- TYPE_ORIENTATION: Measures the yaw, pitch, and roll of the device
- TYPE_PRESSURE: Senses the current atmospheric pressure
- TYPE_PROXIMITY: Provides the distance between the sensor and some object
- TYPE_TEMPERATURE: Measures the temperature of the surrounding area

Not all devices will offer all this functionality, of course.[4]

The SensorTest example, available on the book's website, demonstrates using the Sensor API. Android's SensorManager class is similar to LocationManager, except the updates will come much more quickly, perhaps hundreds per second. To get access to the sensors, you first call the getSystemService() method like this:

SensorTest/src/org/example/sensortest/SensorTest.java
```
private SensorManager mgr;
  // ...
  mgr = (SensorManager) getSystemService(SENSOR_SERVICE);
```

Then you call the registerListener() in your onResume() method to start getting updates and call unregisterListener() in your onPause() method to stop getting them.

Interpreting Sensor Readings

The sensor service will call your onSensorChanged() method every time a value changes.

---

4. Unfortunately, Android 1.5 removed support for the TRICORDER sensor that turned your device into a fully functional *Star Trek* tricorder. Darn it, Jim—I'm a programmer, not an *ovum paschalis*.

It should look something like this:

SensorTest/src/org/example/sensortest/SensorTest.java

```java
public void onSensorChanged(SensorEvent event) {
    for (int i = 0; i < event.values.length; i++) {
        // ...
    }
}
```

All the sensors return an array of floating-point values. The size of the array depends on the particular sensor; for example, TYPE_TEMPERATURE returns only one value, the temperature in degrees Celsius. You may not even need to use all the numbers returned. For instance, if you just need a compass heading, you can use the first number returned from the TYPE_ORIENTATION sensor.

Turning the sensor readings (especially from the accelerometer) into meaningful information is something of a black art. Here are a few tips to keep in mind:

- Accelerometer readings are extremely jittery. You'll need to smooth out the data using some kind of weighted averaging, but you have to be careful not to smooth it too much, or your interface will feel laggy and soft.
- Sensor numbers will come in at random times. You may get several in a row, then have a short pause, and then receive a bunch more. Don't assume a nice even rate.
- Try to get ahead of the user by predicting what they're going to do next. Let's say the last three readings show the start of a roll to the right, with each one a little faster than the last. You can guess with some degree of accuracy what the next reading is going to be and start reacting based on your prediction.

The most challenging use of sensors is an action game that requires a one-to-one connection between how the player moves the device and what happens on the screen. Unfortunately, the emulator isn't going to be much use for this kind of thing.

Emulation Notes

According to Google, it is not possible to test the sensors using the emulator at all. Most computers don't have a light sensor, a GPS chip, or a compass built into them. Sure enough, if you run the SensorTest program in the emulator, it will display no results at all. However, a

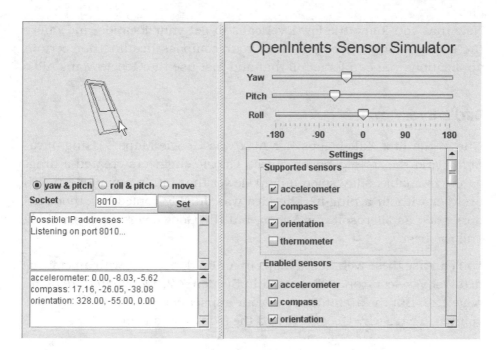

Figure 8.2: FAKING OUT THE SENSORS WITH THE SENSOR SIMULATOR

project called OpenIntents[5] provides an alternate sensor's API that you can call just for testing purposes.

The way it works is that you connect the emulator to another application running on your desktop computer called the Sensor Simulator. The simulator shows a picture of a virtual phone and lets you move it around on the screen with the mouse (see Figure 8.2), and then it feeds those movements to your Android program running on the emulator. If your development computer actually does have sensors of its own (like the Apple MacBook) or you can connect to a Wii remote with Bluetooth, the Sensor Simulator can use that as a data source.

The downside is that you have to modify your source code to make it work. See the OpenIntents website for more information if you want to try it. My recommendation is to forget about sensor emulation and get your hands on a real device. Keep tweaking your algorithms until it feels right.

---

5. http://www.openintents.org

Now that you know the low-level calls to get your location and query the sensors for numbers such as your compass heading, for certain applications you can forget all that and just use the Google Maps API.

8.3 Bird's-Eye View

One of the first "killer apps" for Ajax was Google Maps.[6] Using JavaScript and the XmlHttpRequest object, Google engineers created a draggable, zoomable, silky smooth map viewer that ran in any modern web browser without a plug-in. The idea was quickly copied by other vendors such as Microsoft and Yahoo, but the Google version is arguably still the best.

You can use these web-based maps in Android, perhaps with an embedded WebView control as discussed in Section 7.2, *Web with a View*, on page 126. But the architecture of your application would be overly convoluted. That's why Google created the MapView control.

Embedding a MapView

A MapView can be embedded directly in your Android application with just a few lines of code. Most of the functionality of Google Maps, plus hooks for adding your own touches, is provided (see Figure 8.3, on the next page).

The MapView class can also tie into your location and sensor providers. It can show your current location on the map and even display a compass showing what direction you're heading. Let's create a sample program to demonstrate a few of its capabilities.

First create a "Hello, Android" application using these values in the wizard:

```
Project name: MyMap
Build Target: Google APIs (Platform: 2.2)
Application name: MyMap
Package name: org.example.mymap
Create Activity: MyMap
Min SDK Version: 8
```

Note that we're using the "Google APIs" build target instead of the "Android 2.2" target. That's because the Google Maps APIs are not part of the normal Android distribution. Edit the layout file, and replace it with a MapView that takes over the whole screen.

---

6. http://maps.google.com

Figure 8.3: Embedded map showing your current location

MyMap/res/layout/main.xml

```xml
<?xml version="1.0" encoding="utf-8"?>
<LinearLayout
    xmlns:android="http://schemas.android.com/apk/res/android"
    android:id="@+id/frame"
    android:orientation="vertical"
    android:layout_width="fill_parent"
    android:layout_height="fill_parent">
    <com.google.android.maps.MapView
        android:id="@+id/map"
        android:apiKey="MapAPIKey"
        android:layout_width="fill_parent"
        android:layout_height="fill_parent"
        android:clickable="true" />
</LinearLayout>
```

Substitute *MapAPIKey* with a Google Maps API key that you get from Google.[7] Note that we have to use the fully qualified name (com.google.

---

7.   http://code.google.com/android/maps-api-signup.html

android.maps.MapView) because MapView is not a standard Android class. We also need to stick a <*uses-library*> tag in the <*application*> element of AndroidManifest.xml:

MyMap/AndroidManifest.xml

```xml
<?xml version="1.0" encoding="utf-8"?>
<manifest xmlns:android="http://schemas.android.com/apk/res/android"
    package="org.example.mymap"
    android:versionCode="1"
    android:versionName="1.0">
    <uses-permission
        android:name="android.permission.ACCESS_COARSE_LOCATION" />
    <uses-permission
        android:name="android.permission.ACCESS_FINE_LOCATION" />
    <uses-permission
        android:name="android.permission.INTERNET" />
    <application android:icon="@drawable/icon"
        android:label="@string/app_name">
      <activity android:name=".MyMap"
            android:label="@string/app_name">
        <intent-filter>
            <action android:name="android.intent.action.MAIN" />
            <category android:name="android.intent.category.LAUNCHER" />
        </intent-filter>
      </activity>
      <uses-library android:name="com.google.android.maps" />
    </application>
    <uses-sdk android:minSdkVersion="3" android:targetSdkVersion="8" />
</manifest>
```

If you leave out the <*uses-library*> tag, you will get a ClassNotFoundException at runtime.

In addition to the fine- and coarse-grained location providers, the MapView class needs Internet access so that it can call Google's servers to get the map image tiles. These will be cached in your application directory automatically.

Here's the outline of the MyMap class:

MyMap/src/org/example/mymap/MyMap.java

```java
package org.example.mymap;

import android.os.Bundle;

import com.google.android.maps.MapActivity;
import com.google.android.maps.MapController;
import com.google.android.maps.MapView;
import com.google.android.maps.MyLocationOverlay;
```

```
public class MyMap extends MapActivity {
    private MapView map;
    private MapController controller;

    @Override
    public void onCreate(Bundle savedInstanceState) {
        super.onCreate(savedInstanceState);
        setContentView(R.layout.main);
        initMapView();
        initMyLocation();
    }
    @Override
    protected boolean isRouteDisplayed() {
        // Required by MapActivity
        return false;
    }
}
```

The most important part is that your activity has to extend MapActivity. The MapActivity class spins up the background threads, connects to the Internet for tile data, handles caching, does animations, takes care of the life cycle, and much more. All you need to do is properly set it up and let it go.

Getting Ready

The first thing we need to do is call findViewById() to get access to the MapView and its container. We can do that in the initMapView() method:

MyMap/src/org/example/mymap/MyMap.java

```
private void initMapView() {
    map = (MapView) findViewById(R.id.map);
    controller = map.getController();
    map.setSatellite(true);
    map.setBuiltInZoomControls(true);
}
```

The getController() method returns a MapController that we'll use to position and zoom the map. setSatellite() switches the map into satellite mode, and setBuiltInZoomControls()[8] turns on the standard zoom controls. The MapView class will take care of making the controls visible when the user pans the map and will take care of fading them out slowly when panning stops.

The last step is to tell the MapView to follow your position in the initMyLocation() method.

---

8. Introduced in Android 1.5.

> \\//
> ⌒ **Joe Asks...**
>
> **Why Is MapView in the com.google.android.maps Package and Not android.maps?**
>
> Any code in the android.* packages is part of the Android core. It's open source and available on every Android device. By contrast, maps are proprietary to Google and to the data providers that Google paid for the geological information and imagery. Google provides the API free of charge as long as you agree to certain conditions.* If you're not happy with the restrictions, you can roll your own views and find your own data sources, but it's not going to be easy or cheap.
>
> _____
> *.   http://code.google.com/apis/maps/terms.html

MyMap/src/org/example/mymap/MyMap.java

```
private void initMyLocation() {
    final MyLocationOverlay overlay = new MyLocationOverlay(this, map);
    overlay.enableMyLocation();
    //overlay.enableCompass(); // does not work in emulator
    overlay.runOnFirstFix(new Runnable() {
        public void run() {
            // Zoom in to current location
            controller.setZoom(8);
            controller.animateTo(overlay.getMyLocation());
        }
    });
    map.getOverlays().add(overlay);
}
```

Android provides a MyLocationOverlay class that does most of the heavy lifting. An overlay is just something that is drawn on top of the map, which in this case is a pulsing dot showing your current location. You call enableMyLocation() to tell the overlay to start listening to location updates and call enableCompass() to tell it to start listening to updates from the compass.

The runOnFirstFix() method tells the overlay what to do the first time it gets a position reading from the location provider. In this case, we set the zoom level and then start an animation that moves the map from wherever it's pointing now to where you are located.

If you run the program now, you should see something like Figure 8.3, on page 165. Touch and drag the screen to move around the map, and use the zoom buttons to get a closer look. When you walk around carrying the phone, the dot on the map should follow you.

Emulation Notes

The first time you run the MyMap program on the emulator you may get an Android AVD Error. Follow the directions in Section 1.3, *Creating an AVD*, on page 9 to create a new AVD for the "Google APIs (Google Inc.) - API Level 8" build target called "em22google."

On the emulator, you'll initially see a zoomed-out map of the world and no dot for your current location. As before, use the Emulator Control view in Eclipse (or in the stand-alone DDMS program) to feed fake GPS data to the sample application.

When running in the emulator, the compass inset will not be shown because the compass sensor is not emulated.

8.4 Fast-Forward >>

This chapter introduced you to the exciting new world of location- and environmental-aware mobile computing. These technologies, in combination with trends such as the adoption of broadband mobile Internet and the exponential growth of computing power and storage, are going to revolutionize the way we interact with computers and with each other.

Another way to perceive the world is by looking and listening. Android provides the Camera class[9] for taking photographs using the built-in camera (if there is one), but you can also use it to do other things like make a bar-code reader. The MediaRecorder class[10] allows you to record and store audio clips. These are beyond the scope of this book, but if you need them for your program, consult the online documentation.

Speaking of storage, the next chapter will show you how to use SQL to store structured information (for example, a travel log of locations, photographs, and notes) locally on your mobile phone. If that's not your area of interest, you can skip ahead to Chapter 10, *3D Graphics in OpenGL*, on page 191 and learn how to unlock Android's hidden 3D graphics potential.

---

9. http://d.android.com/reference/android/hardware/Camera.html
10. http://d.android.com/reference/android/media/MediaRecorder.html

Chapter 9

Putting SQL to Work

In Chapter 6, *Storing Local Data*, on page 109, we explored keeping data around in preferences and in plain files. That works fine when the amount of data is small or when the data is all one type (such as a picture or an audio file). However, there is a better way to store large amounts of structured data: a relational database.

For the past thirty years, databases have been a staple of enterprise application development, but until recently they were too expensive and unwieldy for smaller-scale use. That is changing with small embedded engines such as the one included with the Android platform.

This chapter will show you how to use Android's embedded database engine, SQLite. You'll also learn how to use Android's data binding to connect your data sources to your user interface. Finally, you'll look at the ContentProvider class, which allows two applications to share the same data.

9.1 Introducing SQLite

SQLite[1] is a tiny yet powerful database engine created by Dr. Richard Hipp in 2000. It is arguably the most widely deployed SQL database engine in the world. Besides Android, SQLite can be found in the Apple iPhone, Symbian phones, Mozilla Firefox, Skype, PHP, Adobe AIR, Mac OS X, Solaris, and many other places.

---

1. http://www.sqlite.org

> **SQLite License**
>
> The SQLite source code contains no license because it is in the public domain. Instead of a license, the source offers you this blessing:
>
> *May you do good and not evil.*
>
> *May you find forgiveness for yourself and forgive others.*
>
> *May you share freely, never taking more than you give.*

There are three reasons why it is so popular:

- It's free. The authors have placed it in the public domain and don't charge for its use.
- It's small. The current version is about 150KB, well within the memory budget of an Android phone.
- It requires no setup or administration. There is no server, no config file, and no need for a database administrator.

A SQLite database is just a file. You can take that file, move it around, and even copy it to another system (for example, from your phone to your workstation), and it will work fine. Android stores the file in the /data/data/*packagename*/databases directory (see Figure 9.1, on the facing page). You can use the adb command or the File Explorer view in Eclipse (Window > Show View > Other... > Android > File Explorer) to view, move, or delete it.

Instead of calling Java I/O routines to access this file from your program, you run Structured Query Language (SQL) statements. Through its helper classes and convenience methods, Android hides some of the syntax from you, but you still need to know a bit of SQL to use it.

9.2 SQL 101

If you've used Oracle, SQL Server, MySQL, DB2, or other database engines, then SQL should be old hat to you. You can skip this section and go to Section 9.3, *Hello, Database*, on page 174. For the rest of you, here's a quick refresher.

Figure 9.1: SQLITE STORES AN ENTIRE DATABASE IN ONE FILE.

To use a SQL database, you submit SQL statements and get back results. There are three main types of SQL statements: DDL, Modification, and Query.

DDL Statements

A database file can have any number of tables. A table consists of rows, and each row has a certain number of columns. Each column of the table has a name and a data type (text string, number, and so forth). You define these tables and column names by first running Data Definition Language (DDL) statements. Here's a statement that creates a table with three columns:

SQLite/create.sql

```
create table mytable (
    _id integer primary key autoincrement,
    name text,
    phone text );
```

One of the columns is designated as the **PRIMARY KEY**, a number that uniquely identifies the row. **AUTOINCREMENT** means that the database will add 1 to the key for every record to make sure it's unique. By convention, the first column is always called _id. The _id column isn't strictly required for SQLite, but later when we want to use an Android ContentProvider, we'll need it.

Note that, unlike most databases, in SQLite the column types are just hints. If you try to store a string in an integer column, or vice versa, it will just work with no complaints. The SQLite authors consider this to be a feature, not a bug.

Modification Statements

SQL provides a number of statements that let you insert, delete, and update records in the database. For example, to add a few phone numbers, you could use this:

`SQLite/insert.sql`

```
insert into mytable values(null, 'Steven King', '555-1212');
insert into mytable values(null, 'John Smith', '555-2345');
insert into mytable values(null, 'Fred Smitheizen', '555-4321');
```

The values are specified in the same order you used in the **CREATE TABLE** statement. We specify **NULL** for _id because SQLite will figure that value out for us.

Query Statements

Once data has been loaded into a table, you run queries against the table using a **SELECT** statement. For example, if you wanted to get the third entry, you could do this:

`SQLite/selectid.sql`

```
select * from mytable where(_id=3);
```

It's more likely you'd want to look up a person's phone number by name. Here's how you'd find all the records containing "Smith" in the name:

`SQLite/selectwhere.sql`

```
select name, phone from mytable where(name like "%smith%");
```

Keep in mind that SQL is case insensitive. Keywords, column names, and even search strings can be specified in either uppercase or lowercase.

Now you know just enough about SQL to be dangerous. Let's see how to put that knowledge to work in a simple program.

9.3 Hello, Database

To demonstrate SQLite, let's create a little application called Events that stores records in a database and displays them later. We're going to start simple and build up from there. Open a new "Hello, Android" program using these values in the project wizard:

```
Project name: Events
Build Target: Android 2.2
Application name: Events
```

```
Package name: org.example.events
Create Activity: Events
Min SDK Version: 8
```

As always, you can download the complete source code from the book's website.

We need somewhere to hold a few constants describing the database, so let's create a Constants interface:

Eventsv1/src/org/example/events/Constants.java

```java
package org.example.events;

import android.provider.BaseColumns;

public interface Constants extends BaseColumns {
    public static final String TABLE_NAME = "events";

    // Columns in the Events database
    public static final String TIME = "time";
    public static final String TITLE = "title";
}
```

Each event will be stored as a row in the events table. Each row will have an _id, time, and title column. _id is the primary key, declared in the BaseColumns interface that we extend. time and title will be used for a time stamp and event title, respectively.

Using SQLiteOpenHelper

Next we create a helper class called EventsData to represent the database itself. This class extends the Android SQLiteOpenHelper class, which manages database creation and versions. All you need to do is provide a constructor and override two methods.

Eventsv1/src/org/example/events/EventsData.java

```java
package org.example.events;

import static android.provider.BaseColumns._ID;
import static org.example.events.Constants.TABLE_NAME;
import static org.example.events.Constants.TIME;
import static org.example.events.Constants.TITLE;
import android.content.Context;
import android.database.sqlite.SQLiteDatabase;
import android.database.sqlite.SQLiteOpenHelper;

public class EventsData extends SQLiteOpenHelper {
    private static final String DATABASE_NAME = "events.db";
    private static final int DATABASE_VERSION = 1;
```

```
15      /** Create a helper object for the Events database */
-       public EventsData(Context ctx) {
-           super(ctx, DATABASE_NAME, null, DATABASE_VERSION);
-       }
-
20      @Override
-       public void onCreate(SQLiteDatabase db) {
-           db.execSQL("CREATE TABLE " + TABLE_NAME + " (" + _ID
-                   + " INTEGER PRIMARY KEY AUTOINCREMENT, " + TIME
-                   + " INTEGER," + TITLE + " TEXT NOT NULL);");
25      }
-
-       @Override
-       public void onUpgrade(SQLiteDatabase db, int oldVersion,
-           int newVersion) {
30          db.execSQL("DROP TABLE IF EXISTS " + TABLE_NAME);
-           onCreate(db);
-       }
-   }
```

The constructor starts on line 16. DATABASE_NAME is the actual filename
of the database we'll be using (events.db), and DATABASE_VERSION is just
a number we make up. If this were a real program, you would increase
the version number whenever you had to make significant changes to
the database design (for example, to add a new column).

The first time you try to access a database, SQLiteOpenHelper will notice
it doesn't exist and call the onCreate() method to create it. On line 21,
we override that and run a **CREATE TABLE** SQL statement. This will create
the events table and the events.db database file that contains it.

When Android detects you're referencing an old database (based on
the version number), it will call the onUpgrade() method (line 28). In
this example, we just delete the old table, but you could do something
smarter here if you like. For example, you could run an **ALTER TABLE** SQL
command to add a column to an existing database.

Defining the Main Program

Our first attempt at the Events program will use a local SQLite database
to store the events, and it will show them as a string inside a TextView.

Joe Asks...

Why Is Constants an Interface?

It's a Java thing. I don't know about you, but I dislike having to repeat the class name every time I use a constant. For example, I want to just type TIME and not Constants.TIME. Traditionally, the way to do that in Java is to use interfaces. Classes can inherit from the Constants interface and then leave out the interface name when referencing any fields. If you look at the BaseColumns interface, you'll see the Android programmers used the same trick.

Starting with Java 5, however, there's a better way: static imports. That's the method I'll use in EventsData and other classes in this chapter. Since Constants is an interface, you can use it the old way or the new way as you prefer.

Unfortunately, as of this writing, Eclipse's support for static imports is a little spotty, so if you use static imports in your own programs, Eclipse may not insert the import statements for you automatically. Here's a little trick for Eclipse users: type a wildcard static import after the package statement (for example, import static org.example.events.Constants.*;) to make things compile. Later, you can use Source > Organize Imports to expand the wildcard and sort the import statements. Let's hope this will be more intuitive in future versions of Eclipse.

Define the layout file (layout/main.xml) as follows:

Eventsv1/res/layout/main.xml

```xml
<?xml version="1.0" encoding="utf-8"?>
<ScrollView
    xmlns:android="http://schemas.android.com/apk/res/android"
    android:layout_width="fill_parent"
    android:layout_height="fill_parent">
    <TextView
        android:id="@+id/text"
        android:layout_width="fill_parent"
        android:layout_height="wrap_content" />
</ScrollView>
```

This declares the TextView with an imaginative ID of text (R.id.text in code) and wraps it with a ScrollView in case there are too many events to fit on the screen. You can see how it looks in Figure 9.2, on the following page.

Figure 9.2: THE FIRST VERSION DISPLAYS DATABASE RECORDS IN A TEXTVIEW.

The main program is the onCreate() method in the Events activity. Here's the outline:

Eventsv1/src/org/example/events/Events.java

```
Line 1   package org.example.events;

         import static android.provider.BaseColumns._ID;
         import static org.example.events.Constants.TABLE_NAME;
    5    import static org.example.events.Constants.TIME;
         import static org.example.events.Constants.TITLE;
         import android.app.Activity;
         import android.content.ContentValues;
         import android.database.Cursor;
   10    import android.database.sqlite.SQLiteDatabase;
         import android.os.Bundle;
         import android.widget.TextView;

         public class Events extends Activity {
   15        private EventsData events;

            @Override
            public void onCreate(Bundle savedInstanceState) {
                super.onCreate(savedInstanceState);
   20           setContentView(R.layout.main);
                events = new EventsData(this);
                try {
                    addEvent("Hello, Android!");
                    Cursor cursor = getEvents();
   25               showEvents(cursor);
                } finally {
                    events.close();
                }
            }
   30    }
```

On line 20 of onCreate(), we set the layout for this view. Then we create an instance of the EventsData class on line 21 and start a **try** block. If you look ahead to line 27, you can see we close the database inside the **finally** block. So even if an error occurs in the middle, the database will still be closed.

The events table wouldn't be very interesting if there weren't any events, so on line 23 we call the addEvent() method to add an event to it. Every time you run this program, you'll get a new event. You could add menus or gestures or keystrokes to generate other events if you like, but I'll leave that as an exercise to the reader.

On line 24, we call the getEvents() method to get the list of events, and finally on line 25, we call the showEvents() method to display the list to the user.

Pretty easy, eh? Now let's define those new methods we just used.

Adding a Row

The addEvent() method puts a new record in the database using the string provided as the event title.

Eventsv1/src/org/example/events/Events.java

```
private void addEvent(String string) {
    // Insert a new record into the Events data source.
    // You would do something similar for delete and update.
    SQLiteDatabase db = events.getWritableDatabase();
    ContentValues values = new ContentValues();
    values.put(TIME, System.currentTimeMillis());
    values.put(TITLE, string);
    db.insertOrThrow(TABLE_NAME, null, values);
}
```

Since we need to modify the data, we call getWritableDatabase() to get a read/write handle to the events database. The database handle is cached, so you can call this method as many times as you like.

Next we fill in a ContentValues object with the current time and the event title and pass that to the insertOrThrow() method to do the actual **INSERT** SQL statement. You don't need to pass in the record ID because SQLite will make one up and return it from the method call.

As the name implies, insertOrThrow() can throw an exception (of type SQLException) if it fails. It doesn't have to be declared with a **throws** keyword because it's a RuntimeException and not a checked exception. However, if you want to, you can still handle it in a **try/catch** block like any other exception. If you don't handle it and there is an error, the program will terminate, and a traceback will be dumped to the Android log.

By default, as soon as you do the insert, the database is updated. If you need to batch up or delay modifications for some reason, consult the SQLite website for more details.

Running a Query

The getEvents() method does the database query to get a list of events:

Eventsv1/src/org/example/events/Events.java

```
private static String[] FROM = { _ID, TIME, TITLE, };
private static String ORDER_BY = TIME + " DESC";
private Cursor getEvents() {
    // Perform a managed query. The Activity will handle closing
    // and re-querying the cursor when needed.
    SQLiteDatabase db = events.getReadableDatabase();
    Cursor cursor = db.query(TABLE_NAME, FROM, null, null, null,
            null, ORDER_BY);
    startManagingCursor(cursor);
    return cursor;
}
```

We don't need to modify the database for a query, so we call getReadableDatabase() to get a read-only handle. Then we call query() to perform the actual **SELECT** SQL statement. FROM is an array of the columns we want, and ORDER_BY tells SQLite to return the results in order from newest to oldest.

Although we don't use them in this example, the query() method has parameters to specify a **WHERE** clause, a **GROUP BY** clause, and a **HAVING** clause. Actually, query() is just a convenience for the programmer. If you prefer, you could build up the **SELECT** statement yourself in a string and use the rawQuery() method to execute it. Either way, the return value is a Cursor object that represents the result set.

A Cursor is similar to a Java Iterator or a JDBC ResultSet. You call methods on it to get information about the current row, and then you call another method to move to the next row. We'll see how to use it when we display the results in a moment.

The final step is to call startManagingCursor(), which tells the activity to take care of managing the cursor's life cycle based on the activity's life cycle. For example, when the activity is paused, it will automatically deactivate the cursor and then requery it when the activity is restarted. When the activity terminates, all managed cursors will be closed.

Displaying the Query Results

The last method we need to define is showEvents(). This function takes a Cursor as input and formats the output so the user can read it.

`Eventsv1/src/org/example/events/Events.java`

```
private void showEvents(Cursor cursor) {
    // Stuff them all into a big string
    StringBuilder builder = new StringBuilder(
        "Saved events:\n");
    while (cursor.moveToNext()) {
        // Could use getColumnIndexOrThrow() to get indexes
        long id = cursor.getLong(0);
        long time = cursor.getLong(1);
        String title = cursor.getString(2);
        builder.append(id).append(": ");
        builder.append(time).append(": ");
        builder.append(title).append("\n");
    }
    // Display on the screen
    TextView text = (TextView) findViewById(R.id.text);
    text.setText(builder);
}
```

In this version of Events, we're just going to create a big string (see line 3) to hold all the events items, separated by newlines. This is not the recommended way to do things, but it'll work for now.

Line 5 calls the Cursor.moveToNext() method to advance to the next row in the data set. When you first get a Cursor, it is positioned before the first record, so calling moveToNext() gets you to the first record. We keep looping until moveToNext() returns false, which indicates there are no more rows.

Inside the loop (line 7), we call getLong() and getString() to fetch data from the columns of interest, and then we append the values to the string (line 10). There is another method on Cursor, getColumnIndex-OrThrow(), that we could have used to get the column index numbers (the values 0, 1, and 2 passed to getLong() and getString()). However, it's a little slow, so if you need it, you should call it outside the loop and remember the indexes yourself.

Once all the rows have been processed, we look up the TextView from layout/main.xml and stuff the big string into it (line 15).

If you run the example now, you should see something like Figure 9.2, on page 178. Congratulations on your first Android database program! There is plenty of room for improvement, though.

What would happen if there were thousands or millions of events in the list? The program would be very slow and might run out of memory trying to build a string to hold them all. What if you wanted to let the user select one event and do something with it? If everything is in a string, you can't do that. Luckily, Android provides a better way: data binding.

9.4 Data Binding

Data binding allows you to connect your model (data) to your view with just a few lines of code. To demonstrate data binding, we'll modify the Events example to use a ListView that is bound to the result of a database query. First, we need to make the Events class extend ListActivity instead of Activity:

`Eventsv2/src/org/example/events/Events.java`

```
import android.app.ListActivity;
// ...
public class Events extends ListActivity {
   // ...
}
```

Next, we need to change how the events are displayed in the Events. showEvents() method:

`Eventsv2/src/org/example/events/Events.java`

```
import android.widget.SimpleCursorAdapter;
// ...
   private static int[] TO = { R.id.rowid, R.id.time, R.id.title, };
   private void showEvents(Cursor cursor) {
      // Set up data binding
      SimpleCursorAdapter adapter = new SimpleCursorAdapter(this,
            R.layout.item, cursor, FROM, TO);
      setListAdapter(adapter);
   }
```

Notice this code is much smaller than before (two lines vs. ten). The first line creates a SimpleCursorAdapter for the Cursor, and the second line tells the ListActivity to use the new adapter. The adapter acts as a go-between, connecting the view with its data source.

If you recall, we first used an adapter in the Translate sample program (see Translate.setAdapters() in Section 7.4, *Using Web Services*, on page 138). In that example, we used an ArrayAdapter because the data source was an array defined in XML. For this one, we use a SimpleCursorAdapter because the data source is a Cursor object that came from a database query.

The constructor for SimpleCursorAdapter takes five parameters:

- *context*: A reference to the current Activity

- *layout*: A resource that defines the views for a single list item

- *cursor*: The data set cursor

- *from*: The list of column names where the data is coming from

- *to*: The list of views where the data is going to

The layout for a list item is defined in layout/item.xml. Note the definitions for the row ID, time, and title views that are referenced in the TO array.

Eventsv2/res/layout/item.xml

```xml
<?xml version="1.0" encoding="utf-8"?>
<RelativeLayout
    xmlns:android="http://schemas.android.com/apk/res/android"
    android:layout_width="fill_parent"
    android:layout_height="fill_parent"
    android:orientation="horizontal"
    android:padding="10sp">
    <TextView
        android:id="@+id/rowid"
        android:layout_width="wrap_content"
        android:layout_height="wrap_content" />
    <TextView
        android:id="@+id/rowidcolon"
        android:layout_width="wrap_content"
        android:layout_height="wrap_content"
        android:text=": "
        android:layout_toRightOf="@id/rowid" />
    <TextView
        android:id="@+id/time"
        android:layout_width="wrap_content"
        android:layout_height="wrap_content"
        android:layout_toRightOf="@id/rowidcolon" />
    <TextView
        android:id="@+id/timecolon"
        android:layout_width="wrap_content"
        android:layout_height="wrap_content"
        android:text=": "
        android:layout_toRightOf="@id/time" />
    <TextView
        android:id="@+id/title"
        android:layout_width="fill_parent"
        android:layout_height="wrap_content"
        android:ellipsize="end"
        android:singleLine="true"
        android:textStyle="italic"
        android:layout_toRightOf="@id/timecolon" />
</RelativeLayout>
```

This looks more complicated than it is. All we're doing is putting the ID, time, and title on one line with colons in between the fields. I added a little padding and formatting to make it look nice.

Finally, we need to change the layout for the activity itself in layout/main.xml. Here's the new version:

Eventsv2/res/layout/main.xml

```xml
<?xml version="1.0" encoding="utf-8"?>
<LinearLayout
   xmlns:android="http://schemas.android.com/apk/res/android"
   android:layout_width="fill_parent"
   android:layout_height="fill_parent">
   <!-- Note built-in ids for 'list' and 'empty' -->
   <ListView
      android:id="@android:id/list"
      android:layout_width="wrap_content"
      android:layout_height="wrap_content"/>
   <TextView
      android:id="@android:id/empty"
      android:layout_width="wrap_content"
      android:layout_height="wrap_content"
      android:text="@string/empty" />
</LinearLayout>
```

Because the activity extends ListActivity, Android looks for two special IDs in the layout file. If the list has items in it, the android:id/list view will be displayed; otherwise, the android:id/empty view will be displayed. So if there are no items, instead of a blank screen the user will see the message "No events!"

Here are the string resources we need:

Eventsv2/res/values/strings.xml

```xml
<?xml version="1.0" encoding="utf-8"?>
<resources>
   <string name="app_name">Events</string>
   <string name="empty">No events!</string>
</resources>
```

For the final result, see Figure 9.3, on the next page. As an exercise for the reader, think about how you could enhance this application now that you have a real list to play with. For example, when the user selects an event, you could open a detail viewer, mail the event to technical support, or perhaps delete the selected event and all the ones below it from the database.

Figure 9.3: This version uses a ListActivity and data binding.

There's still one little problem with this example. No other application can add things to the events database or even look at them! For that, we'll need to use an Android ContentProvider.

9.5 Using a ContentProvider

In the Android security model (see the discussion in Section 2.5, *Safe and Secure*, on page 27), files written by one application cannot be read from or written to by any other application. Each program has its own Linux user ID and data directory (/data/data/*packagename*) and its own protected memory space. Android programs can communicate with each other in two ways:

- *Inter-Process Communication (IPC)*: One process declares an arbitrary API using the Android Interface Definition Language (AIDL) and the IBinder interface. Parameters are marshaled safely and efficiently between processes when the API is called. This advanced technique is used for remote procedure calls to a background Service thread.[2]

---

2. IPC, services, and binders are beyond the scope of this book. For more information, see http://d.android.com/guide/developing/tools/aidl.html, http://d.android.com/reference/android/app/Service.html, and http://d.android.com/reference/android/os/IBinder.html.

- *ContentProvider*: Processes register themselves to the system as providers of certain kinds of data. When that information is requested, they are called by Android through a fixed API to query or modify the content in whatever way they see fit. This is the technique we're going to use for the Events sample.

Any piece of information managed by a ContentProvider is addressed through a URI that looks like this:

content://*authority*/*path*/*id*

where:

- content:// is the standard required prefix.
- *authority* is the name of the provider. Using your fully qualified package name is recommended to prevent name collisions.
- *path* is a virtual directory within the provider that identifies the kind of data being requested.
- *id* is the primary key of a specific record being requested. To request all records of a particular type, omit this and the trailing slash.

Android comes with several providers already built in, including the following:[3]

- content://browser
- content://contacts
- content://media
- content://settings

To demonstrate using a ContentProvider, let's convert the Events example to use one. For our Events provider, these will be valid URIs:

```
content://org.example.events/events/3  -- single event with _id=3
content://org.example.events/events  -- all events
```

First we need to add a two more constants to Constants.java:

Eventsv3/src/org/example/events/Constants.java

```
import android.net.Uri;
// ...
    public static final String AUTHORITY = "org.example.events";
    public static final Uri CONTENT_URI = Uri.parse("content://"
        + AUTHORITY + "/" + TABLE_NAME);
```

---

3. For an up-to-date list, see http://d.android.com/reference/android/provider/package-summary.html. Instead of using the strings here, use the documented constants such as Browser.BOOKMARKS_URI. Note that access to some providers requires additional permissions to be requested in your manifest file.

The layout files (main.xml and item.xml) don't need to be changed, so the next step is to make a few minor changes to the Events class.

Changing the Main Program

The main program (the Events.onCreate() method) actually gets a little simpler because there is no database object to keep track of:

`Eventsv3/src/org/example/events/Events.java`

```
@Override
public void onCreate(Bundle savedInstanceState) {
    super.onCreate(savedInstanceState);
    setContentView(R.layout.main);
    addEvent("Hello, Android!");
    Cursor cursor = getEvents();
    showEvents(cursor);
}
```

We don't need the **try/finally** block, and we can remove references to EventData.

Adding a Row

Two lines change in addEvent(). Here's the new version:

`Eventsv3/src/org/example/events/Events.java`

```
import static org.example.events.Constants.CONTENT_URI;
    private void addEvent(String string) {
        // Insert a new record into the Events data source.
        // You would do something similar for delete and update.
        ContentValues values = new ContentValues();
        values.put(TTME, System.currentTimeMillis());
        values.put(TITLE, string);
        getContentResolver().insert(CONTENT_URI, values);
    }
```

The call to getWritableDatabase() is gone, and the call to insertOrThrow() is replaced by getContentResolver().insert(). Instead of a database handle, we use a content URI.

Running a Query

The getEvents() method is also simplified when using a ContentProvider:

`Eventsv3/src/org/example/events/Events.java`

```
private Cursor getEvents() {
    // Perform a managed query. The Activity will handle closing
    // and re-querying the cursor when needed.
    return managedQuery(CONTENT_URI, FROM, null, null, ORDER_BY);
}
```

Here we use the Activity.managedQuery() method, passing it the content URI, the list of columns we're interested in, and the order they should be sorted in.

By removing all references to the database, we've decoupled the Events client from the Events data provider. The client is simpler, but now we have to implement a new piece we didn't have before.

9.6 Implementing a ContentProvider

A ContentProvider is a high-level object like an Activity that needs to be declared to the system. So, the first step when making one is to add it to your AndroidManifest.xml file before the <activity> tag (as a child of <application>):

Eventsv3/AndroidManifest.xml

```
<provider android:name=".EventsProvider"
    android:authorities="org.example.events" />
```

android:name is the class name (appended to the manifest's package name), and android:authorities is the string used in the content URI.

Next we create the EventsProvider class, which must extend Content-Provider. Here's the basic outline:

Eventsv3/src/org/example/events/EventsProvider.java

```
package org.example.events;

import static android.provider.BaseColumns._ID;
import static org.example.events.Constants.AUTHORITY;
import static org.example.events.Constants.CONTENT_URI;
import static org.example.events.Constants.TABLE_NAME;
import android.content.ContentProvider;
import android.content.ContentUris;
import android.content.ContentValues;
import android.content.UriMatcher;
import android.database.Cursor;
import android.database.sqlite.SQLiteDatabase;
import android.net.Uri;
import android.text.TextUtils;

public class EventsProvider extends ContentProvider {
    private static final int EVENTS = 1;
    private static final int EVENTS_ID = 2;

    /** The MIME type of a directory of events */
    private static final String CONTENT_TYPE
        = "vnd.android.cursor.dir/vnd.example.event";
```

```
/** The MIME type of a single event */
private static final String CONTENT_ITEM_TYPE
   = "vnd.android.cursor.item/vnd.example.event";

private EventsData events;
private UriMatcher uriMatcher;
// ...
}
```

By convention we use vnd.example instead of org.example in the MIME type.[4] EventsProvider handles two types of data:

- EVENTS (MIME type CONTENT_TYPE): A directory or list of events

- EVENTS_ID (MIME type CONTENT_ITEM_TYPE): A single event

In terms of the URI, the difference is that the first type does not specify an ID, but the second type does. We use Android's UriMatcher class to parse the URI and tell us which one the client specified. And we reuse the EventsData class from earlier in the chapter to manage the real database inside the provider.

In the interest of space, I'm not going to show the rest of the class here, but you can download the whole thing from the book website. All three versions of the Events example can be found in the source code .zip file.

The final version of the Events sample looks exactly like the previous version on the outside (see Figure 9.3, on page 185). On the inside, however, you now have the framework for an event store that can be used by other applications in the system, even ones written by other developers.

9.7 Fast-Forward >>

In this chapter, we learned how to store data in an Android SQL database. If you want to do more with SQL, you'll need to learn about more statements and expressions than the ones we covered here. A book such as *SQL Pocket Guide* [Gen06] by Jonathan Gennick or *The Definitive Guide to SQLite* [Owe06] by Mike Owens would be a good investment, but keep in mind that the SQL syntax and functions vary slightly from database to database.

---

4. Multipurpose Internet Mail Extensions (MIME) is an Internet standard for describing the type of any kind of content.

Another option for data storage on Android is db4o.[5] This library is larger than SQLite and uses a different license (GNU Public License), but it's free and may be easier for you to use, especially if you don't know SQL.

The SimpleCursorAdapter introduced in this chapter can be customized to show more than just text. For example, you could display rating stars or sparklines or other views based on data in the Cursor. Look for ViewBinder in the SimpleCursorAdapter documentation for more information.[6]

And now for something completely different...the next chapter will cover 3D graphics with OpenGL.

---

5. http://www.db4o.com/android
6. http://d.android.com/reference/android/widget/SimpleCursorAdapter.html

3D Graphics in OpenGL

Two-dimensional graphics are great for most programs, but sometimes you need an extra level of depth, interactivity, or realism that isn't possible in 2D. For these times, Android provides a three-dimensional graphics library based on the OpenGL ES standard. In this chapter, we'll explore 3D concepts and build up a sample program that uses OpenGL.

10.1 Understanding 3D Graphics

The world is three-dimensional, yet we routinely view it in two dimensions. When you watch television or look at a picture in a book, the 3D images are flattened out, or *projected*, onto a 2D surface (the TV panel or book page).

Try this simple experiment: cover one eye and look out the window. What do you see? Light from the sun bounces off objects outside, passes through the window, and travels to your eye so you can perceive it. In graphics terms, the scene outside is projected onto the window (or *viewport*). If someone replaced your window with a high-quality photograph, it would look the same until you moved.

Based on how close your eye is to the window and how big the window is, you can see a limited amount of the world outside. This is called your *field of view*. If you draw a line from your eye to the four corners of the window and beyond, you would get the pyramid in Figure 10.1, on the following page. This is called the *view frustum* (Latin for a "piece broken off"). For performance reasons, the frustum is usually bounded by near and far clipping planes as well. You can see everything inside the frustum but nothing outside of it.

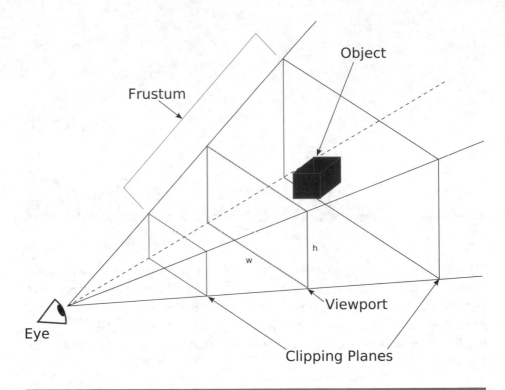

Figure 10.1: Viewing a three-dimensional scene

In 3D computer graphics, your computer screen acts as the viewport. Your job is to fool the user into thinking it's a window into another world just on the other side of the glass. The OpenGL graphics library is the API you use to accomplish that.

10.2 Introducing OpenGL

OpenGL[1] was developed by Silicon Graphics in 1992. It provides a unified interface for programmers to take advantage of hardware from any manufacturer. At its core, OpenGL implements familiar concepts such as viewports and lighting and tries to hide most of the hardware layer from the developer.

Because it was designed for workstations, OpenGL is too large to fit on a mobile device. So, Android implements a subset of OpenGL called OpenGL for Embedded Systems (OpenGL ES).[2] This standard was cre-

---

1. http://www.opengl.org
2. http://www.khronos.org/opengles

> ### Thank You, John Carmack
>
> OpenGL has proven to be very successful, but it almost wasn't. In 1995, Microsoft introduced a competitor called Direct3D. Owing to Microsoft's dominant market position and significant R&D investments, for a while it looked like Direct3D was going to take over as a de facto industry standard for gaming. However, one man, John Carmack, cofounder of id Software, refused to comply. His wildly popular Doom and Quake games almost single-handedly forced hardware manufacturers to keep their OpenGL device drivers up-to-date on the PC. Today's Linux, Mac OS X, and mobile device users can thank John and id Software for helping to keep the OpenGL standard relevant.

ated by the Khronos Group, an industry consortium of companies such as Intel, AMD, Nvidia, Nokia, Samsung, and Sony. The same library (with minor differences) is now available on major mobile platforms including Android, Symbian, and iPhone.

Every language has its own language bindings for OpenGL ES, and Java is no exception. Java's language binding was defined by Java Specification Request (JSR) 239.[3] Android implements this standard as closely as possible, so you can refer to a variety of books and documentation on JSR 239 and OpenGL ES for a full description of all its classes and methods.

Now let's take a look at how to create a simple OpenGL program in Android.

10.3 Building an OpenGL Program

Begin by creating a new "Hello, Android" project as in Section 1.2, *Creating Your First Program*, on page 9, but this time supply the following parameters in the New Android Project dialog box:

```
Project name: OpenGL
Build Target: Android 2.2
Application name: OpenGL
Package name: org.example.opengl
Create Activity: OpenGL
Min SDK Version: 8
```

---

3. http://jcp.org/en/jsr/detail?id=239

> ### Joe Asks...
> #### Will Every Phone Have 3D?
>
> Yes and no. Some low-end devices running Android may not actually have 3D hardware. However, the OpenGL programming interface will still be there. All the 3D functions will be emulated in software. Your program will still run, but it will be much slower than a hardware-accelerated device. For this reason, it's a good idea to provide options for users to turn off certain details and special effects that take time to draw but aren't absolutely necessary for the program. That way, if the user is running your program on a slower device, they can disable some of your eye candy to get better performance.

This will create OpenGL.java to contain your main activity. Edit this, and change it to refer to a custom view named GLView, as shown here:

OpenGL/src/org/example/opengl/OpenGL.java

```java
package org.example.opengl;

import android.app.Activity;
import android.os.Bundle;

public class OpenGL extends Activity {
    GLView view;
    @Override
    public void onCreate(Bundle savedInstanceState) {
        super.onCreate(savedInstanceState);
        view = new GLView(this);
        setContentView(view);
    }

    @Override
    protected void onPause() {
        super.onPause();
        view.onPause();
    }

    @Override
    protected void onResume() {
        super.onResume();
        view.onResume();
    }
}
```

We override the onPause() and onResume() methods so they can call the methods of the same name in the view.

We won't need the layout resource (res/layout/main.xml), so you can delete it. Now let's define our custom view class:

OpenGL/src/org/example/opengl/GLView.java

```
package org.example.opengl;

import android.content.Context;
import android.opengl.GLSurfaceView;

class GLView extends GLSurfaceView {
    private final GLRenderer renderer;

    GLView(Context context) {
        super(context);

        // Uncomment this to turn on error-checking and logging
        //setDebugFlags(DEBUG_CHECK_GL_ERROR | DEBUG_LOG_GL_CALLS);

        renderer = new GLRenderer(context);
        setRenderer(renderer);
    }
}
```

GLSurfaceView is a new class introduced in Android 1.5 that greatly simplifies using OpenGL in Android. It provides the glue to connect OpenGL ES to the view system and activity life cycle. It takes care of picking the appropriate frame buffer pixel format, and it manages a separate rendering thread to enable smooth animation. All GLView needs to do is extend GLSurfaceView and define a renderer for the view.

In the next section, we'll fill the screen with a solid color.

10.4 Rendering the Scene

As we saw in Section 4.2, *Drawing the Board*, on page 71, the Android 2D library calls the onDraw() method of your view whenever it needs to redraw a section of the screen. OpenGL is a bit different.

In OpenGL ES on Android, drawing is separated into a rendering class that is responsible for initializing and drawing the entire screen. Let's define that now.

Here's the outline for the GLRenderer class:

OpenGL/src/org/example/opengl/GLRenderer.java

```java
package org.example.opengl;

import javax.microedition.khronos.egl.EGLConfig;
import javax.microedition.khronos.opengles.GL10;

import android.content.Context;
import android.opengl.GLSurfaceView;
import android.opengl.GLU;
import android.util.Log;

class GLRenderer implements GLSurfaceView.Renderer {
    private static final String TAG = "GLRenderer";
    private final Context context;

    GLRenderer(Context context) {
        this.context = context;
    }

    public void onSurfaceCreated(GL10 gl, EGLConfig config) {
        // ...
    }

    public void onSurfaceChanged(GL10 gl, int width, int height) {
        // ...
    }

    public void onDrawFrame(GL10 gl) {
        // ...
    }
}
```

GLRenderer implements the GLSurfaceView.Renderer interface, which has three methods. Let's start with the onSurfaceCreated() method, which is called when the OpenGL Surface (kind of like a Canvas in regular 2D) is created or re-created:

OpenGL/src/org/example/opengl/GLRenderer.java

```java
public void onSurfaceCreated(GL10 gl, EGLConfig config) {
    // Set up any OpenGL options we need
    gl.glEnable(GL10.GL_DEPTH_TEST);
    gl.glDepthFunc(GL10.GL_LEQUAL);
    gl.glEnableClientState(GL10.GL_VERTEX_ARRAY);

    // Optional: disable dither to boost performance
    // gl.glDisable(GL10.GL_DITHER);
}
```

On line 3, we set a couple of OpenGL options. OpenGL has dozens of options that can be enabled or disabled with glEnable() and glDisable(). The most commonly used ones include the following:

Option	Description
GL_BLEND	Blend the incoming color values with the values already in the color buffer.
GL_CULL_FACE	Ignore polygons based on their winding (clockwise or counterclockwise) in window coordinates. This is a cheap way to eliminate back faces.
GL_DEPTH_TEST	Do depth comparisons, and update the depth buffer. Pixels farther away than those already drawn will be ignored.
GL_LIGHTi	Include light number i when figuring out an object's brightness and color.
GL_LIGHTING	Turn on lighting and material calculations.
GL_LINE_SMOOTH	Draw antialiased lines (lines without jaggies).
GL_MULTISAMPLE	Perform multisampling for antialiasing and other effects.
GL_POINT_SMOOTH	Draw antialiased points.
GL_TEXTURE_2D	Use textures to draw surfaces.

All options are off by default except for GL_DITHER and GL_MULTISAMPLE. Note that everything you enable has some cost in performance.

Next let's fill out the onSurfaceChanged() method. This method is called once after the Surface is created and then again whenever the size of the Surface changes:

OpenGL/src/org/example/opengl/GLRenderer.java

```
Line 1   public void onSurfaceChanged(GL10 gl, int width, int height) {
     2       // Define the view frustum
     3       gl.glViewport(0, 0, width, height);
     4       gl.glMatrixMode(GL10.GL_PROJECTION);
     5       gl.glLoadIdentity();
     6       float ratio = (float) width / height;
     7       GLU.gluPerspective(gl, 45.0f, ratio, 1, 100f);
     8   }
```

Here we configure our view frustum and set a few OpenGL options. Note the call to the GLU.gluPerspective() helper function on line 7. The last two arguments are the distance from the eye to the near and far clipping planes (see Figure 10.1, on page 192).

Figure 10.2: THAT WAS A LOT OF TROUBLE TO GET A BLACK SCREEN.

It's time to draw something. The onDrawFrame() method is called over and over in the rendering thread created by the GLSurfaceView class.

OpenGL/src/org/example/opengl/GLRenderer.java

```java
public void onDrawFrame(GL10 gl) {
    // Clear the screen to black
    gl.glClear(GL10.GL_COLOR_BUFFER_BIT
        | GL10.GL_DEPTH_BUFFER_BIT);

    // Position model so we can see it
    gl.glMatrixMode(GL10.GL_MODELVIEW);
    gl.glLoadIdentity();
    gl.glTranslatef(0, 0, -3.0f);

    // Other drawing commands go here...
}
```

To start with, we set the screen to black. We clear both the color and depth buffers. Always remember to clear both, or you'll get some very

> ### Version 1.what?
>
> OpenGL ES 1.0 is based on full OpenGL version 1.3, and ES 1.1 is based on OpenGL 1.5. JSR 239 has two versions: the original 1.0 and a maintenance release version 1.0.1. There are also some OpenGL ES extensions that I won't get into. All versions of Android implement JSR 239 1.0.1, with OpenGL ES 1.0 and some 1.1. For most programs, the JSR standard will suffice, so that's what we use in this chapter.
>
> Starting with Android 2.2, OpenGL ES 2.0 is supported via the android.opengl package.* You can also call it from the Native Development Kit (NDK).† OpenGL ES 2.0 is defined relative to the full OpenGL 2.0 specification and emphasizes shaders and programmable 3D pipelines. There is no JSR standard yet for OpenGL ES 2.0, and the programming interface is not backwards compatible with 1.0.
>
> *. http://d.android.com/reference/android/opengl/GLES20.html
> †. http://d.android.com/sdk/ndk

strange results left over from the depth information for the previous frame. We also set the starting position for the rest of the drawing commands, which will be completed in the next section.

If you run the program now, you get Figure 10.2, on the facing page. If you're thinking that it's silly to draw the same black screen over and over again in a loop, you're right. This will make more sense later when we talk about animation, so just bear with me for now.

Let's move on and draw something a little more interesting. But first we need to define exactly what we're drawing (the model).

10.5 Building a Model

Depending on the complexity of the objects you want to draw, you will typically create them using a graphical design tool and import them into your program. For the purposes of this example, we'll just define a simple model in code: a cube.

OpenGL/src/org/example/opengl/GLCube.java

```
Line 1   package org.example.opengl;

         import java.nio.ByteBuffer;
         import java.nio.ByteOrder;
5        import java.nio.IntBuffer;

         import javax.microedition.khronos.opengles.GL10;

         import android.content.Context;
10       import android.graphics.Bitmap;
         import android.graphics.BitmapFactory;
         import android.opengl.GLUtils;

         class GLCube {
15           private final IntBuffer mVertexBuffer;
             public GLCube() {
                 int one = 65536;
                 int half = one / 2;
                 int vertices[] = {
20                       // FRONT
                         -half, -half, half, half, -half, half,
                         -half, half, half, half, half, half,
                         // BACK
                         -half, -half, -half, -half, half, -half,
25                       half, -half, -half, half, half, -half,
                         // LEFT
                         -half, -half, half, -half, half, half,
                         -half, -half, -half, -half, half, -half,
                         // RIGHT
30                       half, -half, -half, half, half, -half,
                         half, -half, half, half, half, half,
                         // TOP
                         -half, half, half, half, half, half,
                         -half, half, -half, half, half, -half,
35                       // BOTTOM
                         -half, -half, half, -half, -half, -half,
                         half, -half, half, half, -half, -half, };

             // Buffers to be passed to gl*Pointer() functions must be
40           // direct, i.e., they must be placed on the native heap
             // where the garbage collector cannot move them.
             //
             // Buffers with multi-byte data types (e.g., short, int,
             // float) must have their byte order set to native order
45           ByteBuffer vbb = ByteBuffer.allocateDirect(vertices.length * 4);
             vbb.order(ByteOrder.nativeOrder());
             mVertexBuffer = vbb.asIntBuffer();
             mVertexBuffer.put(vertices);
             mVertexBuffer.position(0);
50       }
```

```
        public void draw(GL10 gl) {
            gl.glVertexPointer(3, GL10.GL_FIXED, 0, mVertexBuffer);

55          gl.glColor4f(1, 1, 1, 1);
            gl.glNormal3f(0, 0, 1);
            gl.glDrawArrays(GL10.GL_TRIANGLE_STRIP, 0, 4);
            gl.glNormal3f(0, 0, -1);
            gl.glDrawArrays(GL10.GL_TRIANGLE_STRIP, 4, 4);
60
            gl.glColor4f(1, 1, 1, 1);
            gl.glNormal3f(-1, 0, 0);
            gl.glDrawArrays(GL10.GL_TRIANGLE_STRIP, 8, 4);
            gl.glNormal3f(1, 0, 0);
65          gl.glDrawArrays(GL10.GL_TRIANGLE_STRIP, 12, 4);

            gl.glColor4f(1, 1, 1, 1);
            gl.glNormal3f(0, 1, 0);
            gl.glDrawArrays(GL10.GL_TRIANGLE_STRIP, 16, 4);
70          gl.glNormal3f(0, -1, 0);
            gl.glDrawArrays(GL10.GL_TRIANGLE_STRIP, 20, 4);
        }
    }
```

The vertices array on line 19 defines the corners of the cube in fixed-point model coordinates (see the "Fixed vs. Floating Point" sidebar). Each face of a cube is a square, which consists of two triangles. We use a common OpenGL drawing mode called *triangle strips*. In this mode, we specify two starting points, and then after that every subsequent point defines a triangle with the previous two points. It's a quick way to get a lot of geometry pumped out to the graphics hardware in a hurry.

Note that each point has three coordinates (x, y, and z). The x- and y-axes point to the right and up, respectively, and the z-axis points out of the screen toward the eye point.

In the draw method (line 52), we use the vertex buffer created in the constructor and draw six different runs of triangles (for the six sides of the cube). In a real program, you would want to combine the calls into one or two strips, because the fewer number of OpenGL calls you make, the faster your program will go.

Now let's use our new class in GLRenderer:

`OpenGL/src/org/example/opengl/GLRenderer.java`

```
private final GLCube cube = new GLCube();
public void onDrawFrame(GL10 gl) {
    // ...
    // Draw the model
    cube.draw(gl);
}
```

> **Fixed vs. Floating Point**
>
> OpenGL ES provides fixed-point (integer) and floating-point interfaces for all its methods. The fixed-point methods end with the letter *x*, and the floating-point ones end with the letter *f*. For example, you can use either glColor4x() and glColor4f() to set the four components of a color.
>
> A fixed-point number is scaled by 2^16, or 65,536. So, 32,768 in fixed point is equivalent to 0.5f. Put another way, the integral part uses the most significant two bytes of a four-byte int, while the fractional part uses the least significant two bytes. This is quite different from the way the native Android 2D library uses integers, so be careful.
>
> In a simple example like this one, it doesn't matter whether you use fixed-point or floating-point arithmetic, so I use them interchangeably as convenient. Keep in mind, though, that some Android devices will not have floating-point hardware, so fixed point might be faster. On the other hand, some developers report it's actually slower than emulated floating point for them. Your mileage may vary.
>
> My advice is to code it first using floating point, because it's easier to program. Then optimize the slow parts using fixed point later if necessary.

Now if you run the program, you'll see the exciting image in Figure 10.3, on the next page. Well, it's more exciting than black.

10.6 Lights, Camera, ...

In real life you have light sources such as the sun, headlights, torches, or glowing lava pools. OpenGL lets you define up to eight light sources in your scene. There are two parts to lighting—a light and something to shine it on. Let's start with the light.

All 3D graphics libraries support three types of lighting:

- *Ambient*: A general glow that the light contributes to the entire scene, even to objects facing away from the light. It's important to have a little ambient light so you can pick out details even in the shadows.
- *Diffuse*: Soft directional lighting, as you might get from a fluorescent panel. Most of the light contributed to your scene will typically come from diffuse sources.

Figure 10.3: DRAWING AN UNSHADED CUBE

- *Specular*: Shiny light, usually from bright point sources. Combined with shiny materials, this gives you highlights (glints) that add realism.

A single light source can contribute all three types of light. These values go into a lighting equation that determines the color and brightness of each pixel on the screen.

The lighting is defined in the GLRenderer.onSurfaceCreated() method:

OpenGL/src/org/example/opengl/GLRenderer.java

```
float lightAmbient[] = new float[] { 0.2f, 0.2f, 0.2f, 1 };
float lightDiffuse[] = new float[] { 1, 1, 1, 1 };
float[] lightPos = new float[] { 1, 1, 1, 1 };
gl.glEnable(GL10.GL_LIGHTING);
gl.glEnable(GL10.GL_LIGHT0);
gl.glLightfv(GL10.GL_LIGHT0, GL10.GL_AMBIENT, lightAmbient, 0);
gl.glLightfv(GL10.GL_LIGHT0, GL10.GL_DIFFUSE, lightDiffuse, 0);
gl.glLightfv(GL10.GL_LIGHT0, GL10.GL_POSITION, lightPos, 0);
```

Figure 10.4: LIGHTING THE SCENE

In our code we define one light source at position (1, 1, 1). It's a white omnidirectional light that has a bright diffuse component and a dim ambient component. In this example, we're not using specular lighting.

Next, we need to tell OpenGL about the materials our cube is made of. Light reflects differently off different materials, such as metal, plastic, or paper. To simulate this in OpenGL, add this code in onSurfaceCreated() to define how the material reacts with the three types of light: ambient, diffuse, and specular:

OpenGL/src/org/example/opengl/GLRenderer.java

```
float matAmbient[] = new float[] { 1, 1, 1, 1 };
float matDiffuse[] = new float[] { 1, 1, 1, 1 };
gl.glMaterialfv(GL10.GL_FRONT_AND_BACK, GL10.GL_AMBIENT,
    matAmbient, 0);
gl.glMaterialfv(GL10.GL_FRONT_AND_BACK, GL10.GL_DIFFUSE,
    matDiffuse, 0);
```

The object will appear to have a dull finish, as if it were made out of paper (see Figure 10.4, on the facing page). The top-right corner of the cube is closer to the light, so it appears brighter.

10.7 Action!

Up to now the cube has just been sitting there without moving. That's pretty boring, so let's make it move. To do that, we need to make a couple of changes to our onSurfaceCreated() and onDrawFrame() methods in GLRenderer.

```
OpenGL/src/org/example/opengl/GLRenderer.java
```

```java
private long startTime;
private long fpsStartTime;
private long numFrames;
public void onSurfaceCreated(GL10 gl, EGLConfig config) {
    // ...
    startTime = System.currentTimeMillis();
    fpsStartTime = startTime;
    numFrames = 0;
}
public void onDrawFrame(GL10 gl) {
    // ...
    // Set rotation angle based on the time
    long elapsed = System.currentTimeMillis() - startTime;
    gl.glRotatef(elapsed * (30f / 1000f), 0, 1, 0);
    gl.glRotatef(elapsed * (15f / 1000f), 1, 0, 0);

    // Draw the model
    cube.draw(gl);
}
```

This code rotates the cube a little bit every time through the main loop. Specifically, every second it rotates 30 degrees around the x-axis and 15 degrees around the y-axis. The result will be a nice, smooth, spinning cube (see Figure 10.5, on the next page).

10.8 Applying Texture

Although the scene is starting to look more interesting, nobody would mistake it for real life. Everyday objects have textures, like the rough surface of a brick wall or the gravel on a garden path. Do you own a laminated table? A wood laminate is just a photograph of wood grain that is glued on the surface of a less expensive material like plastic or particle board.

Figure 10.5: ROTATING THE CUBE

Time-Based Animation

The first version of this example kept track of the current rotation angle and simply incremented it each time through the loop. Can you think of a reason why that was a bad idea?

Since Android can run on a variety of different devices, you can't predict how long it will take to draw a single frame. It might take half a second or 1/100th of a second. If you moved an object a fixed amount every frame, then on slow devices the object would move too slowly, and on fast devices it would move too fast. By tying the amount of movement to how much time has elapsed, you can achieve predictable movement on any device. Faster hardware will draw the animation more smoothly, but objects will get from A to B in the same amount of time.

We're going to do the same thing to our cube using a picture. Unfortunately, the code to do this is fairly long. Don't worry if you don't understand it all right away.

OpenGL/src/org/example/opengl/GLCube.java

```java
private final IntBuffer mTextureBuffer;

public GLCube() {
    int texCoords[] = {
            // FRONT
            0, one, one, one, 0, 0, one, 0,
            // BACK
            one, one, one, 0, 0, one, 0, 0,
            // LEFT
            one, one, one, 0, 0, one, 0, 0,
            // RIGHT
            one, one, one, 0, 0, one, 0, 0,
            // TOP
            one, 0, 0, 0, one, one, 0, one,
            // BOTTOM
            0, 0, 0, one, one, 0, one, one, };
    // ...
    ByteBuffer tbb = ByteBuffer.allocateDirect(texCoords.length * 4);
    tbb.order(ByteOrder.nativeOrder());
    mTextureBuffer = tbb.asIntBuffer();
    mTextureBuffer.put(texCoords);
    mTextureBuffer.position(0);
}
static void loadTexture(GL10 gl, Context context, int resource) {
    Bitmap bmp = BitmapFactory.decodeResource(
            context.getResources(), resource);
    GLUtils.texImage2D(GL10.GL_TEXTURE_2D, 0, bmp, 0);
    gl.glTexParameterx(GL10.GL_TEXTURE_2D,
            GL10.GL_TEXTURE_MIN_FILTER, GL10.GL_LINEAR);
    gl.glTexParameterx(GL10.GL_TEXTURE_2D,
            GL10.GL_TEXTURE_MAG_FILTER, GL10.GL_LINEAR);
    bmp.recycle();
}
}
```

Next we need to tell OpenGL to use the texture coordinates. Add this to the beginning of the draw() method:

OpenGL/src/org/example/opengl/GLCube.java

```java
gl.glEnable(GL10.GL_TEXTURE_2D); // workaround bug 3623
gl.glTexCoordPointer(2, GL10.GL_FIXED, 0, mTextureBuffer);
```

Figure 10.6: APPLYING A TEXTURE

And finally we need to call the loadTexture() method in GLRenderer. Add these lines to the end of the onSurfaceCreated() method:

OpenGL/src/org/example/opengl/GLRenderer.java

```
// Enable textures
gl.glEnableClientState(GL10.GL_TEXTURE_COORD_ARRAY);
gl.glEnable(GL10.GL_TEXTURE_2D);

// Load the cube's texture from a bitmap
GLCube.loadTexture(gl, context, R.drawable.android);
```

This code enables textures and texture coordinates and then calls our loadTexture() method, passing it the Activity context and resource ID so it can load the texture image.

R.drawable.android is a PNG file 128 pixels square that I copied to res/drawable-nodpi/android.png. You can find it in the downloadable code package that accompanies this book. Note the number 128 doesn't

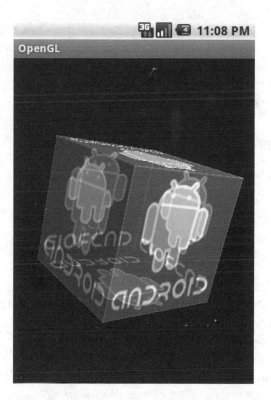

Figure 10.7: THE FINAL VERSION: A SEE-THROUGH CUBE

appear anywhere in the code, so you substitute a larger or smaller image easily.

You can see our progress so far in Figure 10.6, on the facing page.

10.9 Peekaboo

Just for fun, let's make the cube partially transparent. Add this to GLRenderer.onSurfaceCreated():

OpenGL/src/org/example/opengl/GLRenderer.java

```
boolean SEE_THRU = true;
// ...
if (SEE_THRU) {
   gl.glDisable(GL10.GL_DEPTH_TEST);
   gl.glEnable(GL10.GL_BLEND);
   gl.glBlendFunc(GL10.GL_SRC_ALPHA, GL10.GL_ONE);
}
```

This turns off depth testing, because we want to see obscured objects as well as foreground ones. It also turns on a blending mode that lets the opacity of objects be based on their alpha (transparency) channel. The net effect is that the back faces of the cube will appear through the front faces. For the final result, see Figure 10.7, on the previous page.

I'll leave it to you to implement an option to turn that on and off. Try playing around with different blend modes to get cool effects.

10.10 Measuring Smoothness

How smooth is smooth? The smoothness of a game or other graphics-heavy program is defined by how fast it can update the display screen. This is typically measured by counting the number of screens or frames per second (FPS) that are displayed. Different people perceive different speeds as "smooth." 15–30FPS is sometimes acceptable to casual gamers, but more serious players have come to expect a higher rate such as 60FPS or more. I recommend that you make every effort to reach a consistent rate of 60FPS. That corresponds to the maximum refresh rate of most LCD displays and is also the speed used on popular gaming platforms such as Sony's PlayStation and PlayStation Portable (PSP).

Note: This won't always be possible, because some Android phones are fill-rate limited, which means their 3D graphics hardware is under-powered compared to their display resolution. Depending on what you are drawing, they may simply not be able to write pixels on the screen fast enough to achieve 60FPS. The first generation of 800x480+ phones such as the Nexus One and Droid Sholes suffer from this issue. Faster devices are coming out that won't have the problem.

A high frame rate is challenging, because at 60FPS you have only 1/60th of a second (16.67 milliseconds) between calls to onDrawFrame() to do everything that needs to be done, including any animation, physics, and game calculations, plus the time it takes to actually draw the scene for the current frame. The only way to tell whether you're making your FPS target is to measure it.

To do that, try adding this bit of code to the end of the onDrawFrame()
method:

`OpenGL/src/org/example/opengl/GLRenderer.java`

```
numFrames++;
long fpsElapsed = System.currentTimeMillis() - fpsStartTime;
if (fpsElapsed > 5 * 1000) { // every 5 seconds
    float fps = (numFrames * 1000.0F) / fpsElapsed;
    Log.d(TAG, "Frames per second: " + fps + " (" + numFrames
            + " frames in " + fpsElapsed + " ms)");
    fpsStartTime = System.currentTimeMillis();
    numFrames = 0;
}
```

Every five seconds it will display your average FPS number to the Android system log (see Section 3.10, *Debugging with Log Messages*, on
page 58). If this number drops below your target rate, then adjust your
algorithm and try again. Keep iterating until you reach your target.
A profiler such as traceview[4] may also come in handy. Note that you
should avoid the temptation to display this on the screen on top of
your other graphics because the act of displaying it will throw off the
number.

If you try this now, you may notice that the emulator runs much more
slowly than the actual device. In my tests I saw about 12FPS on the
emulator and closer to 60FPS on a real phone. The lesson here is that
for performance testing you can't trust the emulator.

10.11 Fast-Forward >>

In this chapter, you learned how to use Android's 3D graphics library.
Because Android uses the industry-standard OpenGL ES API, a wide
variety of additional information is available if you want to learn more.
In particular, I recommend the Javadoc for the JSR 239 API specifi-
cation.[5] For other graphics tips, check out the developer talks at the
Google I/O conference.[6]

---

4. http://d.android.com/guide/developing/tools/traceview.html
5. http://java.sun.com/javame/reference/apis/jsr239
6. http://code.google.com/events/io/2009/sessions/WritingRealTimeGamesAndroid.html and http://
code.google.com/events/io/2010/sessions/writing-real-time-games-android.html

Part IV

The Next Generation

Multi-Touch

With each new version of Android, new features are added to the platform. In this part, we'll concentrate on those newer features and on making your programs available to others.

In this chapter, we'll learn how to use the new multi-touch features in Android 2.0, warts and all. Then we'll cover home screen widgets, introduced in Android 1.6, and live wallpaper, introduced in Android 2.1. Android's popularity and its rapid pace of development have created a problem with fragmentation, so there's a whole chapter dedicated to dealing with all the different versions and screen sizes you'll encounter in the field. Finally, there's a chapter that discusses how to get your program into users' hands by publishing it on the Android Market.

11.1 Introducing Multi-Touch

Multi-touch is simply an extension of the regular touch-screen user interface, using two or more fingers instead of one. We've used single-finger gestures before,[1] although we didn't call it that. Remember in Section 4.3, *Entering Numbers*, on page 77 when we let the user touch a tile in the Sudoku game in order to change it? That's called a *tap* gesture. Another gesture is called *drag*. That's where you hold one finger on the screen and move it around, causing the content under your finger to scroll.

Tap, drag, and a few other single-fingered gestures have always been supported in Android. However, because of the popularity of the Apple iPhone, early Android users suffered from a kind of gesture envy. The

---

1. Some people use them more than others.

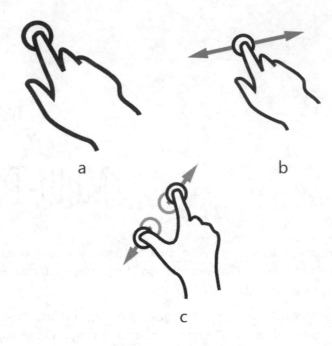

Figure 11.1: Three common touch gestures: a) tap, b) drag, and c) pinch zoom

iPhone supported multi-touch, in particular the "pinch zoom" gesture (see Figure 11.1).

With pinch zoom, you place two fingers on the screen and squeeze them together to make the item you're viewing smaller, or you pull them apart to make it bigger. Before Android 2.0, you had to use a clunky zoom control with icons that you pressed to zoom in and out (see the setBuilt-InZoomControls() method in Section 8.3, *Getting Ready*, on page 167). But thanks to its new multi-touch support, you can now pinch zoom on Android too—as long as the application supports it, of course.

Note: Android 2.2 introduced a new class called ScaleGestureDetector that recognizes the pinch zoom gesture. However, I decided not to use it in order to be compatible with 2.0 and 2.1 devices. If you only need to target 2.2, see the online documentation for more information.[2]

---

2. http://d.android.com/reference/android/view/ScaleGestureDetector.html

> **Warning: Multi-bugs Ahead**
>
> Multi-touch, as implemented on current Android phones, is extremely buggy. In fact, it's so buggy that it borders on the unusable. The API routinely reports invalid or impossible data points, especially during the transition from one finger to two fingers on the screen, and vice versa.
>
> On the developer forums, you can find complaints of fingers getting swapped, x- and y-axes flipping, and multiple fingers sometimes being treated as one. Some of these problems can be traced back to hardware limitations in the touch-screen sensors used in certain phones, but many could be fixed or improved with software updates.
>
> With a lot of trial and error, I was able to get the example in this chapter working because the gesture it implements is so simple. Until Google acknowledges and fixes the issues with multi-touch, that may be about all you can do. Luckily, pinch zoom seems to be the only multi-touch gesture most people want.

If you try to run the example in this chapter on Android 1.5 or 1.6, it will crash because those versions do not support multi-touch. We'll learn how to work around that in Section 13.3, *Evolving with Android APIs*, on page 256.

11.2 Building the Touch Example

To demonstrate multi-touch, we're going to build a simple image viewer application that lets you zoom in and scroll around an image. The finished product is shown in Figure 11.2, on the next page.

Begin by creating a new "Hello, Android" project with the following parameters in the New Android Project dialog box:

```
Project name: Touch
Build Target: Android 2.2
Application name: Touch
Package name: org.example.touch
Create Activity: Touch
Min SDK Version: 8
```

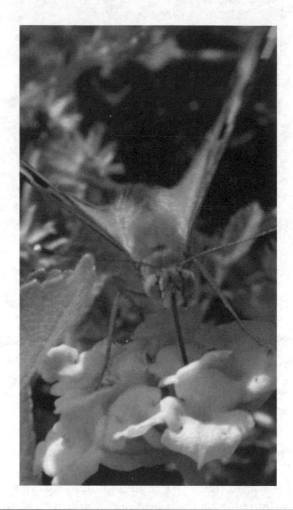

Figure 11.2: THE TOUCH EXAMPLE IMPLEMENTS A SIMPLE IMAGE VIEWER WITH DRAG-AND-PINCH ZOOM.

This will create Touch.java to contain your main activity. Let's edit it to show a sample image, put in a touch listener, and add a few imports we'll need later:

Touchv1/src/org/example/touch/Touch.java

```java
package org.example.touch;

import android.app.Activity;
import android.graphics.Matrix;
import android.graphics.PointF;
import android.os.Bundle;
import android.util.FloatMath;
import android.util.Log;
import android.view.MotionEvent;
import android.view.View;
import android.view.View.OnTouchListener;
import android.widget.ImageView;

public class Touch extends Activity implements OnTouchListener {
    private static final String TAG = "Touch";
    @Override
    public void onCreate(Bundle savedInstanceState) {
        super.onCreate(savedInstanceState);
        setContentView(R.layout.main);
        ImageView view = (ImageView) findViewById(R.id.imageView);
        view.setOnTouchListener(this);
    }

    @Override
    public boolean onTouch(View v, MotionEvent event) {
        // Handle touch events here...
    }
}
```

We'll fill out that onTouch() method in a moment. First we need to define the layout for our activity:

Touchv1/res/layout/main.xml

```xml
<?xml version="1.0" encoding="utf-8"?>
<FrameLayout
    xmlns:android="http://schemas.android.com/apk/res/android"
    android:layout_width="fill_parent"
    android:layout_height="fill_parent">
    <ImageView android:id="@+id/imageView"
        android:layout_width="fill_parent"
        android:layout_height="fill_parent"
        android:src="@drawable/butterfly"
        android:scaleType="matrix">
    </ImageView>
</FrameLayout>
```

The entire interface is a big ImageView control that covers the whole screen. The android:src="@drawable/butterfly" value refers to the butterfly image used in the example. You can use any JPG or PNG format image you like; just put it in the res/drawable-nodpi directory. The android:scaleType="matrix" attribute indicates we're going to use a matrix to control the position and scale of the image. More on that later.

The AndroidManifest.xml file is untouched except for the addition of the android:theme= attribute:

Touchv1/AndroidManifest.xml

```xml
<?xml version="1.0" encoding="utf-8"?>
<manifest xmlns:android="http://schemas.android.com/apk/res/android"
      package="org.example.touch"
      android:versionCode="1"
      android:versionName="1.0">
   <application android:icon="@drawable/icon"
        android:label="@string/app_name"
        android:theme="@android:style/Theme.NoTitleBar.Fullscreen">
      <activity android:name=".Touch"
             android:label="@string/app_name">
         <intent-filter>
            <action android:name="android.intent.action.MAIN" />
            <category android:name="android.intent.category.LAUNCHER" />
         </intent-filter>
      </activity>
   </application>
   <uses-sdk android:minSdkVersion="3" android:targetSdkVersion="8" />
</manifest>
```

@android:style/Theme.NoTitleBar.Fullscreen, as the name suggests, tells Android to use the entire screen with no title bar or status bar at the top. You can run the application now, and it will simply display the picture.

11.3 Understanding Touch Events

Whenever I first learn a new API, I like to first put in some code to dump everything out so I can get a feel for what the methods do and in what order events happen. So let's start with that. First add a call to the dumpEvent() method inside onTouch():

Touchv1/src/org/example/touch/Touch.java

```java
@Override
public boolean onTouch(View v, MotionEvent event) {
   // Dump touch event to log
   dumpEvent(event);
   return true; // indicate event was handled
}
```

Note that we need to return true to indicate to Android that the event has been handled. Next, define the dumpEvent() method. The only parameter is the event that we want to dump.

Touchv1/src/org/example/touch/Touch.java

```java
/** Show an event in the LogCat view, for debugging */
private void dumpEvent(MotionEvent event) {
    String names[] = { "DOWN", "UP", "MOVE", "CANCEL", "OUTSIDE",
            "POINTER_DOWN", "POINTER_UP", "7?", "8?", "9?" };
    StringBuilder sb = new StringBuilder();
    int action = event.getAction();
    int actionCode = action & MotionEvent.ACTION_MASK;
    sb.append("event ACTION_").append(names[actionCode]);
    if (actionCode == MotionEvent.ACTION_POINTER_DOWN
            || actionCode == MotionEvent.ACTION_POINTER_UP) {
        sb.append("(pid ").append(
                action >> MotionEvent.ACTION_POINTER_ID_SHIFT);
        sb.append(")");
    }
    sb.append("[");
    for (int i = 0; i < event.getPointerCount(); i++) {
        sb.append("#").append(i);
        sb.append("(pid ").append(event.getPointerId(i));
        sb.append(")=").append((int) event.getX(i));
        sb.append(",").append((int) event.getY(i));
        if (i + 1 < event.getPointerCount())
            sb.append(";");
    }
    sb.append("]");
    Log.d(TAG, sb.toString());
}
```

Output will go to the Android debug log, which you can see by opening the LogCat view (see Section 3.10, *Debugging with Log Messages*, on page 58).

The easiest way to understand this code is to run it. Unfortunately, you can't run this program on the emulator (actually you can, but the emulator doesn't support multi-touch, so the results won't be very interesting). Therefore, hook up a real phone to your USB port, and run the sample there (see Section 1.4, *Running on a Real Phone*, on page 14).

When I tried it on my phone and performed a few quick gestures, I received the following output:

```
Line 1   event ACTION_DOWN[#0(pid 0)=135,179]
  -      event ACTION_MOVE[#0(pid 0)=135,184]
  -      event ACTION_MOVE[#0(pid 0)=144,205]
  -      event ACTION_MOVE[#0(pid 0)=152,227]
  5      event ACTION_POINTER_DOWN(pid 1)[#0(pid 0)=153,230;#1(pid 1)=380,538]
  -      event ACTION_MOVE[#0(pid 0)=153,231;#1(pid 1)=380,538]
```

```
  -   event ACTION_MOVE[#0(pid 0)=155,236;#1(pid 1)=364,512]
  -   event ACTION_MOVE[#0(pid 0)=157,240;#1(pid 1)=350,498]
  -   event ACTION_MOVE[#0(pid 0)=158,245;#1(pid 1)=343,494]
 10   event ACTION_POINTER_UP(pid 0)[#0(pid 0)=158,247;#1(pid 1)=336,484]
  -   event ACTION_MOVE[#0(pid 1)=334,481]
  -   event ACTION_MOVE[#0(pid 1)=328,472]
  -   event ACTION_UP[#0(pid 1)=327,471]
```

Here's how to interpret the events:

- On line 1 we see an ACTION_DOWN event, so the user must have pressed one finger on the screen. The finger was positioned at coordinates x=135, y=179, which is near the upper left of the display. You can't tell yet whether they're trying to do a tap or a drag.

- Next, starting on line 2, there are some ACTION_MOVE events, indicating the user moved their finger around a bit to those coordinates given in the events. (It's actually very hard to put your finger on the screen and *not* move it at all, so you'll get a lot of these.) By the amount moved, you can tell the user is doing a drag gesture.

- The next event, ACTION_POINTER_DOWN on line 5, means the user pressed down another finger. "pid 1" means that pointer ID 1 (that is, finger number 1) was pressed. Finger number 0 was already down, so we now have two fingers being tracked on the screen. In theory, the Android API can support up to 256 fingers at once, but the first crop of Android 2.*x* phones is limited to 2.[3] The coordinates for both fingers come back as part of the event. It looks like the user is about to start a pinch zoom gesture.

- Here's where it gets interesting. The next thing we see is a series of ACTION_MOVE events starting on line 6. Unlike before, now we have two fingers moving around. If you look closely at the coordinates, you can see the fingers are moving closer together as part of a pinch zoom.

- Then on line 10, we see an ACTION_POINTER_UP on pid 0. This means that finger number 0 was lifted off the screen. Finger number 1 is still there. Naturally, this ends the pinch zoom gesture.

- We see a couple more ACTION_MOVE events starting on line 11, indicating the remaining finger is still moving around a little. If you compare these to the earlier move events, you'll notice a dif-

---

3. Although the idea of 256 fingers may seem silly outside of *Men in Black* headquarters, keep in mind that Android is designed for a wide variety of devices, not just phones. If you have a tabletop-sized screen with several people gathered around it, you could easily have more than a handful of fingers on the display.

ferent pointer ID is reported. Unfortunately, the touch API is so buggy you can't always count on that (see the "Warning: Multi-bugs Ahead" sidebar).

- Finally, on line 13, we get an ACTION_UP event as the last finger is removed from the screen.

Now the code for dumpEvent() should make a little more sense. The getAction() method returns the action being performed (up, down, or move). The lowest 8 bits of the action is the action code itself, and the next 8 bits is the pointer (finger) ID, so we have to use a bitwise AND (&) and a right shift (>>) to separate them.

Then we call the getPointerCount() method to see how many finger positions are included. getX() and getY() return the X and Y coordinates, respectively. The fingers can appear in any order, so we have to call getPointerId() to find out which fingers we're really talking about.

That covers the raw mouse event data. The trick, as you might imagine, is in interpreting and acting on that data.

11.4 Setting Up for Image Transformation

To move and zoom the image, we'll use a neat little feature on the ImageView class called *matrix transformation*. Using a matrix we can represent any kind of translation, rotation, or skew that we want to do to the image. We already turned it on by specifying android:scaleType= "matrix" in the res/layout/main.xml file. In the Touch class, we need to declare two matrices as fields (one for the current value and one for the original value before the transformation). We'll use them in the onTouch() method to transform the image. We also need a mode variable to tell whether we're in the middle of a drag or zoom gesture, and we need the start, mid, and oldDist variables for controlling zooming:

Touchv1/src/org/example/touch/Touch.java

```
public class Touch extends Activity implements OnTouchListener {
    // These matrices will be used to move and zoom image
    Matrix matrix = new Matrix();
    Matrix savedMatrix = new Matrix();

    // We can be in one of these 3 states
    static final int NONE = 0;
    static final int DRAG = 1;
    static final int ZOOM = 2;
    int mode = NONE;
```

```java
    // Remember some things for zooming
    PointF start = new PointF();
    PointF mid = new PointF();
    float oldDist = 1f;

    @Override
    public boolean onTouch(View v, MotionEvent event) {
        ImageView view = (ImageView) v;

        // Dump touch event to log
        dumpEvent(event);

        // Handle touch events here...
        switch (event.getAction() & MotionEvent.ACTION_MASK) {
        }

        view.setImageMatrix(matrix);
        return true; // indicate event was handled
    }
}
```

The matrix variable will be calculated inside the **switch** statement when we implement the gestures.

11.5 Implementing the Drag Gesture

A drag gesture starts when the first finger is pressed to the screen (ACTION_DOWN) and ends when it is removed (ACTION_UP or ACTION_POINTER_UP).

Touchv1/src/org/example/touch/Touch.java

```java
switch (event.getAction() & MotionEvent.ACTION_MASK) {
case MotionEvent.ACTION_DOWN:
    savedMatrix.set(matrix);
    start.set(event.getX(), event.getY());
    Log.d(TAG, "mode=DRAG");
    mode = DRAG;
    break;
case MotionEvent.ACTION_UP:
case MotionEvent.ACTION_POINTER_UP:
    mode = NONE;
    Log.d(TAG, "mode=NONE");
    break;
case MotionEvent.ACTION_MOVE:
    if (mode == DRAG) {
        matrix.set(savedMatrix);
        matrix.postTranslate(event.getX() - start.x,
                event.getY() - start.y);
    }
    break;
}
```

When the gesture starts, we remember the current value of the transformation matrix and the starting position of the pointer. Every time the finger moves, we start the transformation matrix over at its original value and call the postTranslate() method to add a translation vector, the difference between the current and starting positions.

If you run the program now, you should be able to drag the image around the screen using your finger. Neat, huh?

11.6 Implementing the Pinch Zoom Gesture

The pinch zoom gesture is similar, except it starts when the *second* finger is pressed to the screen (ACTION_POINTER_DOWN).

Touchv1/src/org/example/touch/Touch.java

```
case MotionEvent.ACTION_POINTER_DOWN:
   oldDist = spacing(event);
   Log.d(TAG, "oldDist=" + oldDist);
   if (oldDist > 10f) {
      savedMatrix.set(matrix);
      midPoint(mid, event);
      mode = ZOOM;
      Log.d(TAG, "mode=ZOOM");
   }
   break;
case MotionEvent.ACTION_MOVE:
   if (mode == DRAG) {
      // ...
   }
   else if (mode == ZOOM) {
      float newDist = spacing(event);
      Log.d(TAG, "newDist=" + newDist);
      if (newDist > 10f) {
         matrix.set(savedMatrix);
         float scale = newDist / oldDist;
         matrix.postScale(scale, scale, mid.x, mid.y);
      }
   }
   break;
```

When we get the down event for the second finger, we calculate and remember the distance between the two fingers. In my testing, Android would sometimes tell me (incorrectly) that there were two fingers pressed down in almost exactly the same position. So, I added an check to ignore the event if the distance is smaller than some arbitrary number of pixels. If it's bigger than that, we remember the current transformation matrix, calculate the midpoint of the two fingers, and start the zoom.

When a move event arrives while we're in zoom mode, we calculate the distance between the fingers again. If it's too small, the event is ignored; otherwise, we restore the transformation matrix and scale the image around the midpoint.

The scale is simply the ratio of the new distance divided by the old distance. If the new distance is bigger (that is, the fingers have gotten farther apart), then the scale will be greater than 1, making the image bigger. If it's smaller (fingers closer together), then the scale will be less than one, making the image smaller. And of course if everything is the same, the scale is equal to 1 and the image is not changed.

Now let's define the spacing() and midPoint() methods.

Distance Between Two Points

To find out how far apart two fingers are, we first construct a vector (x, y) that is the difference between the two points. Then we use the formula for Euclidean distance to calculate the spacing:[4]

Touchv1/src/org/example/touch/Touch.java

```java
private float spacing(MotionEvent event) {
    float x = event.getX(0) - event.getX(1);
    float y = event.getY(0) - event.getY(1);
    return FloatMath.sqrt(x * x + y * y);
}
```

The order of the points does not matter because any negative signs will be lost when we square them. Note that all math is done using Java's **float** type. Although some Android devices may not have floating-point hardware, we're not doing this often enough to worry about its performance.

Midpoint of Two Points

Calculating a point in the middle of two points is even easier:

Touchv1/src/org/example/touch/Touch.java

```java
private void midPoint(PointF point, MotionEvent event) {
    float x = event.getX(0) + event.getX(1);
    float y = event.getY(0) + event.getY(1);
    point.set(x / 2, y / 2);
}
```

---

4. http://en.wikipedia.org/wiki/Euclidean_distance

All we do is take the average of their X and Y coordinates. To avoid garbage collections that can cause noticeable pauses in the application, we reuse an existing object to store the result rather than allocating and returning a new one each time.

Try running the program now on your phone. Drag the image with one finger, and zoom it by pinching two fingers in or out. For best results, don't let your fingers get closer than an inch or so apart. Otherwise, you'll start to run into some of those bugs in the API I mentioned earlier.

11.7   Fast-Forward >>

In this chapter, we learned how to use the multi-touch API to create a pinch zoom gesture. There's a nice site called GestureWorks[5] that describes a whole library of gestures that have been implemented on the Adobe Flash platform. If you're willing to push the limits of Android's quirky multi-touch support, then perhaps you can find ideas there for other gestures to implement in your Android programs.

Because multi-touch code uses new methods that didn't exist before Android 2.0, if you try to run the touch example on earlier versions, it will fail with a "Force close" error. Luckily, there are ways around this limitation, as described in Section 13.3, *Evolving with Android APIs*, on page 256. You can't teach an old phone new tricks, but you can at least keep it from crashing.

In the next chapter, we'll investigate home screen extensions, including live wallpaper.

---

5. http://gestureworks.com

There's No Place Like Home

No matter how deeply you get into a game or other Android program, it's reassuring to know that you can press the Home button to return to a familiar place—the Android Home screen. It's the central location where you start the web browser, make a phone call, open email, run apps, and do everything else that makes Android fun.

Since you're going to be spending a lot of time there, Android lets you customize the Home screen in many different ways such as setting a static background image and rearranging icons. In this chapter, you'll learn about two more ways: widgets and live wallpaper. Now click your heels together, and let's get started.

12.1 Hello, Widget

Introduced in Android 1.5 (Cupcake), *widgets* are miniature application views that can be embedded in the Home screen. A few widgets are provided with Android including an analog clock, a music controller, and one that just shows a picture. Many developers have created interesting widgets to display the weather, news headlines, horoscopes, and more, and you can too. This section will show you how.

Creating Your First Widget

For this example we're going to create a widget that shows today's date. If you'd like a peek at the final result, see Figure 12.5, on page 238.

Unfortunately, there is no special Eclipse wizard for making a widget, so we'll first create a regular "Hello, Android" application like we did in Section 1.2, *Creating Your First Program*, on page 9 and then tweak it a little. Select File > New > Project... to open the New Project dialog box. Then select Android > Android Project, and click Next. Enter the following information:

```
Project name: Widget
Build Target: Android 2.2
Application name: Widget
Package name: org.example.widget
Min SDK Version: 8
```

Instead of entering a name for the Activity field, leave that field blank, and turn off the check mark next to Create Activity. When you're done, it should look something like Figure 12.1, on the next page.

Click Finish. The Android plug-in will create the project and fill it in with some default files. The files will not be correct for a widget project, so let's fix them up now.

Calling All Widgets!

Our first stop is the AndroidManifest.xml file. Although it's technically possible (and in fact common) to put widgets and activities in the same application, this example will have a widget only. We don't need an *activity* tag, but we do need to add a *receiver* to define the widget. Here is the revised manifest file:

Widget/AndroidManifest.xml

```xml
<?xml version="1.0" encoding="utf-8"?>
<manifest xmlns:android="http://schemas.android.com/apk/res/android"
     package="org.example.widget"
     android:versionCode="1"
     android:versionName="1.0">
  <application android:icon="@drawable/icon"
         android:label="@string/app_name">
    <!-- Broadcast Receiver that will process AppWidget updates -->
    <receiver android:name=".Widget"
          android:label="@string/widget_name">
      <intent-filter>
        <action android:name=
           "android.appwidget.action.APPWIDGET_UPDATE" />
      </intent-filter>
      <meta-data android:name="android.appwidget.provider"
         android:resource="@xml/widget" />
    </receiver>
  </application>
  <uses-sdk android:minSdkVersion="3" android:targetSdkVersion="8" />
</manifest>
```

The *meta-data* tag tells Android it can find the widget definition in res/xml/widget.xml.

Figure 12.1: NEW ANDROID WIDGET PROJECT

Here's the definition:

Widget/res/xml/widget.xml

```xml
<?xml version="1.0" encoding="utf-8"?>
<appwidget-provider
        xmlns:android="http://schemas.android.com/apk/res/android"
    android:minWidth="146dip"
    android:minHeight="72dip"
    android:updatePeriodMillis="1800000"
    android:initialLayout="@layout/main"
    />
```

This specifies a minimum size for the widget, how often it should be updated (more on that later), and a reference to its starting layout.

The layout is defined in res/layout/main.xml:

Widget/res/layout/main.xml

```xml
<?xml version="1.0" encoding="utf-8"?>
<LinearLayout xmlns:android="http://schemas.android.com/apk/res/android"
    android:orientation="vertical"
    android:layout_width="fill_parent"
    android:layout_height="fill_parent"
    android:background="@drawable/widget_bg"
    >
<TextView android:id="@+id/text"
    android:layout_width="fill_parent"
    android:layout_height="fill_parent"
    android:text="@string/hello"
    android:textSize="18sp"
    android:gravity="center"
    android:textColor="@android:color/black"
    />
</LinearLayout>
```

You may have noticed that this layout is almost the same as the one we used for the "Hello, Android" example except that this version specifies centered black text and a background image.

Stretch to Fit

For the background, we could have used any Android Drawable, such as a solid color or a bitmap (see Section 4.1, *Drawable*, on page 64). We could have even left it off to get a completely transparent background. But for this example, I wanted to show you how to use a NinePatch image.

Figure 12.2: DEFINING A STRETCHABLE BACKGROUND WITH THE DRAW 9-PATCH TOOL

A NinePatch image is a stretchable PNG image often used for the background of resizable buttons. You use the Draw 9-patch tool[1] included with the SDK to create one, as shown in Figure 12.2.

A 1-pixel border around the real image contains additional information about how to stretch the image and insert padded content. Lincs on the bottom and right edges tell Android where content should go. If the content doesn't fit in that area (which is usually the case), then the lines on the left and top edges tell Android which pixel rows and columns should be duplicated in order to stretch the image.

The resulting file must use the extension .9.png and be placed in the project's res/drawable directory.

---

1. http://d.android.com/guide/developing/tools/draw9patch.html

Figure 12.3: CUSTOMIZING YOUR HOME SCREEN WITH WIDGETS

The next thing we need is the Widget class.

Embrace and Extend

The Widget needs to extend the AppWidgetProvider class provided by Android. By using that class, we get a bunch of built-in functionality for free, which is always a plus. So, here's the definition for the Widget class:

Widget/src/org/example/widget/Widget.java

```
package org.example.widget;

import android.appwidget.AppWidgetProvider;

public class Widget extends AppWidgetProvider {
    // ...
}
```

We'll come back to fill in this class in a moment, but for now we can just use the default behavior provided by AppWidgetProvider.

Finally, let's get rid of a few pesky error messages by defining these string values:

`Widget/res/values/strings.xml`

```xml
<?xml version="1.0" encoding="utf-8"?>
<resources>
    <string name="hello">Hello World!</string>
    <string name="app_name">Widget</string>
    <string name="widget_name">Widget</string>
</resources>
```

All that's left now is to run it.

Running the Widget

To run your new widget, go to the Package Explorer window, right-click the Widget project, and select Run As > Android Application. Nothing much will appear to happen as Eclipse builds and installs the widget on your emulator or device.

To see the new widget, open the Home screen's context menu: press and hold your finger (or mouse) on the Home screen. A menu will appear with options listing all the types of things you can add (see Figure 12.3, on the facing page).

Select Widgets from the menu, and then select the widget named Widget (clever, huh?). At last, your widget should appear (see Figure 12.4, on the next page).

Try moving it around by pressing and holding your finger on the widget. Rotate the display to see how the widget automatically resizes itself. To remove it, drag it to the trash can icon at the bottom of the screen.

As exciting as that was, let's do it one better by displaying the current date and time in our widget.

Keeping Up-to-Date

In Android 1.5, widget hosts (programs like the Home screen that can contain widgets) send a message to all their little widget kids whenever the widgets should display something. The Android way to send a message is to broadcast an intent. In this case, the intent is android. appwidget.action.APPWIDGET_UPDATE.

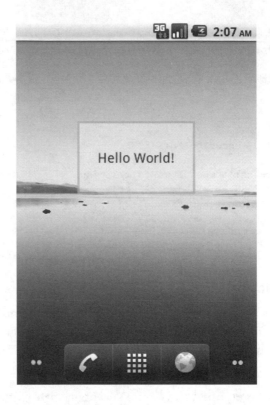

Figure 12.4: HELLO, WIDGET

Back when we set up the AndroidManifest.xml file, we told Android that we could receive that intent and do something interesting with it. Now it's time to fill out the Widget class to do just that:

Widget/src/org/example/widget/Widget.java

```
Line 1  package org.example.widget;

        import java.text.SimpleDateFormat;
        import java.util.Date;
     5
        import android.appwidget.AppWidgetManager;
        import android.appwidget.AppWidgetProvider;
        import android.content.Context;
        import android.widget.RemoteViews;
    10
        public class Widget extends AppWidgetProvider {
            // ...
            // Define the format string for the date
            private SimpleDateFormat formatter = new SimpleDateFormat(
    15          "EEEEEEEEE\nd MMM yyyy");
```

```
      @Override
      public void onUpdate(Context context,
            AppWidgetManager appWidgetManager, int[] appWidgetIds) {
20       // Retrieve and format the current date
         String now = formatter.format(new Date());

         // Change the text in the widget
         RemoteViews updateViews = new RemoteViews(
25             context.getPackageName(), R.layout.main);
         updateViews.setTextViewText(R.id.text, now);
         appWidgetManager.updateAppWidget(appWidgetIds, updateViews);

         // Not really necessary, just a habit
30       super.onUpdate(context, appWidgetManager, appWidgetIds);
      }
   }
```

Whenever the APPWIDGET_UPDATE intent comes in, Android calls our onUpdate() method. On line 21, we format the current date using a SimpleDateFormat created on line 14. This shows the day of the week, day of the month, month name, and year on the first row of the widget, and then the hour, minute, second, and milliseconds on the second row.

Next, on line 24, we create a RemoteViews instance for the new view layout that the widget will display. It just so happens that this example uses the same layout, R.layout.main, when updating as it did when it was started. Line 26 replaces the original "Hello, World" text with the current date and time.

Finally, on line 27, we send our updated view to replace the current contents of the widget. The call to super.onUpdate() on line 30 is just there for code hygiene.

Remove the widget from your Home screen, and reinstall it from Eclipse. When you add it back to the Home screen, you should see something like Figure 12.5, on the following page.

The frequency of updates is controlled by the android:updatePeriodMillis= parameter in res/xml/widget.xml. A value of 1800000 represents 30 minutes, so our widget will be updated twice an hour. Note that this is only an approximate number. The actual update event may be delayed (possibly a long time) because of other things happening on the phone.

Google recommends you set widgets to update infrequently, such as once a day or once an hour, in order to conserve battery power. Starting in Android 1.6, the android:updatePeriodMillis= parameter will not honor any values under thirty minutes. If you need more frequent updates, you'll have to set up your own timer using the AlarmManager class. This is left as an exercise for the reader.

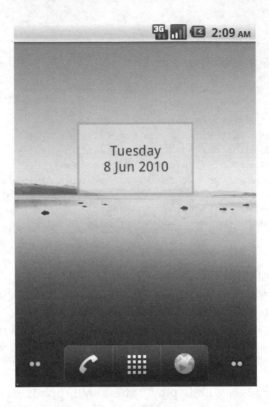

Figure 12.5: DISPLAYING THE DATE AND TIME

Go Wild

Now that you know the basics of widget building, there's no end to the interesting doodads you can create. If you need more advanced features such as responding to events, background processing, and specifying an initial activity for configuration, consult the online documentation.[2] Try to keep your widgets simple and useful, though. By cleverly using widgets, you can make the Android experience more personal and dynamic for your users.

Do you find yourself wishing for a bit more room to express than a widget provides? Then follow the yellow brick road to the land of live wallpapers.

12.2 Live Wallpaper

Regular wallpaper just sits there. It looks nice, but it never changes. *Yawn.*

---

2. http://d.android.com/guide/topics/appwidgets

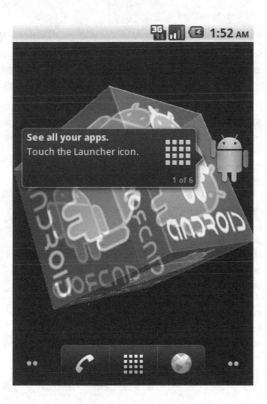

Figure 12.6: THE WALLPAPER EXAMPLE REUSES CODE FROM THE OPENGL CHAPTER.

Live wallpaper is a new feature in Android 2.1 (Eclair Maintenance Release 1). It lets you replace boring static wallpaper images with everything from vibrant and pulsing music visualizations to quiet, meditative ponds that respond to your touch with gentle ripples.

Displaying current weather conditions, slide shows, Magic 8 Balls, and pyrotechnics are just a few of the ideas that are possible. Let's pull back the curtain to see how the magic is done.

Creating the Wallpaper Project

In this example, we'll create a live wallpaper that displays a rotating cube using OpenGL. The final result is shown in Figure 12.6. Start by creating a new Android project using these values in the project wizard:

```
Project name: Wallpaper
Build Target: Android 2.2
Application name: Wallpaper
Package name: org.example.wallpaper
Min SDK Version: 8
```

As with the widget project, leave the activity name blank, and turn off the check mark next to Create Activity. After the project is created, we need to perform some major changes to the AndroidManifest.xml file. Here's what it should look like:

Wallpaper/AndroidManifest.xml

```xml
<?xml version="1.0" encoding="utf-8"?>
<manifest xmlns:android="http://schemas.android.com/apk/res/android"
    package="org.example.wallpaper"
    android:versionCode="1"
    android:versionName="1.0">
  <application android:label="@string/app_name">
    <service android:name=".Wallpaper"
        android:label="@string/service_name"
        android:permission="android.permission.BIND_WALLPAPER">
      <intent-filter>
        <action android:name=
          "android.service.wallpaper.WallpaperService" />
      </intent-filter>
      <meta-data android:name="android.service.wallpaper"
        android:resource="@xml/wallpaper" />
    </service>
  </application>
  <uses-sdk android:minSdkVersion="7" android:targetSdkVersion="8" />
</manifest>
```

The *<service>* tag is new. It defines an Android service that will run in the background and respond to events. The android:permission= attribute means that any program that calls our service will need to have the specified permission. The Android Home screen program already has that permission set, so it will work fine.

The *<intent-filter>* tag tells Android what type of service this is, and the *<meta-data>* tag lets it know where to find extra information about the wallpaper. The android:resource="@xml/wallpaper" setting refers to the res/xml/wallpaper.xml file, which is a new file you should create now using the following contents:

Wallpaper/res/xml/wallpaper.xml

```xml
<?xml version="1.0" encoding="utf-8"?>
<wallpaper xmlns:android="http://schemas.android.com/apk/res/android"
  android:author="@+string/author"
  android:description="@string/description"
  android:thumbnail="@drawable/thumbnail" />
```

The wallpaper metadata specifies the author of the wallpaper (that's you), a short description of what it does, and a thumbnail image. The image and description will appear in a list when the user is asked to pick a wallpaper to display.

Before we get any further, let's define all the strings we'll need for the project in res/values/strings.xml:

`Wallpaper/res/values/strings.xml`

```xml
<?xml version="1.0" encoding="utf-8"?>
<resources>
    <string name="app_name">Wallpaper</string>
    <string name="service_name">Hello, Android!</string>
    <string name="author">Hello, Android!</string>
    <string name="description">Sample live wallpaper
        from Hello, Android!</string>
</resources>
```

You should delete the layout file, res/layout/main.xml, because we won't be using it. We'll fill in the Wallpaper class (Wallpaper.java) after we learn a few things about Android services.

Introducing Services

One of the distinguishing features of Android is the ability to run programs in the background. To contrast them with foreground activities, Android calls these programs *services*.

The main Java class for a service inherits from the Service class. Services have a life cycle similar to activities (see Section 2.2, *It's Alive!*, on page 22) but are a little simpler. There's an onCreate() method that is called when the service is first created and an onDestroy() method that is called when it is destroyed.

In between, Android will call the onStartCommand() method (onStart() prior to version 2.0) when a client requests that the service be started. Services can be sticky or not sticky, depending upon whether you want the service to hang around between requests.

There are a few other methods for things such as low memory conditions that you can implement if you like. See the online documentation for all the gory details.[3]

For the wallpaper example, we don't need to worry about any of these methods because they are all handled by the WallpaperService class, which is a subclass of Service.

---

3. http://d.android.com/reference/android/app/Service.html

Our main class needs to extend WallpaperService like this:

Wallpaper/src/org/example/wallpaper/Wallpaper.java

```java
package org.example.wallpaper;

import android.service.wallpaper.WallpaperService;

public class Wallpaper extends WallpaperService {
    private class MyEngine extends Engine {
        // Engine implementation goes here...
    }

    @Override
    public Engine onCreateEngine() {
        return new MyEngine();
    }
}
```

All we had to do was implement the onCreateEngine() method, which is a single line. It's sole purpose is to create and return another class called MyEngine.

Building a Drawing Engine

The MyEngine class has to be an inner class of Wallpaper, so in Java it's declared inside the enclosing class's curly brackets. MyEngine extends the Engine class provided by Android. Here's the outline for MyEngine with all the methods stubbed out:

Wallpaper/src/org/example/wallpaper/Wallpaper.java

```java
private class MyEngine extends Engine {
    @Override
    public void onCreate(final SurfaceHolder holder) {
        super.onCreate(holder);
    }

    @Override
    public void onDestroy() {
        super.onDestroy();
    };

    @Override
    public void onSurfaceCreated(final SurfaceHolder holder) {
        super.onSurfaceCreated(holder);
    }

    @Override
    public void onSurfaceDestroyed(final SurfaceHolder holder) {
        super.onSurfaceDestroyed(holder);
    }
```

```
@Override
public void onSurfaceChanged(final SurfaceHolder holder,
        final int format, final int width, final int height) {
    super.onSurfaceChanged(holder, format, width, height);
}

@Override
public void onVisibilityChanged(final boolean visible) {
    super.onVisibilityChanged(visible);
}

@Override
public void onOffsetsChanged(final float xOffset,
        final float yOffset, final float xOffsetStep,
        final float yOffsetStep, final int xPixelOffset,
        final int yPixelOffset) {
    super.onOffsetsChanged(xOffset, yOffset, xOffsetStep,
        yOffsetStep, xPixelOffset, yPixelOffset);
}
}
```

Note that every method should always call its superclass method. You can get Eclipse to generate these stubs for you in the Java editor by selecting the class name MyEngine, right-clicking, selecting Source > Override/Implement Methods, and picking the methods you want to create. There's one difference in what Eclipse generates and what was shown earlier, however. I've added the final keyword to every method parameter. That will be needed later so inner classes within those methods can access the parameters. If you forget and leave them out, the compiler will let you know.

During the engine's life cycle, Android will call these methods in a specific order. Here is the entire sequence:

onCreate

    onSurfaceCreated

        onSurfaceChanged (1+ calls in any order)

        onOffsetsChanged (0+ calls in any order)

        onVisibilityChanged (0+ calls in any order)

    onSurfaceDestroyed

onDestroy

We'll be filling out all these methods in the rest of the chapter.

We'll also need a few more **import** statements to prevent compiler errors. I usually let Eclipse create those for me while I'm coding (using Content Assist (⌊Ctrl+spacebar⌋) or Quick Fix (⌊Ctrl+1⌋) or in a batch with the Source > Organize Imports command (⌊Ctrl+Shift+O⌋). But if you prefer, you can just type them all in now. Here's the full list:

```
import java.util.concurrent.ExecutorService;
import java.util.concurrent.Executors;

import javax.microedition.khronos.egl.EGL10;
import javax.microedition.khronos.egl.EGL11;
import javax.microedition.khronos.egl.EGLConfig;
import javax.microedition.khronos.egl.EGLContext;
import javax.microedition.khronos.egl.EGLDisplay;
import javax.microedition.khronos.egl.EGLSurface;
import javax.microedition.khronos.opengles.GL10;

import android.service.wallpaper.WallpaperService;
import android.view.SurfaceHolder;
```

Next we need to borrow some code to draw our cube.

Reusing the OpenGL code

You don't have to use OpenGL for live wallpapers, but I like it because it's faster than the regular Android 2D graphics libraries (see Chapter 4, *Exploring 2D Graphics*, on page 61). Also, we just so happen to have a nice rotating 3D cube example already written from another chapter (Chapter 10, *3D Graphics in OpenGL*, on page 191).

Grab three files from that project now: GLCube.java, GLRenderer.java, and android.png. Put the Java files in the org.example.wallpaper package (in other words, the org/example/wallpaper directory), and place the PNG file in the res/drawable-nodpi directory.

If you haven't done that chapter yet, you can download all these files from the book's website. Unzip the source code archive to a temporary location, and copy the files from the OpenGL project.

You shouldn't have to make any changes to the source code except for the package name at the top of both Java files, which should read as follows:

```
package org.example.wallpaper;
```

Now we just have to figure out how to call the code from our new wallpaper project.

Creating and Destroying the Engine

To begin, let's define a few fields for the engine to use. Put these at the start of the MyEngine class:

`Wallpaper/src/org/example/wallpaper/Wallpaper.java`

```
private GLRenderer glRenderer;
private GL10 gl;
private EGL10 egl;
private EGLContext glc;
private EGLDisplay glDisplay;
private EGLSurface glSurface;

private ExecutorService executor;
private Runnable drawCommand;
```

The most important variable here is executor. In Java, an executor is an object that can run snippets of code (called *runnables*) asynchronously in another thread. When the wallpaper engine is first created, we're going to create one of these executors to handle all interaction with OpenGL.

We have to do that because OpenGL can be called only from a single thread. The service has to create a thread to do drawing in the background anyway, and we can't call some of the OpenGL code in the background thread and some in the foreground thread. So, we use a single executor for everything. The definition of onCreate() shows how to initialize it:

`Wallpaper/src/org/example/wallpaper/Wallpaper.java`

```
@Override
public void onCreate(final SurfaceHolder holder) {
   super.onCreate(holder);
   executor = Executors.newSingleThreadExecutor();

   drawCommand = new Runnable() {
      public void run() {
         glRenderer.onDrawFrame(gl);
         egl.eglSwapBuffers(glDisplay, glSurface);
         if (isVisible()
               && egl.eglGetError() != EGL11.EGL_CONTEXT_LOST) {
            executor.execute(drawCommand);
         }
      }
   };
}
```

Besides the executor, we also create a runnable called drawCommand, which will be used later to draw each frame of the cube animation. This is a Java anonymous inner class, so it has access to all the fields and **final** parameters of its parents. Note that we haven't initialized any of those variables yet (such as glRenderer and glDisplay), but that's OK because we're just defining this code to be run later, after everything is ready.

The opposite of onCreate() is onDestroy(). onDestroy() is called when Android is finished with the wallpaper engine. All it needs to do is shut down the executor we created in onCreate():

Wallpaper/src/org/example/wallpaper/Wallpaper.java

```
@Override
public void onDestroy() {
   executor.shutdownNow();
   super.onDestroy();
};
```

Note that we call super.onDestroy() at the end of the method, not at the beginning like we do in most places. That's just a standard Java idiom to let the superclass clean up after itself in a mirror image of the way creation was done. I don't know if it's really necessary in this case, but by following the convention, we don't even have to think about it.

Managing the Surface

During the engine's lifetime, Android will create a Surface representing the background of the Home screen for the engine to draw on. When the surface is first created, onSurfaceCreated() is called. We use this opportunity to initialize OpenGL and our GLRenderer class that we copied from the other project:

Wallpaper/src/org/example/wallpaper/Wallpaper.java

```
@Override
public void onSurfaceCreated(final SurfaceHolder holder) {
   super.onSurfaceCreated(holder);
   Runnable surfaceCreatedCommand = new Runnable() {
      @Override
      public void run() {
         // Initialize OpenGL
         egl = (EGL10) EGLContext.getEGL();
         glDisplay = egl.eglGetDisplay(EGL10.EGL_DEFAULT_DISPLAY);
         int[] version = new int[2];
         egl.eglInitialize(glDisplay, version);
         int[] configSpec = { EGL10.EGL_RED_SIZE, 5,
               EGL10.EGL_GREEN_SIZE, 6, EGL10.EGL_BLUE_SIZE,
               5, EGL10.EGL_DEPTH_SIZE, 16, EGL10.EGL_NONE };
```

```
            EGLConfig[] configs = new EGLConfig[1];
            int[] numConfig = new int[1];
            egl.eglChooseConfig(glDisplay, configSpec, configs,
                    1, numConfig);
            EGLConfig config = configs[0];

            glc = egl.eglCreateContext(glDisplay, config,
                    EGL10.EGL_NO_CONTEXT, null);

            glSurface = egl.eglCreateWindowSurface(glDisplay,
                    config, holder, null);
            egl.eglMakeCurrent(glDisplay, glSurface, glSurface,
                    glc);
            gl = (GL10) (glc.getGL());

            // Initialize Renderer
            glRenderer = new GLRenderer(Wallpaper.this);
            glRenderer.onSurfaceCreated(gl, config);
        }
    };
    executor.execute(surfaceCreatedCommand);
}
```

It would be nice if Android would provide a helper class to hide some of this OpenGL boilerplate detail from the programmer (something like GLSurfaceView, but for wallpapers), but until then, just hold your nose and copy the code.

The onSurfaceDestroyed() method is called when the background surface is about to go away. This is a good place to terminate all that OpenGL stuff we initialized earlier:

Wallpaper/src/org/example/wallpaper/Wallpaper.java

```
@Override
public void onSurfaceDestroyed(final SurfaceHolder holder) {
    Runnable surfaceDestroyedCommand = new Runnable() {
        public void run() {
            // Free OpenGL resources
            egl.eglMakeCurrent(glDisplay, EGL10.EGL_NO_SURFACE,
                    EGL10.EGL_NO_SURFACE, EGL10.EGL_NO_CONTEXT);
            egl.eglDestroySurface(glDisplay, glSurface);
            egl.eglDestroyContext(glDisplay, glc);
            egl.eglTerminate(glDisplay);

        };
    };
    executor.execute(surfaceDestroyedCommand);
    super.onSurfaceDestroyed(holder);
}
```

While the surface is up, Android calls the onSurfaceChanged() method to tell you its width and height.

Wallpaper/src/org/example/wallpaper/Wallpaper.java

```
@Override
public void onSurfaceChanged(final SurfaceHolder holder,
        final int format, final int width, final int height) {
   super.onSurfaceChanged(holder, format, width, height);
   Runnable surfaceChangedCommand = new Runnable() {
      public void run() {
         glRenderer.onSurfaceChanged(gl, width, height);
      };
   };
   executor.execute(surfaceChangedCommand);
}
```

So far, the surface has not been visible to the user, so we shouldn't draw anything on it yet. That's about to change.

Making the Wallpaper Visible

After the WallpaperService is initialized, the Engine is initialized, and the Surface is initialized (whew!), the only thing left to do is to make the surface visible. When it's ready to do that, Android calls the onVisibility-Changed() method with a boolean parameter that says whether it has become visible or invisible:

Wallpaper/src/org/example/wallpaper/Wallpaper.java

```
@Override
public void onVisibilityChanged(final boolean visible) {
   super.onVisibilityChanged(visible);
   if (visible) {
      executor.execute(drawCommand);
   }
}
```

If it's visible, all we need to do is queue up a call to the drawCommand runnable, which will draw one frame of the animation and, if the surface is still visible, queue itself up again over and over. To save the battery, it is very important that a wallpaper run only while it is visible.

At this point, you should be able to try the example in the emulator or on a real device. Right-click the project, and select Run As > Android Application. As with widgets, the wallpaper will only be installed, not executed, by running it from Eclipse. To really run it, go to the device or emulator, and press and hold your finger (or mouse) on the Home screen. A menu will appear with options listing all the types of things you can add (see Figure 12.3, on page 234).

Select Wallpapers from the menu, and then Live wallpapers. A list of all live wallpapers will appear. Pick the one called Hello, Android! and the wallpaper should start spinning around happily in preview mode (if it doesn't, then follow the instructions in Section 3.10, *Debugging*, on page 58 to diagnose the problem). Touch the Set wallpaper button to make this the wallpaper for your Home screen, or press the Back button to return to the list. For the live wallpaper in action, see Figure 12.6, on page 239.

Responding to User Input

When you use regular, static wallpaper and you pan the Home screen left or right with your finger, the wallpaper moves a little as well. However, if you try that with the live wallpaper example now, nothing happens.

To get that functionality, we have to implement the onOffsetsChanged() method:

Wallpaper/src/org/example/wallpaper/Wallpaper.java

```
@Override
public void onOffsetsChanged(final float xOffset,
        final float yOffset, final float xOffsetStep,
        final float yOffsetStep, final int xPixelOffset,
        final int yPixelOffset) {
    super.onOffsetsChanged(xOffset, yOffset, xOffsetStep,
            yOffsetStep, xPixelOffset, yPixelOffset);
    Runnable offsetsChangedCommand = new Runnable() {
        public void run() {
            if (xOffsetStep != 0f) {
                glRenderer.setParallax(xOffset - 0.5f);
            }
        };
    };
    executor.execute(offsetsChangedCommand);
}
```

If xOffsetStep is 0, it means panning is disabled (for example, in preview mode). For other values, we shift the view based on the xOffset variable. If the offset is 0, the user has panned all the way to the left, and if it's 1, they have panned all the way to the right. Care to guess what 0.5 means?

Now I'm about to go back on what I said earlier about not modifying GLRenderer. Since the OpenGL example did not have any user input, we have to add an extra field and a setParallax() method that sets it to the GLRenderer class:

`Wallpaper/src/org/example/wallpaper/GLRenderer.java`

```
class GLRenderer implements GLSurfaceView.Renderer {
  // ...
  private float xOffset;

  public void setParallax(float xOffset) {
    this.xOffset = -xOffset;
  }
}
```

Then in the middle of the GLRenderer.onDrawFrame() method, we have to change one line to use that new field to translate the model a little to the left or right:

`Wallpaper/src/org/example/wallpaper/GLRenderer.java`

```
public void onDrawFrame(GL10 gl) {
  // ...
  // Position model so we can see it
  gl.glMatrixMode(GL10.GL_MODELVIEW);
  gl.glLoadIdentity();
  gl.glTranslatef(xOffset, 0, -3.0f);

  // Other drawing commands go here...
}
```

We could have moved the eye point instead, but it was easier just to move the cube. That's it! Now try the example again, and you can pan left or right with ease.

There are two other ways to interact with live wallpaper that you can support if you like: commands and touch events. To support commands, implement the onCommand() method, and to support raw touch events, implement the onTouchEvent() method. I'll leave that as an exercise for you.

12.3 Fast-Forward >>

In this chapter, we learned how to jazz up the Android Home screen with widgets and a live wallpaper. The Android Market is full of examples of both that people like you have created. I'd love to see yours there, so read Chapter 14, *Publishing to the Android Market*, on page 269 for directions and encouragement.

Note: If your application provides a widget, live wallpaper, or other home screen enhancement, you should not allow it to be installed from the SD card. See Section 13.6, *Installing on the SD Card*, on page 265 for more information.

When Android first came out, there was only one version and one phone model to worry about. Now there are several dozen devices of various shapes and sizes running at least four different versions of Android. You're not in Kansas anymore, but the next chapter will help you avoid the flying monkeys.

Write Once, Test Everywhere

Today, Android can be found in a bewildering array of mobile phones, tablets, and other devices. This is both a blessing and a curse. It's a blessing for consumers because they can choose between Android-powered devices of different shapes, sizes, and prices. But for developers, it can be a curse to try to support all those variations.

To complicate things, the rapid pace of Android development has left a fragmented trail of devices running different versions of the platform in its wake. The following table shows all the versions of Android ever released:[1]

Version	Code name[2]	API	Released	Comments
1.0	BASE	1	Oct. 2008	No longer in use
1.1	BASE_1_1	2	Feb. 2009	No longer in use
1.5	CUPCAKE	3	May 2009	Widgets
1.6	DONUT	4	Sept. 2009	High- and low-density displays
2.0	ECLAIR	5	Nov. 2009	No longer in use
2.0.1	ECLAIR_0_1	6	Dec. 2009	Multi-touch, no longer in use
2.1	ECLAIR_MR1	7	Jan. 2010	Live wallpaper
2.2	FROYO	8	May 2010	SD card installs

This chapter will cover how to support multiple Android versions and screen resolutions in one program. The first step is testing.

---

1. See http://d.android.com/resources/dashboard/platform-versions.html for an up-to-date chart showing the percentage of devices running each version of Android.
2. Android version codes and API levels are specified in the Build.VERSION_CODES class.

13.1 Gentlemen, Start Your Emulators

For most of this book I've been telling you to target your applications to version 2.2 of the Android platform (also known as FroYo). However, there's one little problem with this advice: your programs may not run on phones that have one of the older versions of Android installed.

The only reliable way of telling whether it will work is to test it. And short of buying one of every Android phone on the market, the best way to test your program on different Android versions and screen sizes is to try it in the emulator.

To do this, you'll need to set up several virtual devices with different versions and emulator skins. A skin specifies the width, height, and pixel density for an emulated device. In addition to the em22 AVD you created in Section 1.3, *Creating an AVD*, on page 9, I recommend that you create the following virtual devices for testing:

Name	Target	Skin	Inspired by Device...
em15	1.5	HVGA (320×480)	HTC G1, Eris
em16	1.6	HVGA (320×480)	HTC Hero
em16-qvga	1.6	QVGA (200×320)	HTC Tattoo
em21-854	2.1	WVGA854 (480×854)	Motorola Droid (Sholes)
em22-800	2.2	WVGA800 (480×800)	HTC Nexus One
em22-1024	2.2	Custom (1024×600)	Notion Ink Adam

You can use the em22 AVD for development and then test your program in the other AVDs before you release the application. And don't forget to try it in both portrait and landscape modes. In the emulator, press Ctrl+F11 or use the 7 or 9 keys on the keypad (NumLock off) to toggle between portrait and landscape.

Unless you have a very powerful desktop computer, you probably won't be able to run all these AVDs at once. In practice, I find that running only one at a time works best. Try it now by starting up the em16 (Android 1.6) emulator. Wait until the emulator comes up to the home screen, and turn off the screen lock if it appears. Now let's see some of the things that can go wrong.

13.2 Building for Multiple Versions

First, we'll try running the "Hello, Android" program from Section 1.2, *Creating Your First Program*, on page 9 in the 1.6 emulator. From the menu, select Run > Run Configurations. Locate the configuration for

HelloAndroid and select it, or create a new Android Application configuration if it doesn't exist. Click the Target tab, and set Deployment Target Selection Mode to Manual. Then click the Run button.

Eclipse will show a dialog asking you to choose a running Android device. You may notice a red *X* next to the emulator name—ignore it. Select the device called em16, and then click OK. The following error will appear in the Console view:

```
ERROR: Application requires API version 8. Device API version
       is 4 (Android 1.6).
Launch canceled!
```

Note: If you get a warning that says "Application does not specify an API level requirement," then you need to specify a minimum SDK version (covered in a moment). If you don't get an error and the application launches in the em16 emulator, it means you've already applied the change in this section. And finally, if Eclipse launches a new emulator window, then you probably have your target selection mode set to Automatic. Change it to Manual, and try again.

The error occurs because we specified version 2.2 as the target version of Android when we created the project. Unless we change something, it won't run at all on older versions. On those devices, it won't even appear in the Android Market. But I happen to know that this program will work just fine on any version of Android. So, how do we tell Android that?

Easy: In the Android manifest, just set your target SDK version to one number and your minimum SDK version to another number. This lets you target a new version of Android but have it still work on phones that have an older version.

To do this, edit the AndroidManifest.xml file, and change the line that says the following:

```
<uses-sdk android:minSdkVersion="8" />
```

to read as follows:

```
<uses-sdk android:minSdkVersion="3" android:targetSdkVersion="8" />
```

If you don't have this line, then add it right before the </manifest> tag.

This tells Android that your program is built for Android 2.2 (API level 8) but will work fine on Android 1.5 (API level 3). Save the file, and try running the project again. It should work this time without any errors. If you get a warning about "Manifest min SDK version (3) is lower than project target API level (8)," just ignore it.

Figure 13.1: THE TOUCH EXAMPLE CRASHES ON ANDROID 1.6.

Unfortunately, for some programs, just saying that we support version 3 doesn't make it so. We'll see an example of that next.

13.3 Evolving with Android APIs

Sometimes you need to use an API that does not appear in all versions of Android. For instance, in the touch example (Chapter 11, *Multi-Touch*, on page 215), we used some new methods of the MotionEvent class that were not there before Android 2.0. If you try to run that example in the em16 emulator, you will get the error in Figure 13.1.

If you then open the LogCat view in Eclipse (Window > Show View > Other > Android Log) and scroll back a little, you'll find a more detailed error message, which will look something like this:

```
Could not find method android.view.MotionEvent.getPointerCount,
    referenced from method org.example.touch.Touch.dumpEvent
VFY: unable to resolve virtual method 11:
    Landroid/view/MotionEvent;.getPointerCount ()I
Verifier rejected class Lorg/example/touch/Touch;
Class init failed in newInstance call (Lorg/example/touch/Touch;)
Uncaught handler: thread main exiting due to uncaught exception
java.lang.VerifyError: org.example.touch.Touch
    at java.lang.Class.newInstanceImpl(Native Method)
    at java.lang.Class.newInstance(Class.java:1472)
    ...
```

The important part is the VerifyError exception. At runtime, Android throws a VerifyError exception whenever it tries to load one class that uses methods that don't exist in a second class. In this case, the Touch class references the getPointerCount() method of the MotionEvent class. MotionEvent exists in 1.5, but the getPointerCount() method was not introduced until version 2.0. Note that it didn't complain about the constants we used like ACTION_POINTER_DOWN because they are baked into our program by the compiler at build time.

It would be nice if we could modify the definition of MotionEvent to add the missing method, but unlike JavaScript or Ruby, Java doesn't support that. We can do something similar, though, using one of three techniques:

- *Subclassing*: We could make a new class that extends MotionEvent and adds the new method. Unfortunately, MotionEvent is final, which in Java means it can't be extended, so that won't work here.
- *Reflection*: Using utilities from the java.lang.reflect package, we could write code to test for the existence of the new method. If it exists, we'd call it, and if doesn't exist, we'd do something else like return 1. That would work, but Java reflection is slow to run and messy to program.
- *Delegation and factory*: We could create two classes, one that will be used on older versions of Android and one that will be used on newer versions. The first one will implement dummy versions of the new methods, while the second one will delegate all calls to the real new methods. Then we pick which class to create using a static factory method (a method the caller uses instead of the **new** keyword to create a class). This technique is simple and can be used to handle most API differences, so we'll use it here.

One of our goals should be to minimize the changes to the original Touch class. We start by replacing all references to MotionEvent with a new class, WrapMotionEvent, like this:

Touchv2/src/org/example/touch/Touch.java

```java
@Override
public boolean onTouch(View v, MotionEvent rawEvent) {
    WrapMotionEvent event = WrapMotionEvent.wrap(rawEvent);
    // ...
}

private void dumpEvent(WrapMotionEvent event) {
    // ...
}
```

```
private float spacing(WrapMotionEvent event) {
    // ...
}

private void midPoint(PointF point, WrapMotionEvent event) {
    // ...
}
```

In the onTouch() method, we take the raw MotionEvent passed in by Android and convert it to a WrapMotionEvent by calling the static factory method WrapMotionEvent.wrap(). Other than these changes, the rest of the Touch class is...untouched.

Now let's create the WrapMotionEvent class. Delegation is a pretty common thing to do in Java, so Eclipse provides a command to make it easy. Click the org.example.touch package in the Package Explorer view, and then select the File > New > Class command. Enter the new class name (WrapMotionEvent), and press Return. Now add a field inside the class for the event we want to wrap. The code should look like this so far:

Touchv2/src/org/example/touch/WrapMotionEvent.java

```
package org.example.touch;

import android.view.MotionEvent;

public class WrapMotionEvent {
    protected MotionEvent event;
}
```

In the Java editor, click the event variable, and then select the Source > Generate Delegate Methods command from the menu. Eclipse will give you a big list of possible methods, but we don't need the whole list, so deselect all of them and select only the ones that are actually used in the program: getAction(), getPointerCount(), getPointerId(int), getX(), getX(int), getY(), and getY(int). When you are done, the dialog should look like Figure 13.2, on the facing page. Click OK to generate the code.

Before doing anything else, save the WrapMotionEvent.java file, and make a copy called EclairMotionEvent.java. We'll come back to that one in a moment.

As it currently stands, WrapMotionEvent calls several methods that don't exist in older Android versions, so we need to replace those. You can tell which ones are a problem by hovering your mouse cursor over each method call.

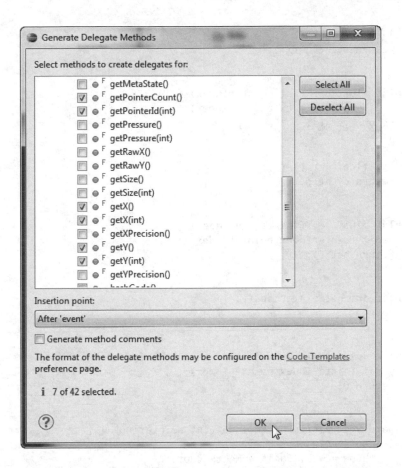

Figure 13.2: LET ECLIPSE CREATE THE DELEGATE METHODS FOR YOU.

The new methods will say "Since: API Level 5," and the old methods will say "Since: API Level 1." Another way to tell would be to temporarily change your build target to Android 1.6, rebuild, and see where the errors are.

Here's the new code that will work under Android 1.6:

Touchv2/src/org/example/touch/WrapMotionEvent.java

```java
package org.example.touch;

import android.view.MotionEvent;

public class WrapMotionEvent {
  protected MotionEvent event;

  public int getAction() {
    return event.getAction();
  }
```

```java
    public float getX() {
        return event.getX();
    }

    public float getX(int pointerIndex) {
        verifyPointerIndex(pointerIndex);
        return getX();
    }

    public float getY() {
        return event.getY();
    }

    public float getY(int pointerIndex) {
        verifyPointerIndex(pointerIndex);
        return getY();
    }

    public int getPointerCount() {
        return 1;
    }

    public int getPointerId(int pointerIndex) {
        verifyPointerIndex(pointerIndex);
        return 0;
    }

    private void verifyPointerIndex(int pointerIndex) {
        if (pointerIndex > 0) {
            throw new IllegalArgumentException(
                "Invalid pointer index for Donut/Cupcake");
        }
    }
}
```

In this version, getPointerCount() will always return 1, indicating there is only one finger pressed. That should ensure that getX(int) and getY(int) will never be called with a pointer index greater than zero, but just in case I've added a verifyPointerIndex() method to check for that error.

Next, we need to add the wrap() method and the constructor for the WrapMotionEvent class:

Touchv2/src/org/example/touch/WrapMotionEvent.java

```java
protected WrapMotionEvent(MotionEvent event) {
    this.event = event;
}
```

```
static public WrapMotionEvent wrap(MotionEvent event) {
    try {
        return new EclairMotionEvent(event);
    } catch (VerifyError e) {
        return new WrapMotionEvent(event);
    }
}
```

The wrap() method is our static factory method. First it tries to create an instance of the EclairMotionEvent class. That will fail under Android 1.5 and 1.6 because EclairMotionEvent uses the new methods introduced in Android 2.0 (Eclair). If it can't create an EclairMotionEvent class, then it creates an instance of the WrapMotionEvent class instead.[3]

Now it's time for us to work on the EclairMotionEvent class that we saved earlier. We'll finish it by making it extend WrapMotionEvent and adding a constructor. We can also take out the getAction() method and the zero-parameter versions of getX() and getY() because they exist in all versions of Android and are already implemented in WrapMotionEvent. Here's the full definition:

> Touchv2/src/org/example/touch/EclairMotionEvent.java

```
package org.example.touch;

import android.view.MotionEvent;

public class EclairMotionEvent extends WrapMotionEvent {

    protected EclairMotionEvent(MotionEvent event) {
        super(event);
    }

    public float getX(int pointerIndex) {
        return event.getX(pointerIndex);
    }

    public float getY(int pointerIndex) {
        return event.getY(pointerIndex);
    }

    public int getPointerCount() {
        return event.getPointerCount();
    }
```

---

3. Design pattern purists will probably deride this code, saying I should have created a separate class to hold the factory method and a common interface for both WrapMotion-Event and EclairMotionEvent to implement. But this is simpler, and it works, which is more important in my book.

```
    public int getPointerId(int pointerIndex) {
      return event.getPointerId(pointerIndex);
    }
}
```

If you try to run the program now, it will work in the 1.6 emulator as well as new versions (2.0 and beyond). On old versions, of course, you'll lose some functionality. Multi-touch is not supported on 1.6, so you won't be able to use the pinch zoom gesture to shrink or grow the image. But you will be able to move the image around using the drag gesture.

In a real program, you might have to implement some alternate way to resize the picture when pinch zoom is not available. For example, you could add buttons to zoom in and out.

Just for fun, start up the em15 (1.5 emulator), and run the program there. It looks OK, but try doing the drag gesture. Nothing happens! We've discovered a bug in Android 1.5.

13.4   Bug on Parade

It turns out that Android 1.5 (Cupcake) has a bug in the ImageView class. The bug prevents the setImageMatrix() method from working when the ImageView is in "matrix" mode, which is pretty ironic if you think about it.

Unfortunately, there is no complete list of bugs, so figuring out this was a bug in Android (as opposed to a bug in our code or a misunderstanding of how something works) took a bit of sleuthing. In case you find yourself in a similar situation, here are the steps that I went through:

1. My first suspect was the new code we just added: the WrapMotionEvent and EclairMotionEvent classes. I put in a few logging statements to verify events were being handled correctly and the transformation matrix was created correctly. They turned up no problems, so I began to suspect something was wrong with the ImageView class or matrix manipulation.

2. Next, I checked the release notes[4] for each version of Android to see whether there were any breaking changes mentioned that

---

4.   http://d.android.com/sdk/RELEASENOTES.html

might affect the ImageView class. Breaking changes are updates that cause code that was working to stop working, or vice versa. I didn't find any that seemed related.

3. Then I searched the Android bug database[5] for the keywords *ImageView* and *matrix*. Unfortunately, the public bug database is incomplete because Google keeps its own private list of bugs, so I didn't find anything.

4. Next, I searched all the Android Developer Forums[6] to see whether anybody else was having the same problem. The groups all have search forms of their own, but the quickest and most accurate way to search the forums is just to use the Google search engine and search the entire Web. Using the same keywords (*ImageView* and *matrix*), I found a posting from 2009 that looked exactly the same. Unfortunately, there was no follow-up or workaround posted, but I knew I was on the right track.

5. Finally, I went to the source.[7] With a few exceptions, all the code for Android is available in a public repository online. I had a clue about where the source to the ImageView class was located in the source tree because one of the earlier searches had revealed the path name. It was in the platform/frameworks/base.git project, under the core/java/widget directory. I opened the history using the repository's web interface.[8] And there it was, a change made on July 30, 2009, with the comment: "Fix a bug in ImageView: The drawing matrix is not updated when setImageMatrix is called." This bug fix was performed in between the Cupcake and Donut versions of Android, which explained why the problem happened in 1.5 but not in 1.6.

In almost all cases, you'll be able to find a solution without resorting to reading the Android source code. But it's nice to know it's there if you need it. By studying the code and trying a few things, I was able to create a workaround for the bug.

---

5. http://b.android.com
6. http://d.android.com/resources/community-groups.html
7. http://source.android.com
8. https://android.git.kernel.org/?p=platform/frameworks/base.git;a=history;f=core/java/android/widget/ImageView.java

Add these lines to the end of the onCreate() method in the Touch class:

Touchv2/src/org/example/touch/Touch.java

```
@Override
public void onCreate(Bundle savedInstanceState) {
    // ...
    // Work around a Cupcake bug
    matrix.setTranslate(1f, 1f);
    view.setImageMatrix(matrix);
}
```

By running the program in the emulator using various versions of Android, you can verify that this fixes the problem in Android 1.5 and doesn't break anything in later versions. Once your program is working with different versions of Android, you should try it at different screen sizes as well.

13.5 All Screens Great and Small

Supporting different screen sizes, resolutions, and pixel densities is important because you want your application to look its best on as many Android devices as possible. Unlike the iPhone, which has just one standard screen (OK, three, if you count the iPad and the iPhone 4), Android-powered devices come in all shapes and sizes.

Android will try to scale your user interface to fit the device, but it doesn't always do a great job of it. The only way to tell is through, you guessed it, testing. Use the emulator skins recommended in Section 13.1, *Gentlemen, Start Your Emulators*, on page 254 to make sure your program works on the most common sizes. If you need to tweak the layouts or images for particular configurations, you can use suffixes in the resource directory names.

For example, you can put images for high-density displays in the res/ drawable-hdpi directory, medium density in res/drawable-mdpi, and low density in res/drawable-ldpi. All the examples do that for their program icons, which will be shown on the home screen. Graphics that are density-independent (that should not be scaled) go in the res/drawable-nodpi directory.

The following is a list of the valid directory name qualifiers, in order of precedence:[9]

Qualifier	Values
MCC and MNC	Mobile country code and optional mobile network code. I don't recommend using this.
Language and region	Two-letter language and optional two-letter region code (preceded by lowercase *r*). For example: fr, en-rUS, fr-rFR, es-rES.
Screen dimensions	small, normal, large.
Wider/taller screens	long, notlong.
Screen orientation	port, land, square.
Screen pixel density	ldpi, mdpi, hdpi, nodpi.
Touchscreen type	notouch, stylus, finger.
Keyboard available?	keysexposed, keyshidden, keyssoft.
Keyboard type	nokeys, qwerty, 12key.
Navigation available?	navexposed, navhidden.
Navigation type	nonav, dpad, trackball, wheel.
Screen dimensions	320x240, 640x480, and so on (not recommended by Google but people use it anyway).
SDK version	API level supported by the device (preceded by lowercase "v"). For example: v3, v8.

To use more than one qualifier, just string them together with a hyphen (-) in between. For example, the res/drawable-fr-land-ldpi directory could contain pictures for low-density displays in landscape mode in French.

Note: In versions prior to 2.1, Android had bugs in how it matched these qualifiers. For advice on dealing with quirks like this, see Justin Mattson's Google I/O presentation.[10]

13.6 Installing on the SD Card

Starting in Android 2.2, you can specify that your application may be installed on the SD card instead of on the phone's limited internal memory.

---

9. See http://d.android.com/guide/topics/resources/providing-resources.html#BestMatch for a full explanation of how Android finds the best matching directory.
10. http://code.google.com/events/io/2010/sessions/casting-wide-net-android-devices.html

To do that, add the android:installLocation= attribute to the <*manifest*> tag in your AndroidManifest.xml file like this:

```
<manifest ... android:installLocation="auto">
```

Valid values are *auto* and *preferExternal*. I recommend you use *auto*, which lets the system decide where it should go. Specifying *preferExternal* requests that your app be installed on the SD card but doesn't guarantee it. Either way, the user can move your application between internal and external storage with the Settings application.

The attribute will be quietly ignored on older versions of Android. If you leave it off entirely, Android will always put your program in internal storage.

So, why aren't SD card installs the default? It turns out that there are many situations where external installation is not a good idea. When you plug your phone's USB cable into your computer to charge it or share files, any running application installed on external storage will be killed. This is especially problematic for home screen widgets, which will simply vanish and never reappear.

Therefore, Google recommends[11] that you do not allow external installation of applications that use any of the following features:

- Account managers
- Alarms
- Device administrators
- Input method engines
- Live folders
- Live wallpapers
- Services
- Sync adapters
- Widgets

As Android 2.2 adoption grows, users will expect everything to be installable on the SD card. If you choose not to allow it, be prepared to explain why to your users.

---

11. http://d.android.com/guide/appendix/install-location.html

13.7 Fast-Forward >>

Supporting multiple versions of Android running on multiple hardware devices with multiple screen sizes is not easy. In this chapter, we've covered the most common issues and solutions to get you started. If you find yourself wanting more, I recommend reading the excellent best-practices document called "Supporting Multiple Screens" at the Android website.[12]

You've worked hard to get your application to this point. Now comes the fun part: letting other people use it. The next chapter will cover how to publish your app to the Android Market.

---

12. http://d.android.com/guide/practices/screens_support.html

Publishing to the Android Market

Up to now you've just been creating software to run in the emulator or to download to your personal Android phone. Are you ready to take the next step? By publishing to the Android Market,[1] you can make your application available to millions of other Android users. This chapter will show you how.

14.1 Preparing

The first step of publishing an application to the Market is, well, to write the application. See the rest of the book for directions on how to do that. But simply writing code is not enough. Your program needs to be of a high quality, free of bugs (yeah right), and compatible with as many devices as possible. Here are a few tips to help you:

- Test it on at least one real device before letting anyone else see it. If you forget all the other tips, remember this one.

- Keep your program simple, and polish the heck out of it. Make your program do one thing well, rather than a lot of things poorly.

- Pick a good Java package name, such as com.yourcompany.prog-name, that you can live with for a long time. Android uses the package name defined in AndroidManifest.xml as the primary identifier for your application. No two programs can have the same package name, and once you upload a program to the Market with that name, you cannot change it without completely removing it, requiring all users to uninstall, and publishing a new program.

---

1. http://market.android.com

- Pick a meaningful value for android:versionCode= and android:versionName= in your AndroidManifest.xml file.[2] Consider future updates, and leave room for them in your naming scheme.

- Follow the Android best practices,[3] such as designing for performance, responsiveness, and seamlessness.

- Follow the user interface guidelines,[4] such as icon design, menu design, and proper use of the Back button.

Compatibility with multiple devices is one of the toughest challenges facing the Android programmer. One issue you'll have to deal with is users having different versions of the platform installed on their phones. See Chapter 13, *Write Once, Test Everywhere*, on page 253 for advice.

Although first impressions and compatibility are important, you'll need to strike a balance between tweaking and polishing your application to make it perfect vs. releasing it in a timely fashion. Once you think it's ready, the next step is to sign it.

14.2 Signing

Android requires that all applications be packaged up into an .apk and signed with a digital certificate before it will consider running them. This is true for the emulator and for your personal testing devices, but it's especially true for programs that you want to publish on the Market.

"But wait," you say, "I haven't been packaging or signing anything up to now." Actually, you have. The Android SDK tools have been secretly building and signing everything using a certificate that Google created using a known alias and password. Because the password was known, you were never prompted for it and probably never even knew it existed. However, the debug certificate cannot be used for applications in the Market, so now it's time to take off the training wheels and make your own certificate.

There are two ways to do it: by hand with the standard Java keytool and jarsigner commands[5] or automatically with Eclipse. I'm just going to cover the Eclipse way.

---

2. http://d.android.com/guide/publishing/versioning.html
3. http://d.android.com/guide/practices/design
4. http://d.android.com/guide/practices/ui_guidelines
5. http://d.android.com/guide/publishing/app-signing.html

Right-click the project in the Package Explorer, and select Android Tools > Export Signed Application Package. The wizard will guide you through the process of signing your application, including creating a new keystore and private key if you don't already have them. You should use the same key for all versions of all your applications and take the appropriate precautions for preventing your private key from falling into the wrong hands.

Note: If you use the Google Maps API (see Section 8.3, *Embedding a MapView*, on page 164), then you'll need to get a new Maps API key from Google because it is tied to your digital certificate. Export the program once, obtain a new Maps API key using the online instructions,[6] change your XML layout file to use the new key, and then export the program again.

When you're done, you'll have an .apk file that is ready for publishing.

14.3 Publishing

The Android Market is a Google-hosted service you can use for posting all your programs. To get started with publishing, you first need to sign up as a registered developer on the publisher's website (also known as the Developer Console).[7] There is a small registration fee.

As an additional step, if you want to charge for your program, you'll need to sign up with a payment processor. The publisher's website will instruct you on how to do that. As of this writing, only Google Checkout is supported, but in the future, other processors such as PayPal may be supported.

Now you're ready to upload. Click the Upload Application link, and fill out the form. Here are three tips:

- Turn Copy Protection off. Android's copy protection is completely insecure and performs no useful function other than to irritate your users. If you're worried about piracy, use the Android Market Licensing service.[8]

- Unless you have a reason not to, set the Locations option to All Current and Future Countries. New countries are being added all

---

6. http://code.google.com/android/add-ons/google-apis/mapkey.html
7. http://market.android.com/publish
8. http://d.android.com/guide/publishing/licensing.html

the time, and this way your application will be available to all of them.

- Do *not* supply your phone number in the application Contact Information. All Market users will be able to see this number, and they will call it when they have problems. Of course, if you have a dedicated number and staff for phone support, then this tip doesn't apply.

Just to give you an example, here's how I filled out the form for an application I published called Re-Translate Pro (an updated version of the translate example from Section 7.4, *Using Web Services*, on page 138):

```
Application .apk file: (select Browse and Upload)
Language: English (en_US)
Title (en_US): Re-Translate Pro
Description (en_US):
   Re-Translate translates a phrase from one language to another and
   then back again so you can make sure you're saying what you meant.

   Try the Lite version to see if you like it first.

   Features:
   - Translates instantly as you type
   - Long press for copy/paste
   - Directly send SMS/Email

Application Type: Applications
Category: Tools
Price: USD $1.99

Copy Protection Off
Locations All Current and Future Countries with Payment

Website: http://www.zdnet.com/blog/burnette
Email: ed.burnette@gmail.com
Phone: (blank)
```

When you click the Publish button, your application will appear *immediately* on the Android Market on all applicable devices. That's right, there is no approval process, no waiting period (other than a few seconds to update the download servers), and no limits to what you can do in your programs. Well, almost. You still have to follow the Android Content Guidelines.[9] Failure to adhere to the guidelines could result in your application being removed from the Android Market. Among

---

9. http://www.android.com/market/terms/developer-content-policy.html

other things, the guidelines say that your content must not be illegal, be obscene, promote hate or violence, or be unsuitable for anyone younger than 18 years of age. In addition, it must not knowingly violate an authorized carrier's terms of service. There have been rare cases of programs being pulled because of user or carrier complaints, but as long as you use common sense, you shouldn't have anything to worry about.

The next section covers updates to already published applications.

14.4 Updating

Let's say your app has been in the Market for a little while and you want to make a change. The simplest kind of change is to the program's metadata, that is, the title, description, price, and all the other information you filled out in the previous section. To change this noncode information, simply select your program from the list on the Developer's Console, make the change, and then click Save.

Do you have a new version of your code? No problem, you can upload it from this page too. Before you do that, however, take a moment to verify that you have changed the two version numbers in your Android-Manifest.xml file. Increment android:versionCode= by one every time you upload (for example, from 1 to 2), and bump the human-readable version number in android:versionName= by the appropriate amount (for example, from 1.0.0 to 1.0.1 for a minor bug fix). Once the version number is correct and the package has been rebuilt and re-signed, select Upload Upgrade; then click Browse, find your new .apk file, and click Upload to send it to the server.

Regardless of the change, you must click the Publish button for your changes to be visible to Android Market users. If you click Save instead, changes will be kept in draft form until you finally commit and click Publish.

If possible, I suggest you perform frequent updates, every two weeks or so. This performs two functions:

- It makes users happy, because they think you are supporting them and listening to their suggestions.

- It keeps your app near the top of the Recently Updated list in the Market. That's one way for new users to discover your program and give it the chance it deserves.

14.5 Closing Thoughts

Here are a few final tips about the Market that I learned the hard way by publishing my own programs there:

- You can make a paid app free, but you can't make a free app paid. If there's any chance you might want to have a free (light) version and a paid (pro) version of your program, then create them both up front. Never take anything away that you put in the free version, or you risk a firestorm of protests.

- In the current version of the Market, you won't be able to buy your own paid application. I hope that will be fixed in a future version.

- Read all the comments left by users, but don't hesitate to report especially rude or vulgar ones as spam. Keep your comment area clean for useful feedback, both positive and negative.

- Don't get discouraged. People can be cruel, especially when posting anonymous comments. A thick skin and a sense of humor are invaluable tools of the trade.

Part V

Appendixes

Java vs. the Android Language and APIs

For the most part, Android programs are written in the Java language, and they use the Java 5 Standard Edition (SE) library APIs. I say "for the most part" because there are a few differences. This appendix highlights the differences between regular Java and what you'll find in Android. If you're already proficient in Java development on other platforms, you should take a close look to see what things you need to "unlearn."

A.1 Language Subset

Android uses a standard Java compiler to compile your source code into regular bytecodes and then translates those bytecodes into Dalvik instructions. Therefore, the entire Java language is supported, not just a subset. Compare this to the Google Web Toolkit (GWT), which has its own Java to JavaScript translator. By using the stock compiler and bytecodes, you don't even need to have the source code for libraries that you want to use in your applications.

Language Level

Android supports code compatible with Java Standard Edition 5 or earlier. Java 6 and 7 class formats and features are not yet supported but could be added in future releases.

Intrinsic Types

All Java intrinsic types including **byte**, **char**, **short**, **int**, **long**, **float**, **double**, Object, String, and arrays are supported. However, on some low-end hardware, floating point is emulated. That means it's performed in software instead of hardware, making it much slower than integer arithmetic. Although occasional use is fine, avoid using **float** or **double** in performance-critical code unless your algorithm really requires floating point or you're sure your application will be running on a high-end device.

Multithreading and Synchronization

Multiple threads are supported by *time slicing*: giving each thread a few milliseconds to run and then performing a *context switch* to let another thread have a turn. Although Android will support any number of threads, in general you should use only one or two. One thread is dedicated for the main user interface (if you have one), and another thread is used for long-running operations such as calculations or network I/O.

The Dalvik VM implements the **synchronized** keyword and synchronization-related library methods such as Object.wait(), Object.notify(), and Object.notifyAll(). It also supports the java.util.concurrent package for more sophisticated algorithms. Use them as you would in any Java program to keep multiple threads from interfering with each other.

Reflection

Although the Android platform supports Java reflection, as a general rule you should not use it. The reason is simple performance: reflection is slow. Consider alternatives such as compile-time tools and preprocessors instead.

Finalization

The Dalvik VM supports object finalization during garbage collection just like regular Java VMs. However, most Java experts advise you not to rely on finalizers because you cannot predict when (or if) they will run. Instead of finalizers, use explicit close() or terminate() methods. Android is targeted toward resource-constrained hardware, so it's important that you release all resources as soon as you no longer need them.

A.2 Standard Library Subset

Android supports a relatively large subset of the Java Standard Edition 5.0 library. Some things were left out because they simply didn't make sense (such as printing), and others were omitted because better APIs are available that are specific to Android (such as user interfaces).

Supported

The following standard packages are supported in Android. Consult the Java 2 Platform Standard Edition 5.0 API documentation[1] for information on how to use them:

- java.awt.font: A few constants for Unicode and fonts
- java.beans: A few classes and interfaces for JavaBeans property changes
- java.io: File and stream I/O
- java.lang (except java.lang.management): Language and exception support
- java.math: Big numbers, rounding, precision
- java.net: Network I/O, URLs, sockets
- java.nio: File and channel I/O
- java.security: Authorization, certificates, public keys
- java.sql: Database interfaces
- java.text: Formatting, natural language, collation
- java.util (including java.util.concurrent): Lists, maps, sets, arrays, collections
- javax.crypto: Ciphers, public keys
- javax.microedition.khronos: OpenGL graphics (from Java Micro Edition)
- javax.net: Socket factories, SSL
- javax.security (except javax.security.auth.kerberos, javax.security.auth.spi, and javax.security.sasl)
- javax.sql (except javax.sql.rowset): More database interfaces
- javax.xml.parsers: XML parsing
- org.w3c.dom (but not subpackages): DOM nodes and elements
- org.xml.sax: Simple API for XML

Note that although the regular Java SQL database APIs (JDBC) are included, you don't use them to access local SQLite databases. Use the

---

1. http://java.sun.com/j2se/1.5.0/docs/api

android.database APIs instead (see Chapter 9, *Putting SQL to Work*, on page 171).

Not Supported

These packages, normally part of the Java 2 Platform Standard Edition, are *not* supported by Android:

- java.applet
- java.awt
- java.lang.management
- java.rmi
- javax.accessibility
- javax.activity
- javax.imageio
- javax.management
- javax.naming
- javax.print
- javax.rmi
- javax.security.auth.kerberos
- javax.security.auth.spi
- javax.security.sasl
- javax.sound
- javax.swing
- javax.transaction
- javax.xml (except javax.xml.parsers)
- org.ietf.*
- org.omg.*
- org.w3c.dom.* (subpackages)

A.3 Third-Party Libraries

In addition to the standard libraries listed earlier, the Android SDK comes with a number of third-party libraries for your convenience:

- org.apache.http: HTTP authentication, cookies, methods, and protocol
- org.json: JavaScript Object Notation
- org.xml.sax: XML parsing
- org.xmlpull.v1: XML parsing

Appendix B

Bibliography

[Bur05]   Ed Burnette. *Eclipse IDE Pocket Guide*. O'Reilly & Associates, Inc, Sebastopol, CA, 2005.

[Gen06]   Jonathan Gennick. *SQL Pocket Guide*. O'Reilly Media, Inc., Sebastopol, CA, second edition, 2006.

[Goe06]   Brian Goetz. *Java Concurrency in Practice*. Addison-Wesley, Reading, MA, 2006.

[Owe06]   Mike Owens. *The Definitive Guide to SQLite*. Apress, Berkeley, CA, 2006.

Index

The Pragmatic Bookshelf

Available in paperback and DRM-free eBooks, our titles are here to help you stay on top of your game. The following are in print as of October 2010; be sure to check our website at pragprog.com for newer titles.

Title	Year	ISBN	Pages
Advanced Rails Recipes: 84 New Ways to Build Stunning Rails Apps	2008	9780978739225	464
Agile Coaching	2009	9781934356432	248
Agile Retrospectives: Making Good Teams Great	2006	9780977616640	200
Agile Web Development with Rails	2009	9781934356166	792
Beginning Mac Programming: Develop with Objective-C and Cocoa	2010	9781934356517	300
Behind Closed Doors: Secrets of Great Management	2005	9780976694021	192
Best of Ruby Quiz	2006	9780976694076	304
Cocoa Programming: A Quick-Start Guide for Developers	2010	9781934356302	450
Core Animation for Mac OS X and the iPhone: Creating Compelling Dynamic User Interfaces	2008	9781934356104	200
Core Data: Apple's API for Persisting Data on Mac OS X	2009	9781934356326	256
Data Crunching: Solve Everyday Problems using Java, Python, and More	2005	9780974514079	208
Debug It! Find, Repair, and Prevent Bugs in Your Code	2009	9781934356289	232
Deploying Rails Applications: A Step-by-Step Guide	2008	9780978739201	280
Design Accessible Web Sites: 36 Keys to Creating Content for All Audiences and Platforms	2007	9781934356029	336
Desktop GIS: Mapping the Planet with Open Source Tools	2008	9781934356067	368
Domain-Driven Design Using Naked Objects	2009	9781934356449	375
Enterprise Integration with Ruby	2006	9780976694069	360
Enterprise Recipes with Ruby and Rails	2008	9781934356234	416
Everyday Scripting with Ruby: for Teams, Testers, and You	2007	9780977616619	320
ExpressionEngine 2: A Quick-Start Guide	2010	9781934356524	250
From Java To Ruby: Things Every Manager Should Know	2006	9780976694090	160
FXRuby: Create Lean and Mean GUIs with Ruby	2008	9781934356074	240

Continued on next page

Title	Year	ISBN	Pages
GIS for Web Developers: Adding Where to Your Web Applications	2007	9780974514093	275
Google Maps API: Adding Where to Your Applications	2006	PDF-Only	83
Grails: A Quick-Start Guide	2009	9781934356463	200
Groovy Recipes: Greasing the Wheels of Java	2008	9780978739294	264
Hello, Android: Introducing Google's Mobile Development Platform	2010	9781934356562	320
Interface Oriented Design	2006	9780976694052	240
iPad Programming: A Quick-Start Guide for iPhone Developers	2010	9781934356579	248
iPhone SDK Development	2009	9781934356258	576
Land the Tech Job You Love	2009	9781934356265	280
Language Implementation Patterns: Create Your Own Domain-Specific and General Programming Languages	2009	9781934356456	350
Learn to Program	2009	9781934356364	240
Manage It! Your Guide to Modern Pragmatic Project Management	2007	9780978739249	360
Manage Your Project Portfolio: Increase Your Capacity and Finish More Projects	2009	9781934356296	200
Mastering Dojo: JavaScript and Ajax Tools for Great Web Experiences	2008	9781934356111	568
Metaprogramming Ruby: Program Like the Ruby Pros	2010	9781934356470	240
Modular Java: Creating Flexible Applications with OSGi and Spring	2009	9781934356401	260
No Fluff Just Stuff 2006 Anthology	2006	9780977616664	240
No Fluff Just Stuff 2007 Anthology	2007	9780978739287	320
Pomodoro Technique Illustrated: The Easy Way to Do More in Less Time	2009	9781934356500	144
Practical Programming: An Introduction to Computer Science Using Python	2009	9781934356272	350
Practices of an Agile Developer	2006	9780974514086	208
Pragmatic Guide to Git	2010	9781934356722	168
Pragmatic Project Automation: How to Build, Deploy, and Monitor Java Applications	2004	9780974514031	176
Pragmatic Thinking and Learning: Refactor Your Wetware	2008	9781934356050	288
Pragmatic Unit Testing in C# with NUnit	2007	9780977616671	176
Pragmatic Unit Testing in Java with JUnit	2003	9780974514017	160
Pragmatic Version Control using CVS	2003	9780974514000	176
Pragmatic Version Control Using Git	2008	9781934356159	200
Pragmatic Version Control using Subversion	2006	9780977616657	248

Continued on next page

Title	Year	ISBN	Pages
Programming Clojure	2009	9781934356333	304
Programming Cocoa with Ruby: Create Compelling Mac Apps Using RubyCocoa	2009	9781934356197	300
Programming Erlang: Software for a Concurrent World	2007	9781934356005	536
Programming Groovy: Dynamic Productivity for the Java Developer	2008	9781934356098	320
Programming Ruby: The Pragmatic Programmers' Guide	2004	9780974514055	864
Programming Ruby 1.9: The Pragmatic Programmers' Guide	2009	9781934356081	960
Programming Scala: Tackle Multi Core Complexity on the Java Virtual Machine	2009	9781934356319	250
Prototype and script.aculo.us: You Never Knew JavaScript Could Do This!	2007	9781934356012	448
Rails for .NET Developers	2008	9781934356203	300
Rails for Java Developers	2007	9780977616695	336
Rails for PHP Developers	2008	9781934356043	432
Rails Recipes	2006	9780977616602	350
Rapid GUI Development with QtRuby	2005	PDF-Only	83
Release It! Design and Deploy Production-Ready Software	2007	9780978739218	368
Scripted GUI Testing with Ruby	2008	9781934356180	192
Seven Languages in Seven Weeks: A Pragmatic Guide to Learning Programming Languages	2010	9781934356593	300
Ship It! A Practical Guide to Successful Software Projects	2005	9780974514048	224
SQL Antipatterns: Avoiding the Pitfalls of Database Programming	2010	9781934356555	352
Stripes ...and Java Web Development Is Fun Again	2008	9781934356210	375
Test-Drive ASP.NET MVC	2010	9781934356531	296
TextMate: Power Editing for the Mac	2007	9780978739232	208
The Agile Samurai: How Agile Masters Deliver Great Software	2010	9781934356586	280
The Definitive ANTLR Reference: Building Domain-Specific Languages	2007	9780978739256	384
The Passionate Programmer: Creating a Remarkable Career in Software Development	2009	9781934356340	200
ThoughtWorks Anthology	2008	9781934356142	240
Ubuntu Kung Fu: Tips, Tricks, Hints, and Hacks	2008	9781934356227	400
Web Design for Developers: A Programmer's Guide to Design Tools and Techniques	2009	9781934356135	300

Grow your Skills

Debug It!

Debug It! will equip you with the tools, techniques, and approaches to help you tackle any bug with confidence. These secrets of professional debugging illuminate every stage of the bug life cycle, from constructing software that makes debugging easy; through bug detection, reproduction, and diagnosis; to rolling out your eventual fix. Learn better debugging whether you're writing Java or assembly language, targeting servers or embedded micro-controllers, or using agile or traditional approaches.

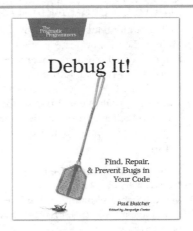

Debug It! Find, Repair, and Prevent Bugs in Your Code
Paul Butcher
(232 pages) ISBN: 978-1-9343562 8 9. $34.95
http://pragprog.com/titles/pbdp

SQL Antipatterns

If you're programming applications that store data, then chances are you're using SQL, either directly or through a mapping layer. But most of the SQL that gets used is inefficient, hard to maintain, and sometimes just plain wrong. This book shows you all the common mistakes, and then leads you through the best fixes. What's more, it shows you what's *behind* these fixes, so you'll learn a lot about relational databases along the way.

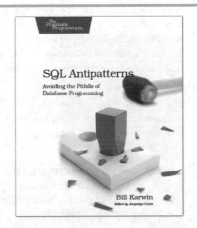

SQL Antipatterns: Avoiding the Pitfalls of Database Programming
Bill Karwin
(300 pages) ISBN: 978-19343565-5-5. $34.95
http://pragprog.com/titles/bksqla

Agile Techniques

Practices of an Agile Developer

Agility is all about using feedback to respond to change. Learn how to • apply the principles of agility throughout the software development process • establish and maintain an agile working environment • deliver what users really want • use personal agile techniques for better coding and debugging • use effective collaborative techniques for better teamwork • move to an agile approach

**Practices of an Agile Developer:
Working in the Real World**
Venkat Subramaniam and Andy Hunt
(189 pages) ISBN: 0-9745140-8-X. $29.95
http://pragprog.com/titles/pad

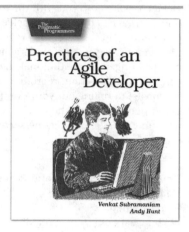

Agile Retrospectives

Mine the experience of your software development team continually throughout the life of the project. Rather than waiting until the end of the project—as with a traditional retrospective, when it's too late to help—agile retrospectives help you adjust to change *today*.

The tools and recipes in this book will help you uncover and solve hidden (and not-so-hidden) problems with your technology, your methodology, and those difficult "people issues" on your team.

Agile Retrospectives: Making Good Teams Great
Esther Derby and Diana Larsen
(170 pages) ISBN: 0-9776166-4-9. $29.95
http://pragprog.com/titles/dlret

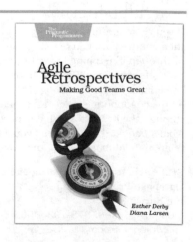

iPhone/iPad

iPhone SDK Development

Jump into application development for today's most remarkable mobile communications platform, the Pragmatic way. This Pragmatic guide takes you through the tools and APIs, the same ones Apple uses for its applications, that you can use to create your own software for the iPhone and iPod touch. Packed with useful examples, this book will give you both the big-picture concepts and the everyday "gotcha" details that developers need to make the most of the beauty and power of the iPhone OS platform.

iPhone SDK Development
Bill Dudney, Chris Adamson, Marcel Molina
(545 pages) ISBN: 978-1-9343562-5-8. $38.95
http://pragprog.com/titles/amiphd

iPad Programming

It's not an iPhone and it's not a laptop: the iPad is a groundbreaking new device. You need to create true iPad apps to take advantage of all that is possible with the iPad. If you're an experienced iPhone developer, *iPad Programming* will show you how to write these outstanding new apps while completely fitting your users' expectation for this device.

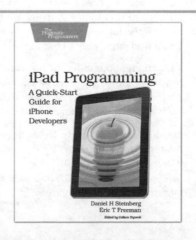

iPad Programming: A Quick-Start Guide for iPhone Developers
Daniel H Steinberg and Eric T Freeman
(250 pages) ISBN: 978-19343565-7-9. $34.95
http://pragprog.com/titles/sfipad

Refactor Your Career

Land the Tech Job You Love

You've got the technical chops—the skills to get a great job doing what you love. Now it's time to get down to the business of planning your job search, focusing your time and attention on the job leads that matter, and interviewing to wow your boss-to-be.

You'll learn how to find the job you want that fits you and your employer. You'll uncover the hidden jobs that never make it into the classifieds or Monster. You'll start making and maintaining the connections that will drive your future career moves.

You'll land the tech job you love.

Land the Tech Job You Love
Andy Lester
(280 pages) ISBN: 978-1934356-26-5. $23.95
http://pragprog.com/titles/algh

Manage It!

Manage It! is an award-winning, risk-based guide to making good decisions about how to plan and guide your projects. Author Johanna Rothman shows you how to beg, borrow, and steal from the best methodologies to fit your particular project. You'll find what works best for *you*.

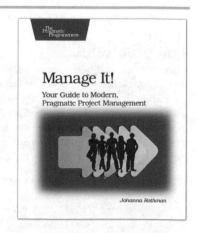

• Learn all about different project lifecycles • See how to organize a project • Compare sample project dashboards • See how to staff a project • Know when you're done—and what that means.

Manage It! Your Guide to Modern, Pragmatic Project Management
Johanna Rothman
(360 pages) ISBN: 0-9787392-4-8. $34.95
http://pragprog.com/titles/jrpm

Refactor Your Career

Pragmatic Thinking and Learning

Software development happens in your head. Not in an editor, IDE, or design tool. In this book by Pragmatic Programmer Andy Hunt, you'll learn how our brains are wired, and how to take advantage of your brain's architecture. You'll master new tricks and tips to learn more, faster, and retain more of what you learn.

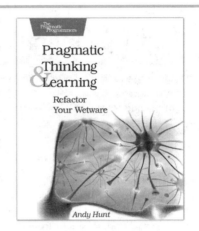

• Use the Dreyfus Model of Skill Acquisition to become more expert • Leverage the architecture of the brain to strengthen different thinking modes
• Avoid common "known bugs" in your mind
• Learn more deliberately and more effectively
• Manage knowledge more efficiently

Pragmatic Thinking and Learning:
Refactor your Wetware
Andy Hunt
(288 pages) ISBN: 978-1-9343560-5-0. $34.95
http://pragprog.com/titles/ahptl

The Passionate Programmer

This book is about creating a remarkable career in software development. Remarkable careers don't come by chance. They require thought, intention, action, and a willingness to change course when you've made mistakes. Most of us have been stumbling around letting our careers take us where they may. It's time to take control.

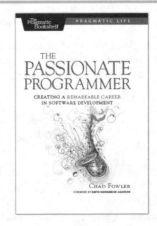

This revised and updated second edition lays out a strategy for planning and creating a radically successful life in software development *(the first edition was released as My Job Went to India: 52 Ways To Save Your Job)*.

The Passionate Programmer: Creating a
Remarkable Career in Software Development
Chad Fowler
(232 pages) ISBN: 978-1934356-34-0. $23.95
http://pragprog.com/titles/cfcar2

The Pragmatic Bookshelf

The Pragmatic Bookshelf features books written by developers for developers. The titles continue the well-known Pragmatic Programmer style and continue to garner awards and rave reviews. As development gets more and more difficult, the Pragmatic Programmers will be there with more titles and products to help you stay on top of your game.

Visit Us Online

Home page for Hello Android, Third Edition
http://pragprog.com/titles/eband3
Source code from this book, errata, and other resources. Come give us feedback, too!

Register for Updates
http://pragprog.com/updates
Be notified when updates and new books become available.

Join the Community
http://pragprog.com/community
Read our weblogs, join our online discussions, participate in our mailing list, interact with our wiki, and benefit from the experience of other Pragmatic Programmers.

New and Noteworthy
http://pragprog.com/news
Check out the latest pragmatic developments, new titles and other offerings.

Save on the eBook

Save on the eBook versions of this title. Owning the paper version of this book entitles you to purchase the electronic versions at a terrific discount.

PDFs are great for carrying around on your laptop—they are hyperlinked, have color, and are fully searchable. Most titles are also available for the iPhone and iPod touch, Amazon Kindle, and other popular e-book readers.

Buy now at pragprog.com/coupon.

Contact Us

Online Orders: www.pragprog.com/catalog
Customer Service: support@pragprog.com
Non-English Versions: translations@pragprog.com
Pragmatic Teaching: academic@pragprog.com
Author Proposals: proposals@pragprog.com
Contact us: 1-800-699-PROG (+1 919 847 3884)